A VIEW FROM
A LAKE

A VIEW FROM A LAKE

BUDDHA, MIND AND FUTURE

NEIL HAYES

Matador
9 Priory Business Park
Kibworth Beauchamp
Leicestershire LE8 0RX, UK
Tel: (+44) 116 279 2299
Fax: (+44) 116 279 2277
Email: books@troubador.co.uk
Web: www.troubador.co.uk/matador

ISBN 978 1784622 176

British Library Cataloguing in Publication Data.
A catalogue record for this book is available from the British Library.

Typeset in Book Antiqua by Troubador Publishing Ltd
Printed and bound in the UK by TJ International, Padstow, Cornwall

Matador is an imprint of Troubador Publishing Ltd

For my family

Contents

Introduction

On the day of my birth, the world was on the brink of full-scale nuclear war. This situation was created entirely by human minds. Although war was averted, there was no apparent impetus to understand how minds might have generated this situation and thereby avoid its reoccurrence.

Half a century later, I took delivery of a new sofa, and with it came an operating manual. Although I recycled this volume unread, I assume that it contained instructions telling me how to sit down without injuring myself. I was grateful that a fellow human being had taken the trouble to consider this matter on my behalf, but it struck me as incongruous relative to the potential nuclear destruction thing.

So many thinking minds throughout our history have considered it appropriate to indulge in thought that might ultimately cause the destruction of the very planet that we inhabit, and yet still the thinking mind roams free. There is a pressing need to understand the thinking mind, because thinking is the cause of so much suffering. This book will take the reader on a journey from ancient India to the Internet age, ending in a wager that we must all make: for a small stake of some highly rewarding mental training, we can bring about both a personal and a communal peace. We will learn that to bet against this outcome by leaving our minds to do what they will makes no sense at all.

The thinking mind is the most formidable apparatus that we will ever wield, and yet we receive little or no education in its safe operation. Of course, very few minds spend their time creating terrible weaponry or plotting global warfare, but generally minds settle for making themselves and others very unhappy. For most of us, all that we notice of the profound delusions in our minds is a constant feeling of some mismatch between where we find ourselves and where we would prefer to be. This perception drives much of our behaviour throughout our lives, and is the primary cause of our own suffering and the harm we do to others. Sometimes, it causes us to think ourselves into debilitating states of anxiety and depression.

Our thinking minds spend much of their time in competition and conflict with other minds. Even the most cursory consideration of this fact suggests that something is wrong, because we are all of the same nature, facing the same challenges. We are born of the same astral matter, and bound by the same fate to become stardust again. Whilst our education system serves to allow us to pour knowledge into our minds, generally the important issues of mind care and mind management are ignored, or rather they are supposed simply to be a matter of acquiring more knowledge. Neither do we receive any practical instruction in the complex subject of how to relate to other minds. We are left to work out for ourselves how we can be happy, and how we can best play our part in the whole universe of being that surrounds us. It is truly bizarre that we are furnished with excessive instruction in how to wield the simplest gadget without causing harm, or indeed how to sit on a sofa, but for the minds we are born with we are on our own.

In order to work out a functional relationship between our thinking minds and the world around us, the tool we use is the thinking mind itself. In addition to the obvious assumption that the thinking mind is capable of understanding itself, there is another, more dangerous, assumption here that for some reason we do not challenge. We assume that if the thinking mind identifies a problem with its own way of relating to the world, then it will work out a solution and implement a change for the better. This may sound plausible in principle, but what if the thinking mind itself is the problem? Or worse, what if the thinking mind is the problem and has a vested interest in not being fixed? The starting point for this book is this very worst case – a thinking mind that by its very nature denies us sustained happiness and harmony, and whose tyranny is opposed to being unseated by more harmonious states of being.

Until we truly understand the nature of our thinking minds, we cannot be free of the suffering that they create. This is not a new insight or starting point, as it is the fundamental principle underlying the teaching of Siddhartha Gautama – who became known as the Buddha, which means "the awakened one" – over two and a half millennia ago. Much of this book draws on the teaching of the Buddha, although it is not intended to be a book about Buddhism. Rather, the Buddha's teachings are used as the most complete and practical guide to mind management that is available today to enable us to understand the nature of mind and how suffering can be transcended. Our journey together will also take in some aspects of contemporary psychology, ideas about the evolution of the thinking mind, and a measure of science fiction, but always with the emphasis on practical guidance to improve our happiness and mental health. The overriding intention is to give a message of hope to all troubled minds that once the task is started it becomes self-sustaining, and naturally leads to increased contentment and compassion.

Psychological theories of mind have until recently been looking in the wrong place for the seat of our wisdom and the most appropriate means of responding to the world around us. They have looked to the thinking mind, the voice in the head, the conscious verbal "I" within us that seeks to control our mental activity and run our lives. We will examine this view closely, and show that the thinking mind is a useful resource to be called upon, but also a tyrant to be tamed. We will expose it as an invader, usurper, deceiver and subjugator, whose expansionist tendencies need to be understood for the good of our species and indeed all beings. However, we will also show that the thinking mind can serve us well once we learn to forge an appropriate relationship with it. We will explore a different mental model and a way of training our minds that leads to lasting happiness, increased wisdom, and better relationships with other beings and the planet as a whole.

Although this book is not about the science of psychology as such, its main purpose is to help break through unhelpful aspects of our psychological make-up that cause us unhappiness and disharmony with the world. To this end, a significant amount of psychological theory and analysis will be imparted, some personal in origin but most from the work of others. Unhelpful and unskilful processes of mind make our mental health fragile, and many of us feel that with the slightest additional impetus we may lose control. The very concept of what it means to be "in control" is difficult for us, because we know that whenever we approach this elusive state it will not last. Even when we are feeling stable, there may be a voice in the head giving us reasons to doubt the tenuous grip on it all that we think we have. Psychologists cannot reassure us here, for their experiments would confirm that although we may think we can predict the future and explain the past, we are often relying on an understanding that is fundamentally false.

If the Buddha were to have been asked about how we can establish the control we seek, he would almost certainly have said that the question is one that does not need to be answered. This is one of the many joys of the Buddha's method: if a question does not help us move towards our liberation from suffering, he taught that we should spend no time in considering it, as to do so would just be unnecessary thinking. "Control" is a largely pointless concept in a universe whose very nature is to change. Nothing, *absolutely nothing,* is stable or lasting, and it is this truth that underpins the whole of the Buddhist relationship with mind.

The mindfulness teachings of the Buddha and their use in modern psychological therapy are themes that are increasingly familiar on our bookshelves and in our mental health organisations. This is unsurprising because consideration of the Buddha's teachings reveals that he taught a psychology, a model of mind that is still vibrantly relevant today. It also becomes clear that this model of mind is complete, in the sense that it appears to need no addition or modification. We are fortunate that it is no dry theoretical model, but rather a highly potent and practical guide that can be put into practice and shown to work. This is evident in the widespread and expanding use of meditation techniques in contemporary mental health therapy. The temptation to dwell in wonder at the Buddha's staggering legacy of mind teachings is perhaps stronger than even the most mindful of us can resist, once it is understood. When his psychological model is put together with the path of mindfulness, wisdom and restraint that he taught, we see the full scale of the man's achievement. We also discover a way of attaining and sustaining mental wellbeing and harmonious living within the human condition.

This book is about training the mind. It is written to some extent backwards from a conventional point of view, in that it deals with the practical aspects of the solution to the problem early on, and then later offers some explanation about what the problem actually is, how it may have arisen, and why the solution is effective. Only from the safe position of initial practical comprehension can we return to elaborate the solution and problem further so that they may be better understood. In an important sense, learning the answer before the question is an effective model for life, in that if we act skilfully and for the benefit of all beings, it surely does not matter all that much what our motivation might be, or indeed whether we have one that we can articulate at all. The behaviour itself is more important. This is not intended to be a book that stimulates thinking, in fact quite the reverse.

The eminent Buddhist monk and scholar Venerable Narada Maha Thera has described the psychological teachings of the Buddha as "dry as dust" for those who read them without understanding. My hope in this book is to offer practical guidance that may help others arrive at a direct understanding of the essence of the teachings, through experience first and explanation second. In Western society, this perspective is particularly difficult to maintain, as our cultural conditioning serves to praise and nourish the thinking aspect of mind, and diminish the awareness aspect. Such veneration of the thinking mind unhelpfully strengthens its identity as "self", whilst marginalising other functions of mind as "not self". In the Buddha's psychological teachings, the concept of "not self" is actually one of the central tenets, although perhaps the one with the most elusive meaning outside direct experience. There is an underlying pressure in the West to "stand up for ourselves", but not necessarily to consider whether this is wise, or even what it really means.

Now let's turn up the heat. Learning about the true nature of our minds is not just a matter of correcting our perspective, it is the response to a crisis. Strong identity with "self", with "I", "me", and "mine", not only causes personal unhappiness and disharmony, but on a global scale it leads to atrocious acts of destruction of our own species, of other beings, and of the very planet we call home. We will discuss how in today's society the sense of self is stronger than it was in the Buddha's time, and how in the last half-century it has strengthened dramatically with technology as its servant. We may be running out of time, in other words. We may also need to keep a wary eye on the servant of computer technology in case it gets big ideas, but more of that later.

The response to the crisis is a way of relating to our minds that will not only bring about our own sustained happiness, but will also enable us to manage the conflict that our minds habitually engage in with others. The model of mind and mind management that is explained in this book draws on the fundamental parts of the Buddha's teaching, although emphasising some aspects more than others, tinkering with some concepts and accepted translations, and omitting some elements entirely. As I have said, this book is not about the religion of Buddhism, and therefore I have felt it acceptable to do this where it suits the message I wish to communicate, although I hope it can be said that I have done this with care and the deepest respect for the original teaching. The book also contains a large measure of personal interpretation, for the Buddha's teaching is more like a set of signposts than a detailed description of the journey. The journey is one we must make and experience for ourselves, because it is only through this direct engagement that insight arises. Likewise, there is a personal bias in the treatment of psychological theory, although this comes from my own thinking mind rather than from a place of deeper wisdom.

The explanation has to be personal, for two reasons. Firstly, and most obviously, using the thinking mind to analyse the mind as a whole is a technique that has its limitations. None of us can claim the perfection of objectivity in such an endeavour. Secondly, and more importantly, it is appropriate only to attempt to pass on that which is truly understood, and that understanding is by its nature personal. That said, the influence of many teachers and fellow truth-seekers can also be traced in the words that follow, and their inspiration is duly acknowledged.

The personal element of this book needs to be carefully handled, and I hope I have done this skilfully. Occasionally,

I will impart my own view based on experience of following the path that I describe, and here I will write in the first person. Insight that derives from a clear mind is much underrated in the West, and yet when it breaks through it is a thrilling experience that brings us wisdom that is long-lasting. I will try to make personal observations as direct as possible, and I have resolved to describe experience as it is and not to use vague similes and metaphors. To this end, I should point out that in the final part of the book "A View From a Lake" is not a metaphor; there is a lake and there is a view from that lake that could save us from ourselves. However, that is a topic for later.

Another matter that needs to be approached with some caution is the subject of mental health and the treatment of its disorders. My experience is that a trained mind can give effective protection against mental health issues such as anxiety and depression, and in the pages that follow I elaborate upon this and refer to sources that support such a view. I also give my opinion on medical approaches to such issues, and on the use of natural supplements that may help with low mood. However, I should emphasise that these are my opinions based on my own personal experience and research, and that I am not a medical professional. Readers should seek professional advice to determine what treatment may be appropriate for them.

The perpetual motion sought by the science of physics may be unattainable, but perpetual happiness is certainly possible. The Buddha developed and taught a method of mental training that led him to enlightenment, which simply means that he was able to see things as they truly are, and with the wisdom, compassion, and equanimity that derives from this viewpoint. Such enlightenment is a lofty goal, but fortunately its attainment is not all-or-nothing. There are benefits all along the way, even when we are taking our first steps on the path. As we learn to manage our minds in the way that the Buddha taught, we see glimpses of clarity, and this creates a perpetual motion in our mental training. We are drawn forward not because we think that we will attain something that we lack, but because we have seen something we instantly recognise to be of great consequence. It becomes instinctively clear that a lasting peace is possible, and also within our reach.

After the Buddha gained his own enlightenment, he gave his first teaching, albeit with some initial reluctance. In doing so it is said that he "set the wheel of truth in motion". This wheel has been turning ever since, sustained only by good intention and generosity. The message of hope in this book derives not just from the perpetual motion of this mind training, but also from just how close to the surface of our minds a joyous state of awareness actually is, and how easy it is to reconnect with it once it has been discovered. We will see that it can be summoned and felt even when our mood is low, and this can turn us away from unhelpful mental states and bring us the happiness we seek. Such wondrous freedom does not come from turning to our thinking minds to work things out, it comes from turning away and letting our thinking minds do what they do whilst we watch from the grandstand of our awareness.

PART ONE

BODY AND MIND

The Feeling in My Body

There is a feeling in my body.

My body experiences sensations. Some of these are responses to something outside of me that makes contact with my body, such as when I feel heat or cold, or am touched by an object that damages my skin. Some are responses to things outside of me that only touch my mind, like when I encounter an angry dog and feel the sensations of fear. Others are responses to events within me that I do not will, such as an ache or being replete with food. Some come from a thought in my mind, like when I recall a memory that embarrasses or angers me, or when I imagine a future that I fear. I perceive all of these sensations to be different. I perceive that I do not have a choice but to experience them.

Stop reading now and consider the following for a couple of minutes:

What sensation can you perceive? (Pick one.)

What is it truly like, independent of your reaction to it or thoughts about it?

Whilst you are considering this, if your thinking mind tries to tell you what the sensation feels like, or tries to judge it (good, bad, etc.), don't listen, just concentrate on experiencing it in the greatest detail possible. There is no need for names

3

or categories; just try to feel it as it truly is, as parts with no sum. Try this exercise for a few different sensations until you have got the hang of it and really penetrated the raw nature of feeling. You have started meditating now, by the way, but for now let's stick with the matter at hand. What is interesting to discover is that actually many of our feelings are remarkably similar when only their physical aspects are considered. This is particularly noticeable with the sensations associated with our emotions, and can be quite astonishing when fully grasped. In emotional responses, there are sensations in a couple of places in the throat, chest and head, some in the midriff, and there are a few that involve the skin and muscles. These few physical impressions in various combinations underlie what we then come to label as emotions, such as elation, contentment, embarrassment, social isolation, sadness and despair.

When emotions arise, it is interesting to consider closely the physical aspects that accompany them and note how they are so that you can say, for example, that sadness feels like *this* (perhaps a certain tightness in the back of the throat, and a heavy sensation at the base of the brain), and happiness feels like *that* (maybe a feeling higher in the throat, and a tingling across the top of the brain). From here we can go on to ask useful questions of our bodies (well, the questions may not seem useful straight away, but bear with me please). We can ask whether the physical experience of wanting a cup of coffee is substantially different from the feeling of happiness. Or, perhaps, whether the physical sensations of dread are significantly different from feeling tired. What does it really mean to say we have a "lump in our throat", or "our heart misses a beat", and the various other similes we use to describe our feelings?

This is the beginning of what the Buddha referred to as "investigation of mental states", and he identified this faculty as one of the seven factors of enlightenment. Indeed, when we are doing this, we are also engaged in concentration and mindfulness, which are two more of those seven. So, we have already started with a form of meditation and now we are making substantial inroads into working with the factors of enlightenment; we are well underway with making a lasting change in our lives.

A crucial question that arises is whether we can be sure that our thinking mind is qualified to make judgements about the nature of our emotions. What if the pattern of sensations were misinterpreted, or maybe there is actually no real need to make any sort of judgement and instead it is better to let the pattern of sensations arise and cease naturally? In allowing our thinking mind to judge our sensations, do we give them legitimacy and extend their life unnecessarily? If so, would the "bad" feelings simply fade away if we did not do this? In analysing our feelings in this way, what we are trying to do is recognise things as they truly are, rather than through the distorting glass of "self". These feelings are not self; if they were they would be with us all the time, but instead, like all things, they arise and they pass away.

By asking these questions of ourselves, we can learn to stop judging, resisting, and getting caught up in our reaction to our feelings. We routinely attach verbal labels, and more importantly value judgements, to physical perceptions, like "hot" or "tingling", but this is a habit we would be wise to unlearn. Rather, we should simply learn to experience things just as they are, with no judgement made or implied. In doing this, we are not trying to deconstruct and unlabel the world; we are just making a determined effort to be within it. Certainly, we will judge a painful feeling to be unpleasant, but the moment we grasp at the judgement we lose the true nature of the feeling. If we can make the effort to experience pure sensation without judgement, then this is the wisdom we are seeking. Actually, even for an 'unpleasant' feeling, when we take away the judging and the resistance that identification with self will produce, we may see that the physical sensation is not as unpleasant as we previously thought, and nor is it as constant.

Your feelings are not you.

Once you have developed in this way a little store of groups of physical feelings that you understand to be associated with a certain label, you can notice better those feelings arising. This will create a small space before your habitual reaction kicks in, and you can actually let the response pass unborn. For unhelpful states of mind in particular, this will be the beginning of a dramatic change in your habitual state of contentment. Another consequence is that you can learn to bring these states to mind to consider them. You can then use them skilfully, e.g. by bringing the happy feeling up and associating it with your current state.

Psychologists agree that a good trick to make ourselves feel happy is simply to smile. This possibility was noted by Darwin in the 1870s when he said that the free expression of outward signs of emotion intensifies that emotion. A little over a hundred years later, this idea spawned a great deal of psychological research strongly indicating that Darwin had been right. We will return to Darwin's wider legacy later, but for now let's stick with this specific idea. The theory is that intentional smiling triggers the feeling of happiness that in other circumstances is the cause of smiling. There is also some evidence to suggest that the effect applies to other facial expressions of emotion, not just smiling. Apparently, making faces in a mirror may increase the effect. Some intense debate can be followed in the psychological literature about the precise mechanism for this, some of it amusingly involving experimental subjects with Botoxed faces to try to determine if it is the intention or the action that causes the effect (Botoxed people don't frown!). Experiments have also shown that gestures such as nodding or shaking the head will affect our tendency to judge something in a positive or negative way. The nature of the bodily mechanisms that are at work here are of no particular importance to us; what matters is that these simple tricks can be taken further, and further still, to yield very useful insights into the nature of our thoughts and feelings, and ultimately to improve our wellbeing. They do this by providing an important instrument with which to survey the landscape of mind and body so that we may then build anew.

The enticing next step is this: to experience the happiness from smiling, one does not have to smile; one can *think* a smile. Stop reading for a moment and try this. Just calm your mind enough to focus on what you are about to do, and think a smile…

What did you experience? Did you experience sensations that you normally associate with happiness? Do it again, and focus now on the nature of the physical impressions that arise. Try to get beyond the fact that they are pleasing, because that is merely a judgement of your mind, and is not contained anywhere in the actual sensations. Scan the chest, the throat, and the head and determine the subtle feelings that have arisen in each. Maybe you felt a tingling somewhere in the top of your head, maybe a lifting and light sensation in the back of the throat, maybe an experience of your chest expanding and warming? Maybe the sensations are not static but flow around? Perhaps they spread to the tongue, shoulders and arms, or further down the body. Go as deep as you can into each of these physical phenomena so that you can know them for what they are. Do not judge or label, just *experience*. Then get to know them as a group, as a pattern that you can associate with the act of smiling, whether or not you are actually doing so.

Now try something different. Instead of thinking the smile, try to summon into your body the pattern of sensations that you associate with smiling. You will find that this is possible, and gives the same result as thinking the smile. Once you have gained some practice in this, the technique can be extended to understand your moods in general. Really, it should not surprise us that we can do this; after all, we can control our limbs and organs with a single thought. When one is in position ready to use the lavatory, for example, how incredible it is that the command to commence evacuation of the bladder or bowel can be given by a thought? The insight here is that we are capable of understanding, and ultimately letting go of, our moods, starting by bringing their sensations into our bodies and allowing them to dwell there for a while. All we have to do is to learn how our moods affect our bodies as raw patterns of feeling. One assumes that actors are adept at this, and psychologists often refer to thinking as being *embodied*, i.e. we think with our bodies, not just with our brains.

Don't just stick to the good moods. Become familiar with the bad ones as well when they arise. You will find that when you look at the sensations that underlie a challenging emotional state, you will tend to become less involved in that state, and it may pass more quickly than usual. You can then call these patterns to mind for a short while to examine them dispassionately, to see them for what they are, to learn not to fear them, and to put them in their place. They are just feelings, they are not you, and they do not need to be your master when they arise.

All this is leading to the insight that what makes moods and emotions your master is your thinking mind, your inner voice. When a feeling of, say, sadness enters your body, your mind will seize upon it and add a thought such as "I failed to achieve such-and-such", or "I am worthless." Before you know it, your thinking mind will have summoned up despair, or worse, and you cannot break the escalating cycle. When you choose to look at the feelings as just feelings, the awareness that this brings may even be sufficient to prevent you falling into the emotional state at all. Or, you may need much more practice before this starts to happen, but it matters not: the important thing is that you have set out on the path to healing. We all differ in the amount of time and effort needed to start to cultivate awareness and peace in our minds.

We may think that to recall bad moods would not be a good idea. Why would somebody want to summon up the physical sensations underlying sorrow or anxiety? The answer is simple: to understand them for what they are and thereby learn a new relationship with them. If they

9

are not labelled by our thinking minds as sorrow and anxiety, or at least not followed up as such, then they are just passing clouds that do not threaten our wellbeing in any way. They also lose their ability to stimulate further negative states. Looked at from this distance, we may even come to see that such patterns can be entirely functional in some circumstances.

The practice of summoning up these impressions is highly potent, because it helps us break the habit of instinctively labelling the pattern and then starting the cycle of thinking that first intensifies the feeling, then leads to further thinking, consumes us, and withdraws us from the present moment. It enables us to establish a *sensation store*, which will be of immense value to us in managing our minds, and will be referred to frequently in these pages. In time, when these sensations arise naturally, we can learn to become detached from them, simply saying to ourselves, for example, "Sadness is like this." In this way, there is no judgement, and no resistance; we are turning away, putting the feeling down gently, and allowing it to subside on its own. Or, we could summon up another emotional state from our sensation store to replace it, or at least suppress it for a while to allow it to lose energy.

The technique of sensation replacement is also very valuable. Try it. Try to cycle through some patterns of feeling from your store of impressions: happy, sad, fearful, embarrassed, isolated – whatever affects you. Jump from one to the other, and back. Make a habit of doing this, to build up your metaphorical muscles of mind wisdom. Perhaps smile at these mental states a little, and hold them in your awareness, without judging, labelling, or becoming them. Roll them around in your mind, play with them, welcome them, but don't jump into them!

You will notice that patterns of sensations called up from the sensation store are not as intense as their naturally arising counterparts, and nor are they as persistent. They are more like the after-images of the "real" feelings, or somewhat distant shadows. We will all differ in how strongly we can experience these summoned impressions, but the intensity does not matter – a mere hint of a sensation is enough to break into an unhelpful pattern of feeling, and may be sufficient to restore mindfulness and thereby prevent us falling into a state of wretchedness.

Now try adding a thought to a feeling you have called up from your sensation store. Stick to the positive feelings when doing this. Generate the impressions of a happy mood and then add a strong happy thought to that mood. You will see that the mind has the tendency then to follow that thought and add others that are related to it. Depending on the strength of the feeling and how evocative the thought is, it may only be a fraction of a second before your mind is away somewhere you did not expect, almost certainly in the past or future. If at the time that you try this you are generally in a bad place emotionally, you will notice that the original set of unpleasant feelings will return, as they are naturally stronger and more pervasively connected than the impressions summoned from the sensation store. But take heart from this: if you were in a bad place, you have managed to interrupt the negative mood and the thought cycle it was generating, even if only for a fleeting moment. You have this power.

This is really important work, for two reasons. Firstly, we can use our sensation stores to generate different emotional states, and these can be employed to break the chain of persistent unhelpful thought that we have learnt to associate with particular states. For example, if we are suffering from low mood, we may call up a joyous state to interrupt the cycle. This is a skilful way of dealing with the immediate mood, but is a mere party trick when compared to the major benefit to be gained. The second reason why working with the sensation store is so important is that considering the physicality of our emotions creates a distance between them and our thinking minds, enabling us to experience things as they really are. Staying with feelings for now, this allows us to view them from our metaphorical cinema seat and therefore not get involved in the action. The cinema seat analogy is actually quite a useful one, as when we watch a film in a cinema it can stir all sorts of powerful emotions such as fear and sadness, and even move us to tears, but we are not taking it personally. Our strong emotions usually arise through empathy with a character on a screen, rather than things that we perceive to be happening to us. It is extremely useful to develop such a distant relationship with our own emotions, and with the "characters", or thought patterns, in our minds. We may even give these characters names, and we will return to this later.

In doing these simple experiments with embodied thought, you have done something courageous and significant: you have stepped into the space between your thoughts, and seized back your natural awareness of the moment from the tyranny of your thinking mind. Through these exercises, we learn that *our feelings as sensations are a different thing from our feelings as reactions to those sensations*. These reactions start with simple judgements of like or dislike, but can turn into a cyclone of thought in which we are hopelessly caught. We create the world that we live in, and the world that we make causes us to suffer as we seek to prolong that which we find pleasurable and resist that which we do not. This is fundamental in the Buddhist outlook. The Buddha taught that we should seek the *uncreated*, which is the pure experience of the present moment, and thereby become at ease in a world where everything is of the nature to change. He taught that such presence of mind has certain foundations, and that understanding the body and its sensations is half of the story. We will now turn to the other half.

The Voice in My Head

There is a voice in my head.

My mind thinks with a voice, sometimes because I will it to do so, but usually just because that is what it seems naturally to do. Often, the inner voice speaks thoughts that I would not choose to think. Sometimes it comments on what is happening right now, but usually it is off somewhere else in the future or past, sounding off about something there. Sometimes I wish it would just shut up. This voice demands to be seen as "me", and yet when I am driving a car or balancing on a board in the ocean, it does not even break its dialogue to check in and see if I am in any danger. When I am feeling anxious or sad, this wannabe self pitches in with further reasons to feel that way, and makes me feel worse. When I am feeling happy, it tries to cling to or relive this feeling, denying me the chance to be content in the new moment that has arrived, or even notice anything about it. Surely, if this voice in my head were really "me", it would know and care more about my happiness and the safety of my body?

Having developed some understanding of the body and its sensations, we now turn to the other half of the Buddha's account of the foundations of mindfulness – the mind and its contents. To improve our happiness, mental wellbeing, and relationships with others, we can train our minds to engage with the world as it really is, rather than

14

through the filter of the voice in the head. If we are driving a car, we can be really driving the car and feeling and knowing every detail of that activity, rather than plotting the downfall of some perceived adversary. If we are surfing on the ocean, we can be totally present in that activity and not worrying about how we look to those on the shore. This is not to say that we are thinking about what we are doing, but rather that we are fully present in the experience of our actions. There is a big difference, and it involves taking a leap of faith and forging a different relationship with what we have come to regard as our "self", i.e. the inner voice, or thinking mind. This inner dialogue is actually not as rational as we perceive it to be, and indeed there are sometimes good reasons not to trust it, and even not to listen to it at all.

Our thinking minds serve us well when there is a problem to be solved, which is unsurprising given that this function of mind evolved for precisely such a purpose. The whys and wherefores of that evolution are useful to understand in order to help with our perspective on the role of thinking in our lives, but we will save that for later. However, when there is no pressing predicament to be addressed, the thinking mind has a tendency to invent one. It will go hunting in our past for something to replay and brood over, or it will travel into an imagined future to consider a problem we do not yet have and indeed almost certainly will never have. This always takes us away from the present moment, in which our minds must have tacitly acknowledged that there is no actual problem. If the present moment did present a challenge, then surely our thinking minds would be right there dealing with it on our behalf? Don't bet on it! It is very common for people to report that in times of extreme crisis, it is instinct, rather than thinking, that pulls them through.

The trouble is, the present moment is the only moment we have; it is *this* moment, the moment that we are alive now, and we are missing out on it if our minds are off doing battle in the past and future. Whether or not the present moment contains a problem, and later we will discuss how perhaps actually it never can, then surely our best option is to be in the moment rather than engaging in hypothetical skirmishes with an unchangeable past or an imagined future?

Because we rely on our thinking minds so much for problem-solving in our daily lives, and have had them praised and criticised all through our formative years, we fall prey to the delusion that unless this aspect of mind is "always on" then we are not in control. Actually, we habitually overestimate the control that we have, which is evidenced by extensive psychological research. Studies show that, when explaining the past or predicting the future, we overestimate our own influence and underestimate the parts played by pure chance and luck. The thinking mind has its place, but in the spaces between the cacophony of thought, and lying behind all of that thought, is the true nature of mind. The desire to control an uncontrollable world is not part of that nature, because the essence of such a desire is resistance to what is. This true mind is at peace with the moment and is not deluded. It is immensely powerful, and is ready to be reawakened and re-established as the guiding light in our lives. The relentless activity of the thinking mind serves to obscure its presence, however.

Sometimes our thinking minds are just pesky, telling us that we "are" the thoughts we are having and therefore we must keep thinking in order to keep being ourselves. Actually, to tell us that our thoughts are "self" is outrageous and unreasonable, as a few moments of contemplation will soon reveal, but we readily submit to it anyway. To illustrate, we can ask ourselves the question "Who are we when we are not thinking?", and of course this will quickly lead us to the conclusion that the inner voice cannot be self. However, if we stop and try not to think for a while, we will find this almost impossible. If you have never tried this before, try it now for a few moments...

What you heard was perhaps a torrent of incessant and mostly unnecessary commentary, right? Or perhaps you started planning or worrying? Whatever happened, there is little chance that you experienced no thoughts at all. Nor is there much chance that you experienced the present moment as a rich and effervescent experience presenting itself to all your bodily senses simultaneously. Try this short experiment a few times, and you will soon notice that the thinking mind is not well equipped to know the present moment fully, if at all. When we try to direct our attention into "right now", the untrained mind tends to fill with commentary that misses out most of the experience of the moment, and soon we will find ourselves travelling in time either forwards or backwards. The thinking mind is essentially limited to the past and the future, and although there are good evolutionary reasons for this that we will come to later, this can be most troublesome. We worry about things that have not happened and most likely never will; at least not in the way we are imagining them. We also dwell on events that have happened in the past, wishing that they had been otherwise, and even reliving them in our heads, making them turn out differently.

What a waste of time! Why do we let our thinking minds get away with this? We do it essentially because we are unaware, and because the runaway train of thinking carries us so fast that any glimpse of awareness is fleeting and blurred. The persistent delusion within us that we *are* our thinking minds is difficult to expose when travelling at such speed, and therefore we spend much of our time allowing our minds to think about whatever they will, no matter how unhappy it is making us, or how much it is causing us to withdraw from the fullness and vibrancy of total contact with the present moment.

Sometimes, our thinking minds are way beyond pesky and they deceive us in more treacherous ways. They tell us that we will only be happy when we obtain something we desire, or manage to avoid something we dislike. Ultimately, any happiness achieved in this way will change to something else and the cycle will start again. Despite the regularity of this type of thinking leading to suffering, the thinking mind still promotes the deception and we continue to fall into it. What is so peculiar is that the insight that happiness cannot be obtained by striving is well within the reach of any normally functioning thinking mind, but for some reason it takes a clarity of mind that few of us can consistently achieve in order to see this truth. With all due respect to the Buddha, it really is not such a deep insight that all things change and lose their ability to satisfy us. Nor is it worthy of a plaque on the wall to realise that we should not pin our happiness on trying to get what we want or avoid what we don't want. There is only one rational explanation as to why such insights seem to elude our species like some sort of genetic blind spot, and why it takes a Buddha mind to penetrate the truth: the thinking mind has a vested interest in keeping us from realising it.

The deceptions of our thinking minds can also turn to much darker purposes. When we are seized by emotional states such as anger, anxiety, or sadness, our thinking minds jump in and start adding thoughts that feed these states. Often, they will do that with the usual calling card of the thinking mind – "I will solve the problem." Typically, there is not a specific problem that is causing our emotional states, and in these cases our thinking minds do the opposite of solving a problem – they create one. As we dwell on why we feel the way we do, our feelings of tension become intensified; our black thoughts of revenge, worry, self-reproach, or whatever shift to overdrive, and before we know it we are consumed by harmful thought. At such points, we become unaware and effectively unconscious. Our entire being is overcome by uncontrollable thinking and we are unable to respond to anything other than the scenario that is playing out in our head. These self-perpetuating cycles can start with a fleeting negative thought or emotional state, but once our thinking minds get involved the thoughts and feelings escalate and we are lost. At worst, our thinking minds can take us into mental states that threaten life itself; it is well documented that ruminative thought is a major factor leading to clinical depression and chronic anxiety. We will not dwell on such matters at this point, but will return to the subject of brooding and ruminative thought at a later stage of the journey to understand our minds.

When the inner voice is silent, or when its commentary is not being heeded, we can observe that there is a mind that is still there and is capable of feats of learning and insight that are truly astonishing. This is the mind of awareness, rather than the mind of thinking. This mind is aware of the inner voice, but is not pushed around by it. In one of the more accessible ancient texts of the Buddha's teachings there is a line that translates to "Difficult is the hearing of the real truth". Here the Buddha was referring directly to this aspect of mind, rather than the inner voice that drowns out the hearing. In Pali, the ancient language of these teachings, this aspect of mind is referred to as *buddho*, which means "the one that knows".

We will leave the voice in our heads for now, although we will return to it frequently as the story develops. It is more than a little odd that we allow the inner voice to assume the title of "self" and control our lives, given that it can be an unwelcome guest, an unreliable witness, a troublemaker, a tormenter, a tyrant, and a false friend. Moreover, when push comes to shove and our lives are in danger, it goes missing. For now, let's simply acknowledge that we have a mind that has contents, and this voice is part of the contents of the mind, not the mind itself. Soon, we will look into our own minds and see this for ourselves, and we will feel the hope that springs from the wisdom that this awakens.

Your thoughts are not you.

Awareness and Choice

I am aware of my body and its feelings.
I am aware of my mind and its contents.
I am the awareness that there are these things.

Let's talk more about awareness. Here, I don't mean dim awareness of the sort that is on the edge of our consciousness when our thinking minds are going about their supposedly important business of thinking, pondering, judging, reminiscing, plotting, daydreaming, fantasising and so on. The sort of awareness I want to point to is the exhilarating feeling of one-pointed awareness when thinking stops dead and we are totally connected to the present moment. This is real awareness.

We do not need to be advanced meditators to experience this state of being, as it is something that is readily achievable in our everyday lives. True, it is a mental destination that can be reached through meditation, and this is a subject we will cover together at length later on. However, it is also an ordinary state, a natural state, indeed the most natural of all states, the real truth that we have forgotten how to hear. It is also a state that we already know how to call to mind without any mental training at all.

One way that this state can arise naturally is when we are awestruck. We all differ in what stimulates such a feeling, but there are two common themes: when we are

21

in the presence of extreme beauty, and when we encounter something wondrous. Beauty is, of course, subjective, but great music and art have the power to inspire this feeling in many of us. It is possible that in 1743 when King George II of England, and then the rest of the audience, reputedly stood on hearing Handel's *Messiah* for the first time, many felt this feeling. Speaking personally, this particular piece of music still has that power, and not just in its famous chorus. Wondrous things are those that simply astound us that such a thing could come into being. Natural scenes can do this, as can great architecture, or other dramatic works of man. For me it is the tombs of great people, but I suspect that this is not a universal phenomenon.

At such times, the present moment acquires extraordinary significance to us and it consumes all of our awareness in such a way that thinking stops. It is as if our awareness is all there is, all there could ever be, without any need or room for thought. We become entirely immersed in the present moment and desire nothing else of it, not even that it may continue. At such times, thinking stops and *being* arises. The sense of self is diminished or absent, and a natural and deep joy surfaces. For me, this feeling often arises when I connect with another person at a profound level, and although I suspect this may be common to other people, and indeed highly significant, we will stay with awe in the face of beauty and grandeur as our reference point. The initial elation will subside in time, but what is interesting is that what it leaves behind is not nothing, but a lasting ease of mind when in the presence of the initial stimulus. Although the first rush of pleasure has gone, the net contentment has not diminished. This elemental state is more satisfying, as it no longer contains the excitement that could otherwise distract us.

This initial elated feeling and then the ensuing fulfilling calm are notable landmarks on the journey we will take in this book, and worthy of a little reflection now. Can you call to mind the feeling of being awestruck, and if so do you remember that you felt a happiness that was like no other? Maybe you are currently in Barcelona on the metro reading or hearing these words, and about to get off to see Gaudi's Sagrada Família for the first time, or maybe you are on an aeroplane over Egypt and are about to glimpse the Pyramids from the window. Maybe you are on the deck of a boat approaching the Norwegian fjords or the coast of Hawaii. If so, you are in luck because you might be about to experience it firsthand, but if not, memory will have to do.

This feeling is of immense significance, and fundamentally different to any other, for two reasons. Firstly, *it has no opposite*. Our more familiar feelings and emotions have opposites, which we experience as highs and lows, and we get blown as if by winds between these extremes. Consider now the uniqueness of a feeling with no opposite. This thought itself may be inspiring enough to provoke the very joy that is being described here; maybe not now, but later when understanding has deepened. Secondly, its locus is *neither mind nor body*. Its beauty seems just to be, and is not as readily analysed as the baser experiences of emotion. The surge of mind and body energy that results from a well-executed yoga stretch has similar qualities, and no doubt touches the same source.

The experience in such situations is essentially an experience of "oneness" with the object being considered, i.e. of there being no apparent separation between subject and object. The narrow experience that is allowed by the thinking mind is suddenly blown apart and filled with awareness, as if with a dazzling light that bleaches out the thinking mind. The thinking mind is there somewhere, but it does not show through, or not so that we notice. It is dumbstruck. The reason that this elation has no opposite is that it is not of the conditioned world, i.e. it is not subject to arising and ceasing, to cause and effect. It just *is*, and it has always been there. This awareness is our true nature, and if the question of "Who am I?" were worth answering, then the answer would be along these lines.

The training offered by the Buddha's path allows us to abide in the joy of this awareness as the proper context for all experience. Through meditation and mindfulness, we can still our minds to the point that this elated feeling arises. The feeling is not the goal, and indeed advanced meditators will tell us that bliss is just a step on the way to a deeper peace, and therefore we should not seek it out as an end in itself. It is not a holiday from the problems of everyday life; it is a perspective upon them. Worldly affairs still surround us, but with awareness we can see them for what they are – as conditions that arise and cease.

Our awareness gives us choices about how we feel and what we think, and about how we engage with the world. We can free ourselves from suffering when we realise that our feelings are just feelings, and our thoughts are just thoughts. The mind of awareness will become our refuge, a place of trust from which we can claim back our minds from the inner voice. The Buddha taught that thoughts and feelings are just *conditions of mind*, and neither need to be heeded nor adopted as self. So, an angry thought is just an angry thought, and a sad thought is just a sad thought. So too with our reactions to the feelings in our bodies, which we may judge to be pleasant or unpleasant. They are just so. He taught that conditions of mind do not require a reaction, and in particular we do not need to become them, to identify ourselves with these feelings of anger or sadness, pleasure or pain, or anything else. For example, to say that we *are* angry or sad is a gross distortion of what we are actually experiencing, and creates the circumstances for inappropriate action on this basis.

Before we start to train our minds well, there is a fact to face, and it is a challenging one. We do not have to swallow it whole at this point, but let's get it out there now – *when we are suffering, we are suffering because we choose to suffer*. This may seem absurd, but it is something we can straightforwardly observe for ourselves. Ask yourself whether you would ever choose to suffer, and almost certainly your thinking mind will tell you that it would not. Well, if you are suffering and this is something that you would not choose and do not desire, then given that there is nobody else in your head, who can it possibly be that is perpetuating the suffering? The outside circumstances do not cause the suffering, they are just conditions that will remain as they are, whether you suffer or not.

When you are upset or angry, try to observe what happens when you attempt to look away from the mental pattern by thinking a smile. This is a straightforward enough experience when we are feeling fine, but something very illuminating happens if we try it when we are feeling down or angry. What happens is that we encounter resistance from the thinking mind. We may even find ourselves thinking thoughts along the lines of "This is not the time for happiness, I am too busy thinking these angry thoughts." We may even find ourselves thinking that we do not want to interrupt our rage, because we feel righteous in our suffering. Don't take my word for it – try it, and see for yourself.

Our distorted view is caused by the thinking mind seizing control of our attention and pulling in all our resources to suit its battle plan. This has the effect of extinguishing our awareness and thereby denying us a choice to do otherwise. However, if we can find a way to be in contact with our natural awareness, then we can choose not to be pulled into habitual suffering. This sounds straightforward enough, but it takes a certain resolution and a deep understanding of mind to achieve with any consistency. As he lay dying, the Buddha saw fit to remind his monks of the need for this resolve, his last words being: "All conditioned things are impermanent. Strive on diligently to achieve your liberation."

It is without question that the thinking function of mind is a very valuable resource, but it is just that much and no more: it is a resource of mind to be called upon when needed. The idea that it is not needed much of the time is abhorrent to it, and as long as it remains in command, it is also abhorrent to us. We can learn when to utilise and heed the thinking mind, and how to recognise those aspects of it that delude us and warp our perception of the world as it really is. We can also learn how to abide in awareness, and thereby not get caught up in the maelstrom of cacophonous thought that our thinking minds create, especially in response to the arising of an emotional state. As our mind-wisdom deepens, we can then utilise the thinking mind for wise reflection and for problem-solving when needed, rather than have it run hither and yonder thinking about things that do not need to be thought about. In this way, we learn that we can choose not to suffer.

You have a choice.

This realisation is of course not an intellectual one. It is not the product of our thinking minds, as that would just be some more thinking. Rather, it is a realisation within the mind of awareness, which is the watcher of our thoughts, not the thinker of them. It is through training the mind of awareness that we achieve this wisdom, or perhaps more accurately, we rediscover it. Reading or hearing words such as these will not get us there, as this is just one thinking mind communicating with another. It is now time to move forward to formal training of the mind.

PART TWO

TRAINING OUR MINDS

Meditation

Sitting Meditation

If you are already meditating, then you may wish to jump over or skim this part of the book, or instead you may choose to compare it with your own experience. As a meditator, you will know that my opinions on the subject are just what they are, but you may nevertheless consider it wise to take a look. Or you may not – you already know what is important. That said, it is common to find that another perspective can re-energise aspects of our own practice. Certainly, that is my own experience, and even after many years of meditation, a new tip, simile, or explanation can be the source of boundless new vitality.

There are many sources of information on how to meditate, and many techniques within these sources. They are all routes up the same mountain, and different people may favour different courses. In the next few pages, we will learn the features of a common and effective method; the very technique that the Buddha himself used. We can surely be in no better company. Since we now have a mountain analogy on the go, we may as well continue with it: we need to understand how not to get lost in the dark, we need to be properly equipped, and, as beginners, we may need a guide. We must be prepared for adverse conditions too, but these will not come from outside. Rather, the bad weather will arise within our own minds.

31

The analogy breaks down when we consider how to react to danger, because for the mountaineer the appropriate response is to engage directly with the danger and act to remove it. For the meditator, the opposite is so, and the right thing to do is simply to look away and let the danger lose interest and pass on its way. So much for analogies.

It is important to be prepared for the fact that when we meditate, the thinking mind will feel its power base threatened, and we will experience it resisting. The inner voice will become persistent. It will tell us we have better things to do and that we must not disregard its important problem-solving activities, which for some reason have to happen right now. It will suggest to us that we are bored or uncomfortable, and it will try to dwell on physical sensations that confirm this. A common trick is to try to convince us that we have only a few minutes left on our timer so we may as well get up now. It is useful to mention this now, because it contains a very valuable lesson. When there are only a few moments left on the timer, this is an opportunity for the wisdom to arise that *each of these future moments will become the present moment when it arrives, and it is only in the present moment that we can become aware.* Therefore, we should look away from the temptation to count down the remaining seconds. The moment will always be now, and if we decide to put off our meditation until another time, then that time too will be now. All we have to do is to be in the present moment.

Another key thing to impart before we get going with meditation is that when we start it is natural to be surprised by how little ability the mind has to stay focused, and we may even come to doubt that this is possible at all. The mind just keeps on going with its chatter regardless of our intention to meditate. It is common to take this personally, i.e. to think that this only happens to us, but we should not be discouraged because the mind is just going about its normal and habitual business. When the mind wanders, then the moment we realise this is actually a moment of awareness, and therefore a moment of learning. Indeed, it is a moment of enlightenment. However, it is also a trigger for one of the more persistent subterfuges of the thinking mind: telling us that we are "getting nowhere" and therefore we should stop and perhaps try again at a better time. We have to be careful of this, as the thought pattern will seek to connect with an avoidance pattern of action. It is essential to understand that *all* meditation is useful, whether it be a meditation in which we think we have "got somewhere" or one in which we feel we have not. It is also important to appreciate that thinking is what minds do – we are not trying to suppress it, just be with it, and so we should not make a drama out of it when it happens.

When the mind wanders and thought acquires primacy, at first this will be all the familiar stuff. However, as we get better at letting go, it is fascinating to observe what comes up in the mind, as things spike up from distant memory like the background radiation of the universe. As we form a new relationship with our minds, we can learn to recognise such subtle changes. The key lesson is that there is nowhere to go in meditation, and nothing to attain – all we are doing is being aware of the present moment. We endeavour to sit in *non-judgemental awareness of the contents of our minds and the sensations in our bodies,* and that is all there is to it. However, it is probably useful to start small, perhaps with ten to fifteen-minute sessions. A personal recommendation is to set a timer for sixteen minutes, and allow the first half-minute or so for any necessary postural adjustments before starting to settle the mind to allow for a quarter of an hour of quality practice.

Here are some guidelines that you may wish to consider. They are not the only way, and the intention is not to be prescriptive, but they do embody meditation techniques that are commonly practised and found to be effective. They follow a simple formula:

Ready

Set

Let go

We teach through language because that is how we communicate with each other, but please bear in mind that the intention of this teaching is to arrive at understanding through *experience*, and that the realisation we seek is not well expressed as verbal concepts. It is not our thinking minds that need to communicate with each other here, and ultimately our outer and inner voices need to become ships on the horizon. The awakening of our awareness comes through the actions that the words suggest, not the words themselves. The words are signposts, not our destination. That said, it is perhaps best to read all three sections – *Ready*, *Set* and *Let Go* – to get a feel for the whole adventure before returning to *Ready* and taking the first step. If this is your first experience of meditation, then this step may well be the most important one you will take in your life, and lead to an enduring change in your world view, and possibly even the world itself. It may be useful to cycle through the steps a few times and return to the text after each cycle.

And always remember two things: there is no such thing as a bad meditation, and your mind is just like everybody else's.

Ready

Meditation is best done regularly, ideally at least once a day, and it can be beneficial to do it at a particular time so it becomes part of a routine.

Select the place in which you will meditate. Ultimately, the hope is to be able to be mindful anywhere at all and in any circumstances, but in the beginning it will be useful to select a pleasant and peaceful place where there are minimal sources of distraction. It helps if the field of vision is uncluttered, although it is not necessary to go as far as some Zen monks who face a blank wall in meditation. That said, I personally have gained great value from that method and use it still when the alternative is to face a disorderly space. If there are objects in your field of view that the thinking mind could seize upon, then it may be best to clear them before you start. On the other hand, the presence of a few potential visual distractions does not have to be a problem. They could simply be something to work with, noticing but not reacting to the thinking mind that is telling you that if only you would get up and move that shoe or straighten that mat, *then* you would be able to get down to some proper meditation.

Formal meditation is usually done in a sitting position. There are alternatives, but let's stick with the mainstream for now, albeit with some customisation for less supple Western bodies. Clothing should be loose and comfortable. The traditional position for sitting is cross-legged on a cushion on the floor. Some bodies may not be flexible enough to adopt this position, but it is worth trying with various numbers and types of cushion before giving up entirely on it and adopting one of the alternatives below. The cushion is important to allow us to sit with our backs straight. This position is good because it is a stable position, and one that does not lead to a drop in energy levels and drifting into sleep.

Sitting cross-legged is a challenge for many or perhaps most Western adults, and there is no shame in not being able to adopt this position naturally. If you need four cushions, then so be it. I personally favour quite a substantial pile of cushions as I lack flexibility in both back and knees. An alternative is to kneel with the knees apart, place the cushions between your legs and under your backside, and then sit gently back, with the lower legs tucked under the upper legs, calves facing the backs of the thighs. In either the cross-legged or kneeling/sitting position, the higher you need your cushions, the more pressure you will place on your knees, so it may help to lay out a soft mat to give you comfort. Such a practice may in any case help you regard this as your meditation space.

These two positions are suitable because they feel dignified, resolute and appropriate for meditation. If you conclude that you are simply not made to sit on the floor in this way, then there are many types of kneeling stools available for meditators to try. These take the general form of a low bench with a tilted seat, which allows the lower legs to tuck under in a kneeling posture whilst the backside is supported by the bench. Of course, you can always sit on a chair, but if you do so then sit erect, not leaning back on a support, else you may fall asleep and ultimately experience the wrong sort of awakening! A cushion set between the base of your spine and the chair can help maintain the spine erect and encourage the body not to relax back into the chair. The goal is not to be uncomfortable, but it is beneficial to adopt a posture that is not your usual position for sitting in comfort. Whatever sitting position you settle upon, all is well; the quality of the mindfulness does not derive from the sitting position. Some people may find it helpful now and again to visualise themselves as being like a mountain in their sitting position, a simile that is useful for the meditator to feel stable, grounded, strong and resolute.

What to do with the hands? Much is written about the symbolic meaning of hand positions in meditation, but it is not really all that important to the experience. The key thing is that you are sitting in a position that you associate with a feeling of being settled, resolute and open. One good position for the hands is to rest one on top of the other in your lap with the palms facing up. If you can associate the upward facing palms with a feeling of receptiveness then that is a helpful thought. A good alternative is to rest them on your knees with your palms downward.

What to do with the eyes? Open or closed? Staring out or down? Many meditate with their eyes closed, many with their eyes open and lowered. As usual, there is no right way or wrong way. As this book is based on personal experience, then the suggestion would be to meditate with the eyes open, and the gaze lowered and fixed a few feet away. That said, the first several years of my meditating life were spent meditating with eyes closed. Closing the eyes can present more of a challenge to those prone to dozing off. It may be that in deep meditation the eyes naturally start to close without our willing it, perhaps stopping before being fully closed, or perhaps closing completely. This can cause a flurry of thought and lose the precious concentration that has been gained – Am I falling asleep? Should I open my eyes again? If it happens, just let it happen and be mindful of your energy and resolve, so that you are alive to the difference between deep meditation and sleep. Don't worry, there is no mistaking the vibrant energy of true awareness, and it certainly feels nothing like sleepiness. If your eyes are closed and you feel truly awake, then it is unlikely that you are asleep. Meditation is about developing wisdom rather than rules, so use your best instinct to work out what is best for your own practice. Trust yourself.

If when meditating with the gaze lowered, a feeling of drowsiness arises that you cannot master by stirring up energy, then it may help to raise the gaze a little. It may also help to observe the body to see if it has slumped, and if so, straighten up. Note that if you do find yourself in this state, you should be aware that the thinking mind will take the opportunity to distract you with some self-reproach or a judgement that this is a poor meditation. As usual, note the thoughts and let them pass on their way.

Adopt your sitting position. Set yourself a timer, preferably one with a pleasant alarm tone so you are not shocked out of meditation. Some meditation apps are available which have beautiful bells and gongs, so there are good alternatives to being jolted out of your meditation by loud and insistent squawking and beeping. The reason it helps to use a timer, rather than consult a watch or clock, is that we are training ourselves to let our thoughts go rather than instinctively follow them, and that needs to include thoughts about consulting our timepiece. The child's persistent question on the family outing "Are we there yet?" is never too far from the surface in later life!

It helps at this point to remind yourself of your resolution to orient your life towards mindfulness through this practice. The practice requires effort and energy, and in order to stir up such vigour it is important to develop a firm resolve. Without such resolution, the mind will always continue to wander. To achieve the one-pointed awareness we are striving for, the mind needs to be directed. Such direction will require our continued effort, although as we advance this effort will become more natural, and indeed will become self-generating and self-sustaining.

The word "effort" sometimes has a negative connotation, but this is only so when we see the source of that effort as being finite and limited. Many of life's most pleasurable activities require effort, but we do not regard them as a struggle because there is abundance in the energy that sustains them. As ever, the thinking mind is the root of the problem here, and psychologists have consistently shown that tasks regarded as effortful are fatiguing, whereas those where we are "in the zone" are not. If the thinking mind suggests that we do not want to do something then suddenly we perceive our resources as limited and we dwell in feelings of lethargy and fatigue. Meditation teaches us not to listen to the thinking mind's ruses, and as a result energy naturally arises. Meditation will lead to feelings of happiness and elation during the practice itself, and then will infuse contentment and equanimity into our daily lives. It is not to be viewed as an obligation like running on a treadmill, but a joy like staring at the stars on a clear night. To think that it is a chore is, of course, just some thinking and as such we are free to choose to ignore it. A common way to drain our energy for the practice is to worry that we are not meditating enough.

Set

Many find it beneficial and effective to spend the first two or three minutes or so establishing the right mindset for meditation. Here, I propose a seven-step technique that helps prime the mind appropriately. The beauty of this technique is that the seven steps can remain the same throughout our practice as it matures, and as our wisdom deepens, each can acquire more meaning and become more personalised. They can also be modified or compressed to suit our deepening experience, but this is a topic for later. Before we go through these steps and how to apply them, here is a summary of them:

1. Cultivation of gratitude for the opportunity to nourish yourself in this way
2. Cultivation of gratitude for the meditation practice itself
3. Generation of positive mental energy towards yourself
4. Generation of positive mental energy towards others
5. Generating forgiveness of others

6. Generating forgiveness of self
7. Resolving to let go

Let us now go into each step. Note that along the way the voice in your head might try to throw in an alternative thought, because you are challenging its hold on your mind. Just note any thoughts, don't pick them up. Show them no interest and let them pass on their way. In time you will start to notice themes in these thoughts and can use these as a basis of deepening your practice as you learn more about your thinking mind and its habits.

1. Reflect for a short while on a thought along these lines: "I am grateful for the opportunity to nourish myself in this way." Try to add a feeling of gratitude during this thought, using what you have learnt in the exercises with the sensation store.

2. Reflect further: "I am grateful for the privilege to be able to use this wonderful means of practice." Again, try to *feel* this gratitude. If you already have experience on the path and have reason to be grateful to any teachers, or to the Buddha himself, then visualising those teachers is useful, as long as you remain aware that attachment to teachers ultimately will not be helpful, as this is *your* path.

3. Turn your attention to your breathing, and for a few breaths reflect thus:
    On the in-breath, reflect, "I nourish myself."
    On the out-breath, say inwardly, "I smile", and think a smile.

41

4. Then for a few more breaths:

> *On the in-breath,* reflect, "I nourish others."
>
> *On the out-breath,* say inwardly, "I smile."

Start by bringing to mind others in your immediate vicinity, whether human or other beings, then progressively widen your perspective to encompass those further afield, and eventually all beings. At the same time as you are verbally projecting this nourishment, try to generate a feeling of the wellbeing that you wish to others. Wishing others to be free from suffering and to find their own path to happiness is not the same as liking or loving them – you are not being asked to be insincere here! In addition to thinking a smile, it may help to add a visualisation of this positive energy emanating from you and encompassing those to whom you are projecting nourishment. Light is a useful visualisation – you choose the colours!

5. For a few more breaths:

> *On the in-breath,* "I forgive others."
>
> *On the out-breath,* "May they be happy", or "I smile" if that feels better.

It can be a good practice here to allow to come to mind somebody with whom you have had recent conflict. Don't spend time in searching for somebody or in thinking, just allow them to come to mind. Note that by saying that you forgive them you are not saying that anything they may have done has your approval; you are just saying that you bear them no ill will. When you do this, you will inevitably feel some resistance to forgiveness now and again, but you know the drill by now – just note the resistance and let it pass.

6. And then for a few more breaths:
    On the in-breath, "I forgive myself."
    On the out-breath, "I smile."
    A key principle is to treat ourselves gently. Often it is said that we need to treat ourselves in the way that a parent may treat a child. It is not a crime to have a naturally restless mind, and so nor is it an occasion for reproach if we fall prey to sloth and torpor and do not get round to meditating. Each moment is a new moment, and we need to forgive ourselves for our imperfections, turn away from any self-criticising thoughts, and re-establish ourselves within our practice.

7. Finally, for a few more breaths, rehearse inwardly your resolution to let go. As insight develops, the nature of your resolve is likely to change, but for now it may be most effective simply to say inwardly, "I will let go", summoning up a feeling of deep determination.

There is a strong theme of conscious and deliberate wishing within the *Set* stage of our meditation practice. Perhaps the word "willing" conveys the intent of the practice better than "wishing", in that we are actively gathering, focusing, and projecting such thoughts outwards. We will give this a name and call it *intentional willing*, as this is a very powerful meditative technique to which we will return frequently.

Our energy for intentional willing may vary from time to time, as may the degree to which we really internalise and mean what we are willing, but it will still have some effect even when it feels perfunctory. It is worth being clear here that the nature of the outcome of this practice is not intended to be some sort of supernatural effect, where the wish in some way travels to its target and has an effect there. This may indeed be possible, who knows, but that would be a benefit over and above what we are trying to establish through our intentional willing. The primary purpose of rehearsing such thoughts is so that they may become habitual, and then start finding their way into our awareness, thoughts, and actions even when we are not in meditation. For example, in a conflict situation at work the thought may come to mind that we wish our supposed assailant to be free from suffering. We are born of our thoughts and actions, and heirs of them as well, and this is a critical element of the Buddha's teaching to which we will frequently return.

Or, we may find ourselves being anxious in our daily lives and wishing we did not have a restless mind. In this case, we may remember the thought we rehearse in our formal meditation: that we forgive ourselves. We can look upon our worrying mind as just so, accept that it is as it is, and forgive ourselves. We don't need to go creating a whole identity out of these anxious thoughts ("I am anxious", or "I am a person who is anxious"), we can just see the thoughts and forgive ourselves for the fact that sometimes our thinking minds get caught up in them.

Now we are set to start the real work of letting go of the mental habits that cause our suffering. For those who are not yet experienced with meditation, it may be beneficial to do a little more to guide the mind into a favourable state, by reflecting on a couple of words of inspiration for a few breaths. At first, we will not know which words will be best to inspire us, so some experimentation may be needed. Two that may be effective are "awakening" and "aware".

"Awakening" may prove a useful word because it points to the fact that we are stirring something that is already within us, and that in doing so we are leaving something behind, which is heedlessness. "Aware" may be good because it points to the ability of the mind to know its own contents, i.e. to note the thoughts and sensations that are arising and ceasing. This reflection may provide a valuable "bridge" for beginners between the resolution to let go, and the actual practice of doing so.

Note that all of the above is offered merely as a guideline and starting point to set the mind. You may choose to modify it to suit your preferences, but of course you should do so after first reflecting to determine whether your choices are wise, or are just more delusions of your thinking mind.

Let Go

Meditation is about *letting go* and really nothing more. Letting go is the motive force behind the whole of the Buddha's path to liberation. Letting go essentially means withdrawing our interest from the reactions of our thinking minds to events that arise at our senses and thoughts that arise in our minds. We include mind here as the sixth sense organ, just as the Buddha did in his psychological teachings. In the same way that the eye has "sight objects" as the mental representation of things in the outside world, the mind has "mind objects", which are the judgements, images, memories, thoughts, and patterns of thoughts that arise in our minds. Some of these mind objects arise in response to something we perceive through our five physical senses, and some arise from within the mind itself. So, letting go means not getting caught up in the events within our minds, or in the sensations within our bodies. A potent image in Buddhist symbology is the conscious mind as a monkey, constantly leaping from one attractive thing to another. The monkey needs to be tamed and taught to be restful.

The concept of a pattern or constellation of thoughts is an important one, and is a fundamental concept in the Buddha's model of mind, which we will examine at length in due course. Our thinking minds naturally develop habitual ways of thinking, in which one thought inevitably leads to a group of related thoughts. These thoughts come as a package, travel as a herd, and are difficult to divide. Meditation lets us break the bonds in such a way that one thought doesn't stimulate a torrent of others. As we have already discussed, some patterns of thought can be damaging to us, and habitual thinking is the root of the problem. Without awareness, we fail to see the humble beginnings of a damaging chain of thoughts, and that each link in the chain represents a choice.

So *how* do we let go? Experienced meditators can do this by simply setting their minds in non-judgemental awareness, where all thoughts and sensations are allowed to be, and are neither judged nor followed. The terms *choiceless awareness* and *vipassana* are often used to describe this type of meditation. However, for inexperienced meditators, this is generally not the best place to start. The basic technique that we are about to learn was the very method the Buddha used in becoming enlightened, and even time-served meditators will frequently return to it, assuming that they ever chose to depart from it. It is the fundamental and universal tool in the meditator's toolbag, and a common view is that it is actually the only tool that is needed.

The essential and indispensable technique is to use a *meditation object* to focus the mind. When the mind is fully focused on the meditation object, it does not react to those things that impinge on the six senses. To attempt to focus on the present moment in all its glory is too tall an order, so we focus the mind on something more straightforward and easy to acquire. The most common meditation object used is awareness of the breath. This sounds incredibly dull and boring, but it is extraordinarily effective, and by no means uninspiring when observed in the right way.

The breath is very suitable because it is always there and is not something we create within in our minds to give us a focus. It is also experienced over quite a large part of the body, so is simple to find. In these respects, the breath is a meditation object that is relatively easy to acquire and to sustain, and equally it is clear when it has disappeared from focus. The idea of the breath as a life force is also beneficial to meditation practice, as is its position in the centre of the dignified sitting posture that we adopt. Far from being dull, the breath becomes interesting and bright as the practice develops, and eventually becomes a peaceable and serene place of abiding to which we find ourselves naturally attracted. We already owe the breath a debt of gratitude for nourishing us physically, and as we progress on our meditation path we will learn a new cause to give thanks.

So let's set off. To acquire the meditation object, we turn our attention to the physical sensation of the breath. Many meditation guides will say something like "at the point at which the breath is most noticeable to you", for example at the nostrils, or in the rising and falling of the diaphragm, or in the filling and emptying of the chest cavity. One view is that the closer the point of concentration is to the place that we experience the mind, the better. This view may favour experiencing the breath in the nostrils and throat. Another view is that it is best to concentrate at the furthest point from the thinking mind, and this would favour concentration on the rise and fall of the diaphragm. I mention these two opposing views to show that there is no right or wrong way to practise, and also to offer a personal preference to concentrate initially on the rise and fall of the diaphragm and the resulting filling and empting of the chest cavity. My own experience is that it is most helpful to distance the point of concentration from the seat of power of the thinking mind. That said, for the first several years of my practice I used the tip of the nose as a reference point, so my overriding opinion is that it probably does not really matter.

Try this for a while, say for fifteen minutes, after going through the *Ready* and *Set* stages described above. Try experiencing the in-breath and out-breath at various points in the body, or as a holistic experience. Whichever feels most natural, go with it and stick with it. Don't experiment too much, because this is likely to lead to unnecessary thinking. If we are focusing on the breath at the abdomen, we can feel a clear connection between the natural fall of the diaphragm and the inevitable drawing in of breath, followed by a transition into the natural raising of the diaphragm as the breath is released, and then a transition into the falling of the diaphragm again.

Be careful to focus only on the awareness of the breath, on the very sensations of the breath, not on thoughts about the breath. The thinking mind is obsessed with providing a running commentary on everything that we do, and we need to learn not to pay attention to this and just let it pass and fade naturally. It is the persistent and unbroken nature of this internal commentary that gives us the illusion that the thinking mind is self, and it is of this "self", or of this illusion of self, that we seek to let go. Another thing for us to watch out for is the thinking mind trying to seize control and make us breathe to its command. The audacity of the thinking mind here is quite preposterous, to think for even a moment that it can fool us into believing that we cannot even breathe without its intervention! Nevertheless, we will all experience this at some point and find ourselves breathing to a rhythm that is not naturally arising. When this happens, as with all things, we just notice it and let it go without judgement.

If we find ourselves passing judgement, e.g. "I should not be doing this", or "I am useless at meditation", we just notice that too without judgement and let it go. Each act of noticing is an important step on the path to our liberation; it is a moment of awareness, and its value is considerable. Our practice of meditation serves to make these moments more frequent, closer together, and longer-lasting. So, rather than judge our lack of awareness when we come to see it, instead we rejoice in our awakening in that moment, and in the next, and in the next...

Pay close attention to the sensations of the in-breath and the out-breath. How do they *really feel*? What are the precise sensations that accompany them? As the Buddha instructed his monks, "When you breathe in short, know that you breathe in short. When you breathe in long, know that you breathe in long." Just let your awareness fall into these sensations – there is no need to label them with thoughts, just experience them fully. If you are focusing on the sensations of the breath in the abdomen, let your awareness sink down there and leave your thoughts behind. Feel the sensations as being just as they are – *like this*. They are *just this way*; that is all you need to know. Don't pick up your sensations and thoughts, just leave them where they are; you don't need them. Your only goal is to let go, as you promised yourself during the *Set* phase.

Notice not just the in-breath and the out-breath, but the points at which one becomes the other. What happens at these transitions? Is there a gap, or is it a continuous feeling of flow? Don't label it with thought; just let your awareness experience how it really feels. And what of the rhythm of the breath? Observe that the rhythm is always there, waiting for your awareness to reconnect with it when your mind has wandered. Don't try to influence the rhythm in any way by breathing consciously, just let awareness sink into the rhythm that is already there.

Thoughts will arise, because thinking is what minds do. Just return to the breath when this happens. Don't pass judgement, just reacquire the meditation object. If the thoughts are of a particular type such as worrying, judging, or daydreaming, then it can be helpful to note this with a word spoken internally ("worrying"; "judging") as you gently return your attention to the breath and let the thought pass and fade. Don't engage in self-admonishment for your loss of concentration, because the thinking mind is just doing what it habitually does. It is perfectly natural to become lost in thought. It is not at all useful, but it is completely ordinary.

It is worthy of frequent emphasis that each time you

become aware that you are thinking, you are growing as a meditator and as a being, and this is why there is no such thing as a bad meditation. When this happens, it is the mind of awareness emerging from behind the clouds of your thinking. It is important to internalise such analogies in order to focus the mind on where it is going, not where it has been. In noticing your mind thinking when it should be concentrating on the breath, you have become aware of and detached from the contents of your mind, which is exactly what you set out to do at the beginning of your practice. There is no "way it is supposed to be" in meditation, there is just the way it is. Remember how during the Seven Steps you generated forgiveness for yourself? Well, what you are forgiving yourself for is the habits of your mind. Your mind may be an anxious mind, an angry mind, a daydreaming mind – whatever, it matters not. All that matters is to notice your thinking, and return to the breath.

Sometimes the thoughts in your mind may be reactions to physical sensations that arise from perceived discomfort in the body whilst sitting still. This too is usual and ordinary, but be aware that the crafty thinking mind will seek to direct your attention to minor aches or itches in order to try to get you to stop meditating and start thinking. You need to use some skill here, but in general it is appropriate just to note the physical sensation as being just as it is, and let it be until it passes, *which it inevitably will*. It is essential to cultivate this insight – even the most intense itch or twinge will just pass if it is not nourished with the energy of our attention. The only way to learn this is to experience it firsthand. When we rise from a period of formal meditation, it is instructive to look back and remember just how much larger than life that itching sensation on the forehead or pain in the knee felt at the time. But where did it go? At the time it bothered us so much that we lost our concentration, and yet although we did not scratch the itch or move the knee the sensation left all on its own.

The thinking mind has a tendency to regard discomfort as *permanent*, and this is the foundation of the tower of resistance that the mind then begins to build. The judgement of permanence is intimately bound with making the feeling into a self – "I am this discomfort" – and in this way it dominates our experience of the world. Try to sit through any perceived irritation in the resolute knowledge that it will pass, and notice too how it comes and goes rather than stays constant.

You are not your discomfort.

This is not to say that meditation is about endurance. Sometimes, if pain is significant, it is wise to change position. Meditation on the sensations of pain can be useful, but is a more refined practice that need not concern us here. The occasional change in posture is perfectly acceptable, as long as we do it wisely. If the body slumps in meditation, it is always sensible to revise the posture to become more upright. There is sound reason for this, as it makes us more energised and less prone to drowsiness. So too should there be a wise basis for other changes of posture, and here we should note that we will not penetrate the true nature of suffering without experiencing a little of it, and that wisdom does not arise from restless fidgeting.

An important distinction here is between endurance and *patient endurance*. With practice, you will learn to apply the distinction effortlessly, but at this point some explanation is appropriate. If you are sitting in an uncomfortable position and a part of your body is telling you so, then this feeling of discomfort will present itself to your mind. We will go deeper into this later in the book, but with all feelings there are four distinct aspects:

1. *The raw sensation itself*
2. *An evaluation* – a feeling of pleasantness or otherwise
3. *A discrimination* – labelling it, for example, as stiffness or pain
4. *A reaction* – an instinctive response, such as to move away from pain

When discomfort or pain arises, try to greet it as just a sensation in your body, perhaps welcoming it with the thought "This is a sensation in my physical being in this moment." Most thoughts and feelings will just pass away on their own and we do not need to get involved to make them subside. If pain or discomfort is more persistent, then it may be appropriate to change position mindfully, but always do this without dwelling in judgement of yourself about whether this is the right thing to do. With practice, we can come to embrace these sensations and even feel some gratitude for their ability to teach us about their nature. Although the term "patient endurance" is common in Buddhist literature, the term *patient forbearance* is better, as it implies less resistance. A point that we will return to is that dealing with the body's niggles is a walk in the park compared to those of the mind.

Note that a ruse of the thinking mind regarding discomfort is to invent stories around it. For instance, if you are experiencing numbness in a leg, then the thinking mind might tell you that you have cut off your blood supply and are in danger of needing your lower leg amputated. Just note the story as a parent would note the fantasies of an imaginative child, and let the thoughts be as they are until they dissipate naturally. It is highly unlikely that you are in any immediate danger – there have been no amputations to my knowledge directly resulting from meditation!

On emerging from sitting meditation, it is helpful to generate a feeling of thankfulness towards yourself and the practice. You have just done something meritorious, and that should be acknowledged. Some may find that a helpful gesture of respect and gratitude is to raise the hands in *anjali* to the heart or to the brow. In *anjali*, the palms are pressed together with the fingers pointing up, as if in prayer. If the association with religious practice bothers you, then don't do it – it is the gratitude, not the gesture itself, that matters. The Buddha made this gesture to the tree at whose foot he had sat before his enlightenment, and this image may best frame the meaning of the action and break the religious connotation. Of course, thoughts about *anjali*, about the practice of meditation, or indeed about anything else are not what matters for you to make progress.

Keep Letting Go

Once you have learnt to let go of your thoughts, even if only for a fleeting moment, then all that remains to do is to keep doing this until it becomes instinctive. Then you will be able to concentrate for longer periods and more readily notice when your mind has strayed from your meditation object. As this happens, the benefits will start to come, satisfaction will deepen, and this will naturally feed the improvement in your practice. Keeping letting go will become natural and self-sustaining.

A very powerful way to enhance your practice is to train your mind to regard the breath as a joyful place for the mind to abide. The nature of the thinking mind is not to rest in any state, but to wander. It seeks out those things that give energy to its wanderings, such as sensual pleasure, worry, planning and so on. Such things are like food to the thinking mind, and when starved of them its ability to suppress our natural awareness becomes weakened. The untrained mind will regard awareness of the breath as unsatisfying and so will tend to draw away from it and towards the thought energy it craves, but by cultivating enjoyment of breath awareness you can bring the mind back to it more easily.

So now you are sitting, focusing your mind on the breath, with your mind momentarily still and peaceful because it is abiding in a joyous place and is not being distracted by thought. If you have reached this point, even for an instant, then the wheel has turned for you. Then you notice that you have lost concentration and have been worrying about something, planning some future event, or reacting to some physical or mental discomfort. If you have trained your mind to regard the breath as a joyful place of abiding, then you will *want* to bring your mind back to this place.

This is not a mere meditator's trick. In doing this you are not fooling your mind to think that the breath is an exalted abiding place, and thereby creating an artificial association between meditation and pleasure. On the contrary, the breath genuinely *is* a joyful place for your awareness to dwell and you will start to see the empty protestations of the thinking mind as just so. Silently comparing the peace and delight of awareness to the turgid ratiocination of the thinking mind is an opportunity for the deepest learning imaginable.

Nor is it an escape to rest within the joy of awareness. Even if we are at a point in our lives where we need to use our thinking minds a great deal for solving a particular set of problems, we will still benefit immeasurably from grounding ourselves in this way. Indeed, it is especially at these points in our lives that meditation can be most valuable. As your meditation practice deepens, you will start to notice a natural joy arising in your mind. This is your true and underlying nature, the very elation that you touch when you are awestruck. It is pure awareness, boundless and deeply satisfying. The tendency we all experience is to react to this bliss with thinking and judging, at which point it vanishes and we become lost in our thoughts again. This is because our thinking minds try to take control of the pleasure we feel, labelling it, judging it, analysing it, and thereby extinguishing it. This is the normal and natural behaviour of our thinking minds, and our practice must now focus on keeping letting go at the very point that we realise we have initially let go. It is especially at this vulnerable point that we need to learn to let go of thought.

The next frontier is to learn simply to be aware of the joy of awareness and let it be as it is, just as we let any thoughts in our mind be as they are. By not grasping at the feeling with thinking, it is left to develop on its own.

Thinking and pondering are still very much present at this stage, but they are detached and free-floating, and they are not fed with the energy of thinking.

And Keep On Letting Go!

It is essential that we do not regard our formal meditation practice as disconnected from the rest of our daily lives. Certainly it is different, but its purpose is to train our minds for all eventualities, not just what happens to us when we are sitting on our cushions. Being wise and aware when we are sitting in meditation is a beginning, but counts for little if its lessons are not applied in our everyday activities. Furthermore, managing our thinking minds in sitting meditation is considerably more straightforward than doing so when in the thick of everyday working and living.

An analogy that has been used by others compares the formal and informal aspects of meditation to the two legs we use to support us when walking freely. According to this analogy, formal meditation is like one of these legs. Without the other leg, our motion is circular and unsupported. The other metaphorical leg is the awareness we bring into our daily lives, and once this is present our locomotion is balanced and purposeful. It is essential to understand at a deep level that *all* of our time should be used for mindfulness practice, not just the part spent in formal seated meditation. There are opportunities for learning and understanding in all that we do, and in all that we do not do. It is said that the great Thai forest monk Ajahn Chah would judge his disciples not so much on how well they were meditating, but how well they dealt with busy celebration days in his monastery when huge and noisy crowds of people would visit.

Bringing mindfulness into our daily lives can be a challenge, because there are so many sources of distraction and so many openings for the thinking mind to seize control and suffocate our awareness with an impenetrable veil of commentary and irrelevant chatter. Not for nothing did the Buddha describe the household life as a "jungle", with creepers of craving constantly seeking to grasp at us. You should seek always to reserve a part of your attention to be aware of what you are doing, and to watch out for the ruses of the thinking mind. For much of the time, to do this may require more mental discipline than you can muster, and therefore you need to be resourceful about how you may remind yourself to be mindful. Your own inventiveness is your only limitation here.

Here are ten ideas that I personally have experienced to be useful:

1. Frequently pause to engage in short periods of meditation in between your daily activities. You don't need to go anywhere, just pause and lower your gaze or close your eyes. A few minutes is sufficient. If you really don't have a few minutes, then one minute will still be helpful. If not one minute, then a few seconds.
2. Turn your attention to the sensations in your body when your mind is busy. Indeed, keep your attention on the sensations of the body as much as possible regardless of what is going on in your mind.
3. Frequently call up feelings of happiness and awareness from your sensation store.

4. Practise flipping between sensations from your sensation store to remind your mind and body that sensations are separate from thoughts.

5. Put things in your way that may bring you up short and remind you to be mindful. A Post-it note with a suitable message attached to a mirror works well. You choose the message; perhaps something along the lines of "Breathe", or "Awaken". Perhaps a simple "!" or "?" would be enough.

6. Make a change to your habits so that each time you encounter your usual response you are reminded to be mindful. Giving up something that you like is a good technique, particularly if it is something that is bad for your mind and body. Total renunciation is an option, but setting limits will also work. Caffeine drinks and alcohol are good candidates here.

7. Another good renunciation skill concerns the use of speech, as speech and thought are intimately linked. Try renouncing gossiping or speaking badly of others. Tell others what you are doing if you feel that they have expectations of you that you would prefer not to meet. Speak little for a while – no meditation master will ever advise you that you are not speaking enough!

8. Ask yourself frequently, "What is the truth of how I feel?" For example, why do you think you feel jealous, afraid, anxious, or angry? Sometimes you may be able to answer such a question honestly and learn something new about yourself, but at other times the main benefit may simply be to interpose a gap between feeling and thought, or between thought and action, or between thought and feeling.

9. Use objects with which you are in regular sense contact
   to inspire you. This may be a picture in your house or
   on your desk, or your own personal interpretation of
   a knotted handkerchief. I will share some examples
   that I use, although we are all different and my choices
   may serve only to amuse you: I have a pair of Buddha
   cufflinks; I have a small Buddha statue in my line of
   sight in my car; and in certain social situations that I
   find difficult, I wear a bracelet with an inscription that
   inspires me.

10. Resolve to notice things more as you go about your
    business. Don't just strive to get from A to B –
    experience the journey. If you are walking outside, are
    you aware of all the trees that you pass? Are there birds
    in the sky? Consider some of these things more closely
    to notice more about them. Touch a tree – go on, just
    let the feeling of embarrassment go if others are
    looking. How does it feel? Is it warmer than you
    expected? Try to see things just as they really are, as if
    you are looking at them for the first time, but without
    any need to judge or categorise.

Regardless of how busy you really are, or how busy your
thinking mind is telling you that you are, it is important
always to bear in mind that when we are at our most busy
and agitated, this is precisely the time that mindfulness
will help us most. Even if you can only manage a short
meditation, do it. A useful tip is to do it after you have just
taken a lavatory break – you are never too busy to do *that*,
now, are you?

Walking Meditation

If you have ever visited a Buddhist monastery, you may have seen monks endlessly walking back and forth, along paths worn into the ground by their footsteps. This is walking meditation. Some monks will do this for several hours at a time. The Buddha was an advocate of this practice and indeed his own walking path is still visible at the place of his enlightenment in Bodh Gaya, northern India. As with meditation on the breath, if the technique was good enough for the Buddha, then it is surely good enough for us.

Although the breath is an excellent meditation object, it is not the only way, particularly when our energy is low or we are feeling drowsy. When tiredness and lassitude have us in their grip, a form of practice that energises the body may be helpful, and here walking meditation can be effective. A more physical form of meditation is also useful when we are at the other end of the spectrum of mental energy, feeling agitated and unable to settle. In such circumstances, we can find ourselves exerting too much mental effort to focus on the breath, which further stirs up our aroused state. Here, expending energy through walking may help allow the mind to settle.

Walking meditation is not just an antidote to problems of too little or too much energy, but is also a useful technique in its own right. Essentially, walking meditation is about focusing the mind fully on the act of walking. That is actually as complete an explanation as any, but some practical advice may help clarify. As before, the *Ready, Set, Let Go* formula is used.

Ready

Choose a secluded and reasonably flat area for a path of twenty paces or so. It is important that the path is not in too stimulating an environment, such as a public place. The length of the path you choose to walk is not critical, but you should select a length that allows you a chance of being mindful for its entire duration. The Buddha's own path that has been preserved in Bodh Gaya is seventeen paces, so there is no better starting point to try than this. Decide how long you will spend in walking meditation and set a timer on your person which will gently alert you when you have reached the end of the session. As with sitting meditation, the goal is not staying power; in meditation, quality is always more important than quantity.

Stand facing your path, and clasp your hands in front of you. The position of the hands is not critical or symbolic in any way, but holding them like this is a practical technique used by monks to give a posture that is different from going for a stroll. It is also a pose that has a feeling of purposefulness about it, and it helps to visualise it in this way. Lower your gaze to a few steps in front of you. Whilst you are walking you need to see where you are going, but also need to avoid unnecessary peripheral stimulation from your environment. Now you are ready.

Set

The suggested method of setting the mind for meditation is the same whether sitting or walking, and hence the techniques already described are appropriate here. It is important to set a mind of gratitude, positivity, forgiveness and resolve in order to benefit most from any meditation practice. Just as this resolve transmits itself into the "mountain" pose of the sitting practice, so too can it inform a determined bearing in walking.

Let Go

Start to walk at a relaxed pace, being fully aware of each step, until you reach the end of your path. Some people slow down their natural pace considerably, but this is probably unnecessary. Reducing your pace a touch is likely to be beneficial, so you can fully focus on the sensations of walking. It is unlikely that a faster pace will be favourable, although there are some that find it so. Feel free, therefore, to find your own pace.

Focus first on the sole of one of your feet. Notice fully the sensations there. Consider the feeling as the heel area strikes the ground. Observe then the roll of the foot towards the placement of the ball of the foot to leave the ground, maybe with a slight clench of the toes. Do this for a while focusing on one foot, until you are ready to concentrate on both feet together. When you are ready, move your attention into both feet and feel the ever-changing sensations there.

It is worth sticking with this basic method until you are well-practised at calming your thinking mind and settling into the mind of awareness whilst walking. Once you feel ready, move your attention into the feeling of the bones and muscles in the feet, and then up the legs.

Observe how the legs work together. Notice whether there is a time when both feet are on the ground, for instance. At this point, you may notice thoughts of wonder pass through your mind; how amazing it is that we can perform such a complex action. As usual, just let thoughts pass on their way, even when they are pleasing.

When you reach the end of your path, stop, turn mindfully, and then pause to examine the contents of your mind. If your mind has wandered, re-establish your awareness and resolve, set off again, and keep walking mindfully up and down your path like this until your timer tells you that you are done. Again, at the end of a period of formal meditation, it is helpful to generate gratitude towards yourself, the practice, and the path that has hosted you. If a gesture of *anjali* feels appropriate, then allow yourself to do that simultaneously. Perhaps a bow of respect may seem to be in order, but of course the gesture does not matter if the sentiment is there.

Those are the basics of walking meditation. Of course, walking is an activity that occurs naturally and frequently in our everyday lives, so it is highly useful to be able to bring mindfulness to it whenever we do it. It complements sitting meditation in that it is more active and involves more sensory input, and therefore presents a different challenge to mindfulness. There are other physical meditative techniques, and I confess with due respect to the Buddha that I find yoga to be more beneficial than walking meditation, and sitting to be better than anything. The important thing is to find the path that works best for *you*, and whether that be walking, yoga, tai chi, or whatever else, it matters not, as long as it is done with maximum mindfulness. As we will learn in the next section, we need to be resourceful in our mindfulness practice, because the ingenuity of the thinking mind in dulling our awareness can seem to be without limit.

Reflection

It is essential not to throw the baby out with the bathwater by believing that all thinking is problematic. Indeed, we have already discussed the fact that the Buddha included "investigation of mental states" amongst the seven factors of enlightenment. Certainly, the thinking mind is the root of our suffering, but it is also part of the means of our liberation, and this is what makes the path to liberation so subtle and challenging. Of course, meditation is not targeted at destroying the thinking mind, or even at silencing it, but rather at developing insight about it. The Buddha taught that thinking can be a powerful means of developing wisdom, if used skilfully. Such thinking is specifically targeted at the truth of our thoughts and behaviour, at seeing through our delusions, and ultimately at unravelling the knots of thought that we create. The Buddha compared wise reflection to seeing the mind as if a mirror were held to it, and stressed the importance of maintaining this view at all times, not just when we are meditating.

Clearly, there is care needed here if we are to use the thinking mind to solve a problem that it creates itself. Although science generally accepts that the mind can be used to understand itself and the world at large, it does seem rather curious that we accept this so readily. In fact, let's not beat about the bush, it is ridiculous. At best, to do this is a potential source of confusion, but at worst it can lead to perilous delusion. Often we may think we are sitting in contemplation of some important aspect of our human condition, whereas in fact we are just brooding unhelpfully on our perceived problems, which are probably for the most part created by our minds anyway.

It is appropriate, therefore, to be cautious at first when using wise reflection. The key is always to know that we are thinking, to know what we are thinking about, and to know why we are thinking about it. Not just to have a superficial view, but truly to *know*. This may sound somewhat trite, but it is extremely potent. The reason we need to be ever-vigilant is that our thinking minds can run away with themselves and take us to all sorts of places we do not need to go. It is no coincidence that we have several words in our language to describe out-of-control thinking: daydreaming, reverie, brooding, fantasising, and perhaps even the vacuous modern word "chilling". Being vigilant means that there should always be a part of the mind that is watching, and therefore that we should never give ourselves over completely to thinking. It is this detached watchfulness that is the awareness that we are cultivating through meditation. Once we get the hang of it, our lives are fundamentally changed.

Using wise reflection, we will come to notice that really quite a lot of our everyday thinking is pointless, and much of it is actually harming us. For instance, a strong habit of mind is fear. Here, the mind will present us with various hypothetical scenarios for us to consider, stirring up further alarm and dread, and thereby inciting more and more terrifying imaginary states to present themselves in our minds. The resultant terror may start merely as feelings of tension in our bodies, to which our thinking minds add habitual escalating chains of thought. Or, it may start as a fleeting and isolated worrying thought, to which the thinking mind adds self-perpetuating cycles of apprehension. We can use wise reflection to diffuse this by observing the process at work, and this is where meditation helps us in identifying sensations and thoughts at their point of origin. In addition, we can reflect upon how often in our lives the dreaded scenarios actually come to pass. In the vast majority of cases, the answer will be that they do not occur at all, and what actually does happen is nowhere near as bad as our minds imagine. We can begin to learn, therefore, the true value of worry.

Another habit of mind is rehearsing conversations we are going to have with others, particularly when the exchange is likely to be emotionally charged. Because conversation involves other parties who will not behave exactly as we expect, the chances of the conversation going the way we have planned it are near zero. As soon as the actual conversation starts, we will find ourselves working without a script. These are opportunities to use wise reflection to determine the usefulness of such musing, and indeed the extent to which we can predict and control the future.

A related habit of mind is talking about our problems to others, and this too is worthy of closer scrutiny. Certainly, there are occasions when an earnest discussion with a close friend may help us get a different perspective on problems we are working through, and sometimes it may help us to share a burden with someone we trust and who may be able to help. However, generally when we talk about our problems we are not doing anything nearly so constructive, and actually we are merely telling somebody our problems in order to be able to keep thinking and talking about them. Our thinking minds like to brood on problems, deluding us into thinking we are solving them, but actually they are just rehearsing them and making us feel worse. In general, if thinking or talking about problems is not related to an action that we are immediately about to take to bring about a resolution, then it is likely that the thinking is doing nothing other than lowering our mood. In such a case, we should perhaps question why we are doing it, but certainly we should let the thoughts pass and not take an interest in them. If we lack the resolve to do this, simply distracting ourselves is good enough. This is a perspective that psychologists are now using in the treatment of patients with depression.

The most powerful use of wise reflection is to direct it at determining the truth of our feelings. Whatever we are feeling, we simply ask ourselves what is the truth of that feeling. It may be best to start with a feeling where the passions are not overly aroused, such as boredom. Here, we would ask ourselves what it really means to be bored, and why we judge that to be undesirable. What is it really *like*? What is wrong with the present moment that requires us to be distracting ourselves from it? The answers we find through investigating such questions can be illuminating. Boredom is actually nothing more than thoughts about boredom, and as such it has neither substance nor guaranteed future. There may be some physical sensations associated with the perception of boredom, but in and of themselves they do not amount to much, and may be judged differently without the thoughts.

A note of caution is that in order to use wise reflection skilfully, we need to be gentle with ourselves, and again the analogy of the parent-child relationship is useful. When we uncover a truth about ourselves by reflecting on our thoughts or behaviour, this is an opportunity for compassion and forgiveness, not for self-reproach. For example, if we find ourselves getting angry or defensive, we may find the answer in our past, for example in playground humiliation or in aspects of our upbringing. Or, we may come to realise we have a problem with an addiction, whether to something physical like alcohol or something more cerebral like praise. We may not be able to penetrate all of our emotional responses in this way, but it will be revealing nevertheless to determine which of our habitual responses are the most resistant to such scrutiny.

In his bestselling book *The Power of Now*, Eckhart Tolle introduces the evocative concept of a *pain body*. He explains that as we go through our lives we accumulate pain, and we carry this pain with us, adding to it as we go. He suggests that the pain body is inside of us, and can be activated by any stimulus that causes us emotional pain, at which point we add this hurt to the pain body we have been carrying around. Tolle explains that we can develop the habit of living our lives through this pain body, and that the pain body will consume us completely if we let it. He describes how it requires thinking to sustain itself, as it feeds on the energy of our thoughts. For Tolle, as for the Buddha, the remedy is to experience the present moment fully, which effectively crowds out both the thinking and the pain body. Tolle's concept of the pain body, or indeed any of Tolle's writing, is an immensely potent source of wise reflection.

Perhaps the most important point to make about the Buddha's teachings on wisdom is that it is a *process* rather than a state. The ancient Pali word that is commonly translated as "wisdom" does not have the sense of a static store of knowledge like the modern concept, but rather points to an active process of *discernment*. It is, therefore, primarily a way of seeing and relating to the world, and our store of acquired knowledge merely supports that purpose. So, one who is wise is one who discerns, who sees the true nature of things as they are actually happening in the moment. To understand after the event is a lesser attainment.

Hindrances

In this section we will explore some of the mental obstacles that can impede our progress in meditation and mindfulness. As usual, it is appropriate to refer to the Buddha's teachings, as he is surely the authoritative source. The Buddha used the term *hindrances* to describe five common mental processes that limit the essential qualities of meditation, which are *serenity* and *insight*. These hindrances arise in us all, and so it is important not to take them personally and regard them as our own failings. The hindrances are a very small aspect of the Buddha's psychological teachings, but are a perfect place to start. As we go along, we will build up a more complete picture of his analysis of the workings of mind, and in this way see the enormity of his achievement. His teaching on the hindrances, like all of his teaching, is as appropriate and full of life today as it was in his time.

In dealing with the hindrances, the first step is always the same, which is simply to note in our minds that the hindrance has arisen. The Buddha spoke of starving the hindrances of that which nourishes them, and the nourishment to which he was referring is the energy of our interest. He explained that generally we are heedless of where we let our minds wander, and through carelessly directing our attention we are allowing the hindrances to feed themselves and grow strong. When we learn to recognise what feeds our attention, both in the physical realm and the mental realm, we are on the road to starving the hindrances. This is a profound insight, and we can learn much from observing where our six senses are instinctively drawn. If we can direct our attention with care, our energies can then be used to nourish those factors that lead to our liberation. In freeing ourselves from the pull of the hindrances, we reclaim an inner peace and can behave with discernment and wisdom.

Before we consider each of the five hindrances in turn, it is important to emphasise that we should take a suitably expansive view of them. They do not just hold back our formal meditation practice, but they also impede the fruits of the practice in all aspects of our lives.

Sensual Desire

Sensual desire is a feeling of need to gratify the senses. In common usage, the word "sensual" has a strongly sexual connotation, which, although a facet of this hindrance, is by no means all of it. For example, the desire to hear something pleasant – or not to hear something unpleasant – is just as much a part of this hindrance as is the desire for sexual contact. For this reason, the more neutral term "sense desire" is also used when describing this hindrance.

Sensual desire causes arousal, and through this arousal a strong identification with self arises – *I* must have that attractive thing, or *I* must avoid that repulsive thing. This strengthening of "I" creates a feeling of a gap between how things are and how we desire them to be, and our thinking minds attempt to seize control of our behaviour to close the gap. When self-view is aroused in this way, then if we are heedless we will act instinctively, habitually and unconsciously. This is the nature of the hindrance of sensual desire.

Sensual desire can make our attention selective, reducing and distorting our experience of the world. The Buddha talked about "guarding the sense doors" to avoid stirring up sensual desire, and many of the rules of the monastic form that he defined for his monks are aimed at doing just this. For example, one rule is that a monk may not take that which is not offered, and it is clear to see that this is aimed at cutting off the instinctive reaction to certain desires of the senses, or more specifically, the desire to reach out and grasp. However, for those of us who do not live a life of monasticism and renunciation, and probably for many who do, the problem of sensual desire looms very large. Unless we are very advanced in our meditation practice, we need to accept that there will always be things that impinge on our six senses that we find pleasing, and to which we are therefore attracted and may become attached. Likewise, there will be things that we perceive to be unpleasant and to which we are therefore inclined to distance ourselves, in which case we may become attached to the absence of such things.

The Buddha's essential teaching is that it is this attachment that causes suffering. If we get what we desire, we suffer when we lose it. If we get what we do not desire, we suffer until we lose it. All things are impermanent, and therefore suffering always follows attachment. Worldly pleasure is by its nature transient, and as such is clearly a form of suffering even if it feels good at the time. If delight and dislike are absent or unheeded, then there is no bondage. That is the Buddha's teaching in a nutshell. The Buddha likened sensory desire to taking out a loan; any pleasure gained through the senses must be repaid through the suffering when the pleasure is ended and replaced with a feeling of loss.

So, we need to deal with sensual desire at the moment that it arises, and before evaluation, discrimination, conceptual proliferation, and instinctive action kick in. Sensory input is just so: it is just a set of conditions in the mind. The rest is the result of thinking and choices. Meditation is all about creating a space around the initial contact so that we let it go by without feeding it with judging, labelling, thinking, and acting. If the initial reaction happens without our mindfulness catching it, then we can catch it later in the process that leads to action. Or, if we do not manage to penetrate the cycle with awareness, then we can just observe this and bring to mind a strengthening resolve.

Meditation is a good way to learn not to react to conditions that impinge on the senses, whether they be pleasurable or otherwise. Pleasing things are easier to dismiss, for example if a dog strays past us whilst we are meditating outside we may note a loving feeling for another being and let it pass. Unpleasant things are much harder, for example if we are meditating in the early morning in a public nature spot then the dreaded fitness "boot camp" may come near, with its shrieking exhortations and whooping encouragement. We may feel irritated by this because we think they are disturbing us, but examining the truth of such a feeling will quickly lead us to the conclusion that actually *we are disturbing ourselves*. The behaviour of others is what it is, it is just so. It is what is happening in the moment, and no amount of us wishing it to be otherwise could possibly change this.

Overcoming the hindrance of sensual desire is not all about renunciation. It is perfectly acceptable to enjoy something that gives us sensory comfort, providing that we are mindful in doing it, are not attached to it, and do not fear its loss. As with all things in the Buddha's teachings, the correct way is one of balance, or the "middle way" as he called it.

Anger and Ill Will

This hindrance arises when feelings of anger, hostility and malice are directed either towards others or towards ourselves. The Buddha likened this hindrance to an illness, in that it denies us our health.

When we feel this way, our thinking minds tend to present us with a tale by which we can dwell in righteous justification of such feelings. The fabrication can be very seductive and convincing, because when we are angry or bearing somebody ill will there is a very strong feeling of a separate self. There needs to be – how can we bear somebody malice if we feel any sense of connection with them, and how can we plan their humiliating downfall without the creativity and direction of the thinking mind? Before we know it, our anger and ill will has intensified, as our thoughts feed our feelings and vice versa, and we waste our time rehearsing hypothetical scenarios in which we emerge triumphant. We may then do a lap of honour, by starting a cycle of self-reproach for not having done, or not having the courage to do, all the great deeds of revenge or malice that our thinking minds have just concocted. We may bring in other negative states such as guilt and feelings of worthlessness. Such feelings are also ill will, but in these cases are turned inwards.

When we are meditating, thoughts of anger and ill will may arise in our mind and we may become lost in them. The negativity can then spread towards the meditation itself, and we may feel that rather than meditating we should instead be doing the important work of ruminating about how we can hurt others, or indeed about actually doing them harm. Thoughts may then arise that we should stop meditating and get down to some serious plotting. What can be seen very clearly here is the hindrance working to bind us to our self-view. The anger is not self – it is something we temporarily become, and it arises as a result of a myriad of preceding conditions and responses of mind. We have a choice in how to react to all these previous conditions, although at the critical moment (now!) we may not have the awareness and wisdom to exert any choice. However, we must never lose sight of the fact that we do have a choice, in this moment and in the next.

All hindrances are overcome by being mindful and looking at the thoughts and feelings with wise awareness. Ill will has an additional remedy, which is the cultivation of opposite states: kindness, compassion, and good will. The person with whom you are angry has virtues and good qualities, in the same way that you do. They are on a path towards awakening, in the same way as you are, albeit at a different stage, maybe less advanced, perhaps more. They arrived in the moment that they hurt you as a result of the conditions in their lives up to that point, in the same way that you did. In all these respects you are not separated from them, and you share the same right to happiness and the same right for others to wish this for you. Regardless of how somebody has behaved towards you, you have no reason to wish them anything other than freedom from suffering, or if not this, the opportunity to improve themselves on their path. They may have upset you because of their own suffering, and to wish for them an end to that suffering is surely wiser than to cause them and yourself further suffering through a negative action.

Cultivation of feelings of kindness is difficult, but is essential for our own development. Developing a heart of kindness allows us to see more in another person than the specific act that caused us insult or anger, and allows us to weaken our attachment to that pain. If we refuse to dwell in ill will towards somebody, then the cycle of them hurting us further through the memory of their deeds is broken. Much of the hurt we feel regarding the actions of others is added by our minds through brooding after the event.

Feelings of kindness also need to be directed towards ourselves, because the hindrance of ill will can just as easily be turned inwards as outwards. We need to see ourselves as more than the sum of our perceived faults, and find the strength to forgive ourselves for any failings, real or merely supposed. If we can learn lessons from our mistakes and misdeeds, then this is all we need and the rest can be allowed to fade. We may do things that we do not like from time to time, and we may even do them repeatedly, but still we need to forgive and improve without abiding in ill will towards ourselves. Self-reproach and guilt serve no purpose. To regard ourselves positively is a big stretch for many of us, but it needs to be accomplished, and without conditions being attached.

Where there is ill will towards the meditation object itself, we need to work on a feeling of joy in connecting with that meditation object. If this object is the breath, then when we reunite our awareness with the breath we associate delight with that union. It is also always essential to be grateful for the point that we have reached on our path. OK, so we are not enlightened, but through meditation we are treating ourselves well and doing the best thing we can do for our own wellbeing and that of others. That is worthy of the greatest respect.

Worry and Flurry

Worry and flurry is perhaps the most evocative description of this hindrance. A longer version might be "restlessness, remorse, brooding, anxiety and worry", or indeed any list of states that stir up the mind and deny it calm. The Buddha described this hindrance in terms of the mind being like a slave that always has to jump to the demands of a domineering master who requires constant perfection. Some of us are more prone to worry than others, and there are times when we are more vulnerable to such fanciful flights of anxious thought, for instance in the middle of the night.

A defining feature of this hindrance is the tendency of the mind to move rapidly away from the present moment into trying to control imagined futures, or rerunning past events. Our minds habitually generate problems for us to consider, but only rarely are they real ones that actually need to be addressed. When our minds do this, our bodies react to provide the mood music, adding feelings of foreboding and tension to the scene playing out in our minds. Sometimes there is a genuine problem that can be straightforwardly resolved, but even then the mind may choose instead to dwell in elaborating the problem, scaring us with possible outcomes if solutions fail, or with ever more fanciful and catastrophic imagined causes of the problem that may require a more intricate form of response. Even when the problem does not yet exist, and may never exist, our thinking minds will still demand that we give thought to it, often at the expense of sleep or other acts of personal kindness.

As we have already discussed, it is important to recognise that a worrying thought, like any other thought, is just a thought. Indeed, the feeling of worry that accompanies the thought may often already be there as an unaccompanied sensation before the thought arises. Worry and flurry is a means by which our thinking minds try to convince us not to relinquish their control. They tell us that our problems, whether real or imagined, require their constant attention, at appropriate times or otherwise. Of course, the attention that the inner voice demands is always required *now*, whether or not there is an immediate problem to be solved in this moment. In following such thoughts, the present moment becomes invisible to us and we are therefore unconscious. We cannot be mindful if the mind is in turmoil with such thoughts, which in turn will stir up the bodily sensations of anxiety, which will then lead to more intense worry and flurry, and so the cycle continues. Rather than us starving the hindrance as the

Buddha instructed, we allow the hindrance to starve us of present moment awareness, and therefore of the ability to be happy, wise, and compassionate.

Again we see a hindrance binding us to a sense of separate self and to the mind object that is the hindrance. We are prey to the delusion that our problems are us, in other words. We can gain a sharp perspective on this through meditation, where we will frequently notice that we may start worrying about something, catch it and return to mindfulness, and then start worrying about something else. The worry is still there, but it has selected a different object. After meditation is over, we may not even remember what it was that we were worrying about. There can surely be few more profound, and indeed amusing, insights into the nature of mind than this. It may be worth an indulgent inner smile at this point at the foolishness of the unruly child, the thinking mind.

Turning to more practical considerations, if there is a problem to be solved, then it is always good practice to get on and solve it straight away, or if not then to decide when we are going to do so. If we do this, then nothing, *nothing at all*, is achieved by further worry and flurry. As the saying goes, there are two types of things not to worry about: those that we can do something about, and those that we can't. Careful contemplation of our worrying tendencies will show us just how often worry is useful problem-solving rather than wasted time.

There are other positive ways of dealing with worry and flurry. Just as for anger and ill will, the sensation store can be consulted to investigate the feelings and overlay them with other feelings for comparison. This is a way of training ourselves that they are not self. A more direct method can be used if we have cultivated a heart of compassion towards ourselves and are comfortable with a bit of light-hearted self-mockery. We can think a thought along the lines of "My problems are the worst that anybody has ever had throughout the whole history of human suffering." This can be an effective trick to break the cycle of worry and flurry, and may be best accompanied by thinking a smile at the same time, or even actually smiling. The chances are that the thought itself will be enough to make us smile and break the cycle of worry.

The "flurry" part of worry and flurry may be much more minor than the states of anxiety we have considered thus far. It may be simple restlessness, which can result from our thinking minds whipping us up into a state of needing to be doing something, including progressing more quickly down our path to enlightenment. As we will discuss in some detail later, there is something unique about the human condition that entails a need to feel that life is "going somewhere". Of course, restless thoughts, like all thoughts, are just thoughts, and we can be content simply to notice them. As previously noted, some walking meditation or other physical form of meditation may be a useful response to a restless mind or body.

Sloth and Torpor

This hindrance is partly about lacking motivation to meditate, and partly about feelings of tiredness that may have a real cause. The Buddha's analogy was being locked in a cramped and dark cell which prevents us from moving freely in the sunshine outside.

Sloth and torpor is a hindrance that we can expect to encounter frequently. It helps if we can learn to recognise it as a familiar friend in need of some guidance on their way, and then to show it the way and let it leave us be. We need to guard against reacting to it with aversion, because this just consumes more energy and compounds the problem. The antidote is to learn to recognise its signs, detect them early in their onset, and then stir up energy to allow us to let it dissipate.

Summoning energy is a challenging skill, and we may not always be successful. The energy needed comes from two sources, and is supported by the sensation store. The first source of the energy is our resolve. We generate this at the start of our meditation, and we can call it back to mind at times when we are flagging. The second source is the joy and loving kindness we associate with our meditation object, which potentiates an energised return to it. Outside of formal meditation, energy comes from taking an interest in the task at hand, whether it be sweeping a floor, walking between tasks, drinking a glass of water, or whatever.

With skill, the approach of sloth and torpor during meditation can be noticed by a mindful individual and headed off with a slight change of posture, or perhaps a visualisation of energy or light. The signs are easy to spot with practice, and where tiredness is only slight, the feelings themselves can be merely noted and not followed up with thoughts of how tired we feel. If drowsiness conquers us totally whilst we are sitting and we find ourselves actually falling asleep, then we need to take a different course of action, which may be to get up and do some walking meditation or yoga.

There may be genuine causes of bodily tiredness, and it is wise to avoid those that are avoidable. Just as what goes on in the body is largely attributable to what goes on in the kitchen (or sweet vending machine, or petrol station snack shop), so it is with the mind; there are certain patterns of eating and drinking that lead to a dip in energy and descent into sleepiness and low mood. This is not a book about food and nutrition, so we will leave it there with a recommendation to address these aspects of lifestyle, not necessarily to the point of complete denial, but certainly to the point of conduciveness to mindfulness. Of course, some causes of tiredness and mental dullness are deep seated, such as fever and jet lag, and in such circumstances stirring up energy for any sort of meditation is likely to be unproductive. However, wise investigation of mental states is always within our reach no matter how our bodies are feeling.

Doubt

Doubt is a very interesting hindrance in that it manifests itself in different forms at different points along the path of our practice. The Buddha likened the hindrance of doubt to being lost in a desert and not recognising any landmarks. We find our way through this wilderness by means of resolve and effort, and through the progressive improvement of our ability to identify landmarks in a terrain that at first seems devoid of them.

Initially, the object of the doubting mind may be the meditation practice itself. Is this method of mind training right for us? Does it work? Has it lost its relevance after over two and a half millennia? With some initial experience of meditation and exposure to the teachings of the Buddha, it will become clear that the path has real meaning, and this will give some impetus to our efforts to start out. As we begin to engage in regular meditation we will learn more about the nature of our minds and feel we are making real progress in managing them, and so we will leave behind our initial doubt.

When we have gained more experience with meditation, we may encounter a new set of doubts regarding whether we can ever let go of our incessant thinking and its identification with self. As the popular sound bite goes, this too shall pass. We will begin to glimpse stillness, and our ability to concentrate in that stillness will gradually improve. The doubt may still be there, but so too will there be an energy to progress that causes the doubt to recede further. It will no longer attract our interest. We will also come to realise that the path to our liberation is a *gradual* awakening, and that we experience benefit at all stages. We do not need to wait for any particular attainment before we can say that we are advancing.

Once we have glimpsed the pure awareness of the mind, the next time we encounter our doubt is highly illuminating. As we sit in meditation on the brink of letting go into stillness, our thinking mind will return and hold us on that threshold, as if fearing to let us enter. This is doubt again, but of a profoundly different kind. We will find ourselves oscillating between stillness and thought, as the thinking mind questions whether we should let go that final time and enter the state of absorption, of one-pointed concentration, or *samadhi* as it is in the language of the Buddha's time. The thinking mind is highly resistant to letting go, because it fears that in doing this it will surrender its seat of supreme power in our minds.

The way to overcome this doubt is to let go completely, but this is unlikely to happen in an instant. Each time we approach the critical point we will be able to work with letting go, and over time we will be successful, even if the thinking mind comes straight back, as it inevitably will, with commentary like "Is this it then? Am I really meditating now?" Of course, we need to learn to let go of that too. The feeling of rapture experienced in letting go even for a moment will be enough to expel the doubt and give us confidence in the path of our practice. As we have previously observed, our liberation is not an absolute that is developed in one Damascene instant, but is a vessel that fills drop by drop, to use another of the Buddha's analogies.

PART THREE

MODERN DELUSION, ANCIENT WISDOM

Going Forth

Two Men, One Goal

Now that we have experienced for ourselves, at least a little, the workings of our own minds through meditation and wise reflection, there will be a clearer insight into how the mind functions. This is the deepest sort of insight, one based on direct and personal experience rather than secondhand scholarship. With the stage now set through this refined view of our mental processes, we will now proceed to examine two very different but globally influential models of mind, each of which has had an immeasurable impact on human history. Firstly, we will consider the common model of mind that has underpinned most of Western education since the Scientific Revolution, and secondly we will explore the model that can be derived from the Buddha's original teachings. Some potentially startling conclusions may become apparent in this comparison, sufficient to doubt the value of the Western view.

Before looking closely at these differing views of mind, we will take a short but potentially illuminating historical detour into their origins. The stories of great discoveries often show interesting idiosyncrasies and similarities, and the origins of Western and Eastern views of mind do not disappoint in this regard. The model of mind that is most familiar to us in the West can be traced to the work of the man who is often called the founder of modern Western philosophy, René Descartes, a Frenchman whose most significant output was published when he was in his early forties during the first half of the 17th century. The alternative we will explore is, of course, from Siddhartha Gautama, an Indian man teaching at a similar age, almost 2,200 years previously.

It is fascinating to compare the lives of these two men in the period leading up to the insights that they were to proclaim to the world. Both started life having lost their mothers, and both had dominant and successful fathers with strong views about the futures of their sons. These early parallels may have had some influence on the destinies of these two great men, but there are three more remarkable coincidences that are particularly revealing. The first is that both men held and declared an extraordinary resolve to penetrate the nature of reality. The second is that this resolve led them to leave their homes and wander in the world in search of truth. The third is that in order to achieve their insights, the method they chose was to look deeply into their own being, because they were both resolute that within us there is a "natural light" that can become obscured.

The French philosopher and mathematician René Descartes was born in 1596 and lived to be fifty-three. He was the son of a government legal official and went to study law when he was twenty, in line with his father's wishes. He came to realise that a career in law was not for him, and that the only things he considered to be of value were philosophy and mathematics. On leaving university, he decided to join the army to see some of the world, having made a striking resolution, which he later described along these lines:

I resolved to consider no knowledge other than that which I could discover in myself or else in the great book of the world. I spent the rest of my youth travelling, visiting courts and armies, engaging with people of diverse character and rank, gathering the most variety of experiences, assessing myself in the diverse situations that fortune presented to me, and above all, always reflecting upon my experiences to secure my own improvement.

Siddhartha Gautama was born in what is now Nepal around 563BC and lived to be eighty. He was the son of the leader of a large clan, the equivalent of a county or state, and brought up in great wealth and luxury as a prince. His father, the noble Suddhodana, is often referred to in historical texts as a king, which although not strictly accurate does give a suitable indication of the opulence of the young Siddhartha's life. At the age of twenty-nine, Siddhartha also went forth from home to homelessness, or more accurately from homes to homelessness, for he had divided his time between three palaces. When he was a young boy, there had been a prophesy that he would become either a monarch of high influence or a great sage. As Suddhodana preferred the former, he shielded his son from even seeing any suffering, lest he started to question the nature of the human condition.

However, it is said that despite his father's controlling efforts, Siddhartha managed to take a few trips outside the palace and on these trips he saw how less privileged people lived. He witnessed for the first time sickness, old age, and death, and this affected him so deeply that he questioned how anybody could lead the sort of hedonistic life that he did when such suffering awaited all people. He resolved to leave home and seek enlightenment. He wandered as a beggar and an ascetic, seeking great sages, and denying himself all pleasure. After six years of this life in which he had not found what he sought, he sat down at the foot of a tree and made the following resolution, similar in nature to that of Descartes but even more passionate:

> *Let my skin and sinews and bone become dry... and let the flesh and blood in my body dry up, but never from this seat will I stir until I have attained complete and absolute wisdom.*

Cogito Ergo Sum

Modern philosophy originated in Western Europe in the 17th century. Its beginnings set the predominant psychological model in the West for the next few hundred years. Many of us will know the famous dictum associated with this point in history, "I think therefore I am", or its equally familiar Latin version "Cogito ergo sum", or "the Cogito" as it is popularly called. This phrase was coined by René Descartes in 1637.

The Father of Modern Philosophy, as Descartes has come to be called, continues to be studied in university philosophy courses almost four centuries later. His system of coordinates, now referred to as the Cartesian coordinate system, is pervasive in modern algebra, geometry and cartography, and many of his other intellectual contributions still survive today in some form. Descartes was a genius, philosopher, mathematician, physicist, visionary, and a friend of royalty. He was also a key figure in the Scientific Revolution that had begun with Copernicus a hundred or so years previously, and this is our interest here. Previously, the Scientific Revolution had been broadly confined to astronomy, anatomy, and medicine, but with Descartes came a focus on the philosophy of *mind*.

Through his writings on the mind, Descartes became the begetter of a Western intellectualist delusion that exists to this very day in our everyday view of mental life. His mathematics introduced us to the concept of the "straight curve", which is surely sufficient reason to be mistrustful of him! In general, before the time of Descartes, philosophy consisted of Christian theologians drawing on the works of Plato, Aristotle, and the writings of the Church. Descartes decided to set all of this aside and start again, dispensing with anything that could be regarded as mere belief, and accepting only that of which he could be certain. The tool he selected for this analysis was his own thinking mind, and he did not appear to question the appropriateness of this choice. His analytical method was that if he could doubt something, then he would not believe it unless it could be proven. Whether or not Descartes actually doubted that he existed is not known, but he nevertheless felt compelled to set out to prove this before moving on to anything else. One may only speculate that his assumption here was that if he did not exist then there would be no point in carrying on any further. For Descartes, if he was to reconstruct the universe based only on certainty, then his first task was to be certain of his own place within the system that he was about to recreate. He eventually arrived at his famous statement, the Cogito, as the proof of his own existence. His argument was that if he was thinking, then at that moment he must exist. Doubting his own existence actually became the proof he was looking for that he existed.

Although the Cogito has been analysed to death since it was first created, it is instructive to spend a short while exploring Descartes' reasoning, because it is so representative of Western thinking, and so diametrically opposed to the model of mind that the Buddha expounded, and which we will soon set out to explore. The Cogito is a beautifully succinct illustration of the delusional bias that exists within the thinking mind, and the very delusion that the Buddha had penetrated over two millennia before. The fact that this misapprehension emerged in Descartes' analysis is not surprising, because it is inherent in the tool of his analysis, i.e. the thinking mind itself. It may be considered strange that such a flawed model went on to become so influential, or that such a great thinker came up with it, but actually it is not so hard to explain, because this model reflects a persistent bias that exists within us all. In other words, it was there all the time.

Let us go through the Cogito piece by piece, as doing this not only reveals the misconception within it (and within untrained minds), but also helps us identify the elements of a more appropriate mental model. The first part, "I think", or perhaps better, "I am thinking", shows that the thinker "I" has an awareness of a mental process that he conceptualises as being "thinking". The important point here is that this awareness must of necessity be separate from thinking, otherwise it could not experience thinking. This awareness is what Descartes seems to have overlooked; it is the watcher, as opposed to the thinker. It is *buddho*.

The next clause begins with the logical operator "therefore", which means that a conclusion is about to be drawn on the basis of the preceding term "I think". The conclusion is the simple phrase "I am", by which he means "I exist". This statement actually contains another inference that is not stated. What has been established is not that the *thinker* exists, but rather that *thought* exists, and from this the thinker is deducing that there must be somebody there doing the thinking, and as that somebody is Descartes, then he exists. There is no comment on the awareness within which all this thinking and concluding is taking place, however. Another interesting, and again unstated, assumption of Descartes' analysis is that thought is to be believed. The idea that the thinking mind can be deluded or deluding does not seem to have been entertained by Descartes. Rather, his view was that if thinking is clear, then it is true, and much of his analytical philosophy depended on this view.

So, although it is a lot less punchy, and probably would not look too well in Latin, what the Cogito is saying is this:

I am aware of a mental process that I conceptualise as being thinking; the fact that I am aware of this thought proves that it exists; the fact that my thoughts about thinking are clear means that they are true; the fact that it is I who is doing the thinking proves that I exist.

Seemingly satisfied that he existed and could trust his thinking, Descartes then went on to build up his impressive oeuvre of philosophical and mathematical analysis, and so began what is now called Modern Philosophy. He even included a proof of the existence of

God using the same method of rational introspection based on clear perception. The fact that Galileo had been tried by the Church for heresy only three years previously no doubt gave impetus to Descartes' decision to come up with a proof of God's existence!

The Sum Total

Of course, the issue here is not whether we exist. Let's take a philosophical risk and just assume that we do, following the Buddha's example of not wasting thought on questions that do not advance our practice. Rather, the issue is the delusion of the thinking mind, and Descartes' Cogito is a superb instrument for demonstrating the key aspects of this pervasive delusion, which is supported by these four fundamental beliefs about the nature of mind:

The thinking mind is the only source of knowledge
The thinking mind and self are equivalent and continuous
Awareness is merely a supporting quality of mind
Thoughts do not deceive us

Descartes constructed the rational basis of his very existence from the fact that his mind could think. When starting to assemble his world from nothing, he selected his thinking mind as the only tool of his analysis, and ended by concluding that it was himself, the only remainder being his body. He explicitly dismissed evidence from any other source, such as his other senses, which he stated to be unreliable.

As we noted earlier, for the Buddha there were four

foundations of mindfulness: the mind and its contents, and the body and its sensations. These foundations were the stable base from which the Buddha analysed human experience. For Descartes, there was no distinction between the mind and its contents, i.e. between awareness and thoughts, and the body and its senses were just a mechanism to host his thinking. He did not entertain the possibility that there could be any other mental resource to analyse the nature of reality than the thinking mind itself, even though it must have been clear to him that there is a part of mind that is aware even before the thinking mind has thought a thought. He did not judge worthy of consideration the times when he was not thinking, or the gaps between his thoughts. Did he stop existing at those points? Of course he didn't. Did he still exist when he was dreaming? Of course he did.

As it was for Descartes, so it is for us all. It is abundantly clear that there is more to the nature of mind than thinking, and yet the strongest habit of our minds is to regard the thinking mind as having the highest mental rank – the rank of *I* and *me*. This delusion is very powerful. Even when we see evidence of another mode of mind in the instinctive decisions we make outside of our rational thinking mind, we will still habitually fall back on the thinking mind when there is a problem to be solved, or when we want to learn how to swing a golf club, or indeed whenever there is anything at all to be learnt or done. As we have previously remarked, we also turn to it when there is nothing to be thought or done, in which case we are in danger.

When looking inside his own mind, Descartes did not question who it was that was aware, or what it was that was aware. Rather, he just accepted his awareness, as if it were merely an impotent bodily sense of no importance. As awareness is still present at times of no thinking, surely this is a better starting point for analysis of the nature of our being than the ephemeral thinking process? This was something that Siddhartha Gautama considered very closely, and with world-changing results. Even the most cursory study of our bodies shows that every single aspect is a thing of wonder, and we will explore in this book how our own awareness is the most wondrous of all our assets. Following the Buddha's example, these very questions of who and what is aware are often used in meditation and wise reflection to penetrate further into the nature of mind and body. Certainly, many a Buddhist monk the world over will spend hours contemplating just these subjects, and it is common to hear monks chanting the parts of the ancient texts that expound the Buddha's teachings in these areas.

Furthermore, Descartes' analysis was being directed by his will, which we have already established was notably strong, but again this aspect of mind does not enter into Descartes' view of self. To be gentle with him, perhaps he regarded all this as "thinking", although of course one does not need to be thinking to be resolute and determined. Observation of any sportsperson at the top of their game will show that thinking is exactly what they are *not* doing, and yet their will does not waiver. It is as if Descartes simply did not acknowledge that there may be functions of mind that exist in addition to the rational, verbal intellect, or the thinking mind.

Finally, Descartes did not acknowledge that his thinking mind might be an unreliable source of truth. Certainly, it is clear from his mathematical insight that his thinking mind was capable of much more than most others, and therefore he had some reason to be proud of it. However, even for Descartes there must have been times when it steered him wrongly. It is well documented that many of the great thinkers in history have come about their discoveries not only by logical thought, but also through other more creative, even capricious mental qualities. A wonderful account of this is given in Arthur Koestler's book *The Sleepwalkers*, in which Koestler observes that what the greatest so-called thinkers have in common is not so much a logical ratiocinating mind, though they certainly have those, but a steely determination to find their goal. Koestler describes how this determination motivates acts of creativity that might make these great thinkers stumble across their discovery from an unforeseen direction, sometimes even without fully realising their quest had ended. The important point here is that the most dazzling achievements that we associate with great thinkers may have come from a facility of mind other than conscious logical thought.

Descartes used the term "clear and present perception" to refer to things that appeared to him (to his thinking mind) as being beyond doubt, and therefore as necessarily true. A degree of careful introspection shows us that many functions of the thinking mind are delusions, but nevertheless they also appear to us as clear and present perceptions. The fact that the babble of commentary in our thinking minds is continuous presents us with a clear perception that it is self. It is not. At the point that we buy ourselves the latest item that we crave, there is clear and present perception that this will make us happy, but this too is a delusion.

In short, the delusion of the thinking mind is that *it is mind itself*, and it is this that holds us back from valuable insight into the nature and power of mind. The reason our journey has taken us back to the early 17th century is to illustrate that this intellectualist and rationalist bias occurred at a turning point in the history of Western thought, and that from this point the West was destined to venerate thinking to its certain detriment. It may be somewhat unfair to place all of the blame with Descartes for our modern delusion, as there are roots of this way of thinking prior to Descartes and there have been many since who have perpetuated the delusion. The reason for singling out Descartes is his place in history; Modern Philosophy was born at this time, when the dominance of the great thinkers in science was beginning.

So, how could we rephrase the Cogito? Either of these would do nicely:

"I think therefore I might be deluded", or
"I think therefore I need to let go."

I Teach About Suffering

When the Buddha was asked what he taught, his response was simple and along these lines: "I teach about suffering and the way out of suffering." In the Buddha's time, a common view amongst the spiritual teachers of the day was that suffering was caused by attachment to things that bring pleasure, and it was therefore common for people to leave their home lives to become ascetics, renouncing worldly things. They lived as beggars, wandering in search of truth. Many went without clothes, and they engaged in very austere practices to deny themselves all comforts. They prophesied that by breaking their bonds with pleasure, they would liberate themselves from suffering.

When the Buddha set out from his palace, he set out on such a path, shaving off his hair and beard and donning a simple beggar's robe. He was homeless and begging for alms to sustain himself – a far cry from the life of luxury that he had left behind. Along the way, he sought out and consulted renowned teachers, but did not find inspiration in their ideas. As was the custom at the time, he is said to have taken to the ascetic practices of self-mortification with enthusiasm, at one point almost starving himself to death. After six years of this life, he realised that in embracing these extreme practices, the ascetics of the day were merely replacing clinging to pleasure with clinging to its converse. He sought a "middle way" between the hedonism of his previous existence and the stark austerity of this new life of asceticism. This middle way was, of course, to become the foundation of one of the world's great religions.

Siddhartha, then aged thirty-five, decided to try to penetrate the very nature of his own mind to understand how suffering arises and so how it may pass away. He sat at the base of the bodhi tree of legend and resolved not to move until he had achieved this understanding, this enlightenment. He determined to investigate the whole process from the moment that an object or thought arrives at the senses, through to the sensations that are stimulated, the feelings that arise, and to the thoughts and actions that follow. In this way, he intended to divine the true nature of suffering and attachment in this world. Legend has it that he did not stir from his seat made of kusha grass for forty-nine days, at which point he achieved enlightenment.

After his enlightenment, at first the Buddha was reluctant to teach. He saw the extent of delusion in the world but doubted that his insight could be communicated in a way that anybody would comprehend. It is understandable that he felt this way, because his newfound wisdom was based entirely on experience and practice, and therefore did not lend itself to being taught in the conventional verbal way. The usual spoken mode of teaching is the output of the teacher's thinking mind, and yet the knowledge that the Buddha needed to describe did not come from that source. Similarly, the receiver of conventional instruction is the thinking mind of the person being instructed, but what the Buddha needed to teach is not readily graspable within that medium. How could the Buddha show people that their thinking minds were deluding them, and that they needed to meditate, to concentrate, to let go, and to reflect wisely? How could he show them the limitations of the thinking mind, when the act of verbal instruction would nourish that very entity? Fortunately for us all, he managed to find the answers to these questions.

In a deer park in the small village of Sarnath in northern India, the newly awakened Buddha gave his first teaching. He started by addressing the small group of men who had been with him in his previous years as an ascetic. These five men had left him in disgust when he moved away from the austere practices by taking some food and drink. At the time, he was near death from hunger and dehydration, but still they thought he had sold out in favour of the pleasures of the flesh. They considered him a quitter and no longer worthy of their respect, and on his reappearance before them they made their feelings known. However, they could see something very different in his deportment, and this made them receptive to hearing what he had to say, although they remained sceptical. On hearing the Buddha's teaching, these men became instant followers, and from this small beginning a worldwide phenomenon began.

Soon, the Buddha had hundreds of followers and had established the monastic discipline that still exists and flourishes to this day. His teaching ministry continued for a further forty-five years throughout India and Nepal until his death at the age of eighty. His doctrine was passed by word of mouth, until it was eventually written down in the *suttas* about 450 years after his death. The Pali word *sutta* literally means "thread"; representative of how the *suttas* thread together the Buddha's various discourses and responses to questions. Most of the original *suttas* begin "Thus have I heard" to reflect their original verbal form, memorised and passed down in recited form from the words of the Buddha himself.

The Buddha's teachings offer a comprehensive psychological model of human nature, together with a means of practice to live joyfully and harmoniously within it. Fortunately, there is no need for blind faith here, as we can verify the Buddha's view for ourselves, as did his first five followers, despite their initial cynicism. We too can witness at first hand that there is no area of experience, worldly or otherwise, to which the teachings do not apply. Of course, this is the only way the Buddha would have wanted us to learn: by putting his teaching into practice.

For those of us who do not live in a Buddhist country, starting out on this path usually follows a clear decision to do so, as opposed to simply adopting a way of life that is already around us. Some turn to the practice after a significant reversal in their life situations, and for these people it may have been necessary first to reach a state of despair in order to find the motivation to transform their lives. Others may approach the teaching feeling more mentally whole, but are no less deluded for feeling so. Some may just be curious about the workings of the mind, and others about the key messages of one of the world's major religions. Whichever is the case, all are brothers and sisters in the pursuit of truth, and it is in this regard that the mind teachings of Buddhism are so unique and nourishing.

The Buddha can be viewed as the first successful psychologist, and indeed, it is no exaggeration to extend this view to state that he is the most accomplished psychologist that there has ever been. It is then only a short and defensible step to the statement that all of psychology is lengthy footnote to his teaching.

The Buddha taught not just the nature of suffering and the role of the thinking mind in creating and perpetuating it, but also a path leading to the liberation from these bonds. He laid down a strict way of training to be followed by a monastic community to achieve the end of suffering, comprising over two hundred rules that are still followed today and chanted regularly in their source language in all continents of the world. Clearly we cannot all become monks or nuns, and so we are fortunate that the teachings are there for lay practitioners to follow as well. The monastic form is designed to challenge its followers at all times and in all aspects of the path. For the rest of us, it could be argued that the path is actually harder to follow, as its boundaries are not so clearly defined. Its pursuit requires effort, but hey, we can do effort, particularly if it is joyful, and the path certainly stirs up joyful energy. Resolution is the key here, and this is why we remind ourselves of our goal and our resolve at the beginning of each formal meditation, and why we are encouraged to find ways of reminding ourselves of this resolve throughout the rest of our day.

On Lists and Languages

No discussion of the Buddha's teaching can avoid "the lists". The Buddha's own teachings, and the teachings that they inspired in the wider Buddhist vehicle, are awash with numbered lists; there are three of these, eight of those, ten of these, thirty-two of those (and these – there are at least two lists of thirty-two), sixty-two of these, and so it goes on. It may seem that almost any number imaginable has one or more lists associated with it in the Buddhist teachings. I find this quite an endearing quality of the teachings, but it took me many years to stop applying energy to learning lists when I should be practising mindfulness. In this book, I have spared the reader almost all of these lists whilst still explaining the essence behind several of them. In the detailed descriptions in this book, there are three lists of three, three fours, three fives, two eights, and a ten, and that is all. For those familiar with Buddhism, the reaction to such pruning may be a high five or a deep six, although I hope the intent is appreciated. To add a little interest for Buddhist travellers on this journey, some of the lists I have chosen to describe may not be the ones you expect. This particularly applies to the threes, the fours, possibly two of the fives and one of the eights. I have also contributed a few lists of my own.

When the Buddha's teachings were finally written down for the first time, they were written in the Pali language. Pali is quite close to the language the Buddha would have used when teaching ordinary people, although when at home in his palaces Sanskrit would have been the correct form. Although Pali is not used as a language now, its study has been preserved through the ages in order to gain access to the original Buddhist scriptures. Sometimes in this book, an original Pali term will be used where the English translation is felt to be lacking in some way. Often, a single Pali word may require a clumsy English phrase to render its meaning, and even then the real essence cannot be determined. The dictionary translation of the French word "croissant" is usually something like "crescent-shaped roll", and for similar reasons a croissant is simply called a croissant wherever it crops up in the world, because it is what it is. When a Pali word is used, diacritics are omitted (diacritics are such things as horizontal bars above letters and dots below, and are used to represent certain sounds that cannot be expressed with the limited Roman alphabet). They have been excluded in this text simply to make the text more accessible to readers. Sometimes using the original Pali word just *feels* right; we are learning something new and beyond our everyday experience, and it can therefore be better to use words that carry no baggage in our minds. When a particular mental state arises, we can greet it with a single name that brings with it no analysis or conceptual proliferation. It is easy to become distracted by learning all the Pali terms and the language itself, and here again I plead guilty, and can only offer the advice not to follow my lead.

The Everyday Model of Mind

How the Mind May Appear To Be

Psychology was not recognised as a separate discipline from philosophy until 242 years after Descartes' famous book containing the Cogito was published. However, from the birth of psychology in Wilhelm Wundt's Leipzig laboratory in 1879, the die was cast – the Cartesian delusion had behavioural science in its grip. Wundt's laboratory exploded into life, with experiments in which trained subjects inspected the contents of their own thinking minds whilst carrying out various tasks. Again, we see an underlying and unchallenged model of mind in which the thinking mind is in control of all knowledge and behaviour, and is viewed as both a trusted commander and a reliable witness. The great significance of Wundt's work was the laboratory setting, lending to this bias an air of scientific respect.

This set the scene for most of the next hundred years of the new science of psychology, until an event in a seemingly unrelated field programmed the collective delusion deeper and pushed psychology further off course for half a century more. It may seem bizarre, but this episode was the invention of the digital computer. The reason this machine did so much to intensify the popular misconception of mind was that it provided it with a ready-made metaphor, and this metaphor of mind fitted in perfectly with the Cartesian delusion. In other words, our fascination with the computer played straight into the hands of the thinking mind in its bid for top mental rank. We will see later that the computer was not just a beguiling companion for the vanity of the thinking mind, but was also to provide it with a means to extend its reach and influence.

It is not too cynical to say that throughout its history, psychology has often adopted the latest technology as a model for mind. Whilst such things as hydraulic feedback, the telephone exchange, and quantum mechanics have been flirtations, the relationship with the digital computer was, and is, the real thing. Since the development of this marvel at the end of the Second World War, it could be said that the computer and modern psychology have grown up together. The results of their special relationship can be seen in the development of both.

Although modern computers look remarkably different today to their historical counterparts, the essential internal design has not changed, and this design is often referred to as the von Neumann architecture after one of its leading pioneers. The model of mind based on the von Neumann architecture acquired particular dominance in the 1970s when the branch of psychology called *cognitive science* was given a name. Essentially, cognitive science is the study of the thinking mind. It was initially founded on the view that *thinking is information processing*, i.e. mental life consists of rule-based manipulation of symbols whose meanings relate them to their counterparts within the real world. The computer analogy here is very clear. Although the bias towards this type of view was given significant impetus by Descartes in the middle of the Scientific Revolution, now it accelerated because there was a whole new language of description flowing from the computer metaphor, and this branch of science had a name.

Cognitive science had many followers, and here the word "followers" is carefully chosen because the new mind science had the feeling of a movement rather than simply a branch of psychology. The titles of books published in that period reflected the energy and hope of the movement – *The Language of Thought*, *The Architecture of Cognition*, and *Cognition and Reality*, to name but three. Indeed, at the time Daniel Dennett, the American philosopher and cognitive scientist, referred to a faction of the proud new science as "High Church Computationalism". From these origins, the companion discipline of Artificial Intelligence, the search for the thinking machine, was born. Cognitive science and computer science had not only formed an enduring bond, but had begotten a new joint discipline.

The use of the computer as a metaphor for mind resonates with our habitual view of mind, which is profoundly based on the Cartesian delusion. This view is so pervasive and instinctive that we will term it the *Everyday Model of Mind*. The everyday model has been at the basis of the majority of psychological research since Wilhelm Wundt's time, and is the view that underlies most educational systems and much of our familiar language. Like the computer, it has been refined and developed, but the same model is still present and incorrect. We will now look closely at its features, which are represented diagrammatically in Figure 1.

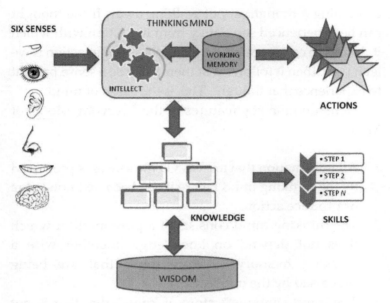

Figure 1 – The Everyday Model of Mind

Before we start to explore the model in detail, it is worth reminding ourselves that although in the West we are brought up to believe we have five senses, in the Buddha's psychology we have six. This sixth sense is represented in Figure 1 by a picture of a brain, and we will refer to it as the sense of "mind". It will be clear even from a limited experience with meditation that the Buddha was right that awareness of the contents of our minds is a distinct and most vital sense. What the sense of mind perceives is "mind objects", which can originate through contact with the outside world via one of our five physical senses, or through contact with thought that arises in the mind. For example, a thought that tells us to stand up and walk away when we are sitting in meditation is simply a mind object containing a thought about walking away. If the thought can be experienced separately from the action with which it desires to connect, and if it does not result in action if we let it pass, then it follows that there must be a sense present to experience that thought. This is the sense of mind.

Here are nine key features of the Everyday Model of Mind:

1. All information that arrives via the senses is processed by the thinking mind before it can become knowledge or produce action.
2. The thinking mind consists of a pure intellect which does not depend on knowledge, together with a working memory to store items that are being processed by the intellect.
3. The mind contains a store of knowledge that is not subject to capacity limits.
4. The thinking mind has access to all of our stored knowledge.
5. Thinking is intentional. It is directed by will.
6. Wisdom and insight result from thinking and knowledge; they cannot arise independently.
7. Knowledge about the thinking mind can only arise through the thinking mind itself.
8. Actions are under the control of the thinking mind unless they are repetitively performed, in which case they may become skills.
9. Skills are automated actions. They are initially learnt stepwise by the thinking mind, and as proficiency is achieved these learned steps are gradually "automated". Once learning is complete, the thinking mind relinquishes control to action procedures in the body.

The von Neumann machine metaphor can be overlaid quite straightforwardly on top of the everyday model shown in Figure 1. In both models, there is a database of knowledge that is common to all input and output processes, and there is a central processing element that is subject to capacity limitations. A working memory is provided in which data can be held temporarily whilst it is being processed for input to the database, or to be output as behaviour. There are also various input and output peripheral devices. For computers, these may be printers or robotic arms, and for the mind they are thought, speech, and action. When carrying out tasks, some types of instruction are interpreted *declaratively*, in which case their steps are explicitly represented in programme steps that can be read and understood. Others, like skills, are interpreted *procedurally*, in which case the declarative steps have been encapsulated into a procedure that is called by name or address and whose contents are no longer visible.

It would be unfair to leave the description of cognitive science here, as it has moved on in important ways since the euphoria of its early relationship with the digital computer. Fortunately, cognitive science did not get completely stuck in the computer metaphor, although it is perhaps fair to say that it did tarry in these waters for too long and may be still somewhat held back by the experience. For instance, an exciting development that gathered pace in the 1990s has enthusiastically embraced *mindfulness* as a means of treating patients stuck in debilitating mental states such as anxiety, compulsion and depression. We will return to this breakthrough later, but for now the essential point is that despite advances in scientific thinking and practice, the everyday model of mind, and its partner the von Neumann metaphor, are still persistent and pervasive.

Like all other organisms that have been successful in evolution, the thinking mind has developed elaborate and highly successful defence mechanisms. What is so intriguing about the everyday model is that it is clearly unsatisfactory as a theory of mind, and yet its hold on us is unyielding. Even when the evidence of its inadequacy is staring us straight in the face, our thinking minds conspire to prevent us from seeing this. For instance, we watch children pick up knowledge and skills at an alarming rate without ever knitting their brows, locked in inner verbal problem-solving. Taking another example, we are able to make instant judgements that would require laboriously complex mathematical computations to work them through sequentially, such as whether we have time to overtake whilst driving towards oncoming traffic. It is clear that our human condition bestows rich and abundant powers of learning upon us, but when it comes to learning about the thinking mind itself, it appears that either we cannot learn, or that we will not.

No matter how often we are exposed to the shortcomings of the thinking mind, there is an armour-plated habit that just seems to bring us straight back to trusting it implicitly. Many have challenged its suitability for command, and have given compelling enough examples of its limitations, but its dominance and influence in science, education, and life in general seems unassailable. It is as if there is a natural belief system within us that supports it, and we tend to fall back on that belief system unless we exert significant energy to refrain from doing so. Even when we decide to apply our energies to being mindfully aware, our thinking minds are able to creep back into control and take over without us even noticing.

Perhaps the most extraordinary defence mechanism of the thinking mind is the way that it presents our own awareness to us. Our awareness is viewed by the thinking mind as just something that supports our thinking, rather than as a powerful capability in its own right, or indeed as it rightfully is, *the* most potent capacity of mind. As we find in meditation, the thinking mind is highly resistant to letting the mind of awareness fly solo even for the briefest instant. For the thinking mind to marginalise our most formidable mental resource as mere supporting cast is both folly and deceit on a grand scale, and yet somehow we are not predisposed to recognise this. Even when René Descartes, one of the greatest minds in recent history, stared into his own being he did not even seem to notice his own awareness. Likewise, at the birth of the science of psychology, when Wilhelm Wundt instructed his subjects to analyse the contents of their minds, he did not question at all the tool that he had picked up to do this work, which was awareness itself.

Given all this, the Buddha's achievement can be seen as all the more remarkable, in that he penetrated straight through his thinking mind and saw *only* his own awareness. Later, we will indulge in some speculation about the evolution of the thinking mind and the nature of this perplexing defence mechanism, but before this there is plenty more of the journey into mindfulness and mental health to cover.

Limitations of the Everyday Model

Let us now explore the limitations of this model of mind that appears so beguiling to us, and whose nine key features we explored earlier. Understanding its shortcomings helps us see the role of the thinking component of mind in its proper context, and gives us an insight into the power of the faculties of mind that we may habitually disregard. In this way, we can feed our wise reflection and understand better why being able to let go of thinking is a skill worth cultivating.

Two Persistent Biases

These are the two fundamental views underlying the everyday model that are pervasive but highly problematic. They are as follows:

Thinking is intentional and purposeful.
Awareness is unintentional and powerless.

We habitually regard thinking as being under the control of the will, i.e. that it occurs because we wish it to and takes the form that we direct. We see it as an effective basis for all problem-solving, even when the source of the difficulty is manifestly the thoughts we are thinking. In contrast, our bias is to look upon awareness as just being there in the background, serving no other function than to support our thinking. Awareness is not commonly viewed as a potent force within the mind; nor indeed one that could dramatically improve the quality of our lives.

If we try for a moment to peek around the thinking mind's defences, we will see the error in these views. Thinking is more often unintentional than intentional, and is frequently purposeless rather than purposeful. Sometimes it is purposeless because we are thinking about the past or the future with no chance of influencing either, and sometimes it is because our thinking is just random mind chatter. Often, we will find ourselves turning over the same old stuff, with no real prospect of making a decision on what to do about it. Much of the time, we are just thinking because it seems unavoidable.

Consider this for a while: how much of our time do we spend actually thinking through a matter that actually needs to be resolved in this moment? Even when we are distracting our thinking minds with listening to the radio or reading a book, how frequently do we find ourselves realising that we have become lost in thought and taken nothing in? When we examine the contents of our thoughts, do they really need to be thought at this time, or are we just daydreaming? When we are worrying about the future or analysing the past, we may delude ourselves that this is intentional and purposeful thinking, but do we really intend to be thinking these thoughts, or are we just being carried along with the habits of our minds? When we become anxious, do we make ourselves less anxious by trying to think things through? When we fail at something and then find ourselves lost in self-reproach and self-deprecation, do we actually *decide* to spend our time criticising ourselves in this way, or does it all just sort of happen? Indeed, can we really believe that we would ever choose to suffer in these ways?

In fact, when we stop to analyse how little of our time

we spend in purposeful thought, we realise just how much of our thinking serves no purpose at all. This is wise reflection. Meditation supports this insight, of course, because it gets us used to seeing our thoughts come and go as mere mental events. Moreover, when our awareness is fully focused on the breath, it can be surprising what thoughts we see passing by. We see that when thinking is detached from our will and awareness, it still continues to happen, and seems to be constantly throwing out bait to try to recapture our interest. We can learn much, and amuse ourselves a little, by watching this process at work. Ultimately, we can learn to quieten the thinking mind's attention-seeking, but all stages on the way to this are also precious.

So, thought is not the controlling king homunculus in our heads that the everyday model of mind supposes it to be. Rather, most of the time it is just a lot of noise that we are better off trying to ignore. On the surprisingly few occasions when we can direct our thinking minds to solve a problem, then of course it is a powerful ally, but its own agenda will take us over if we do not train ourselves to be mindful. So much for the first bias of the everyday model that thought is intentional, purposeful, and productive.

What of the second bias: that awareness is passive and impotent? The key insight here is that just as we can direct our thinking minds, so too can we direct our minds of awareness. The vast majority of potential experience passes us by without our noticing, but we can change this, and when we do our lives are transformed for the better. When we direct our awareness, we experience richness in the world that was previously unavailable to us: tastes, smells, sounds, textures and appearances that we did not notice before. Our sense of awe and wonder of the world returns, and with it may come feelings of gratitude and openness. By experiencing the present moment, we create gaps in habitual patterns of thought, which otherwise might connect together to take us elsewhere. The sixth sense of mind allows us to become aware of the mind's contents, and this is where the potential of the mind really starts to be tapped. We are no longer lost in thought; we are fully present, centred, and ready to experience the world as it really is. When we are fully aware, it is as if the world comes flooding into the mind as a raging torrent, and the richness of the experience seems to be completely without bounds.

So, far from being passive and impotent, awareness is vibrant and liberating. It is significant that when we are in a state of focused awareness, the question of whether we are happy or otherwise is of no interest, and this is a subject we will come to later.

Knowledge We Have Lost or Knowledge We Never Had?

Now let's travel to Japan a couple of decades after the turn of the 20th century, where large numbers of people were starting to be trained in the art of sexing day-old chicks. To this day, the Japanese remain the elite in this specialist craft, for which national championships have been held and astonishing records set. At the time, the demand for female chicks from commercial egg producers was large, and so too was the cost to poultry farms of rearing twice as many chicks as they needed until they could be sexed at around five weeks by their adult plumage. Male chicks were useless to both parties. Training in the art of chicken sexing took two years or so, and was generally done by a student watching a skilled sexer and absorbing the complex pattern of up to a thousand cues that might be relevant to the decision. Although one chick's back end looks very much like another, even to a trained expert, these experts can hit close to a hundred per cent accuracy when sexing around a thousand chicks an hour. What they cannot do is say too much about how they do it.

The problem of inarticulate expertise is well documented in the psychological literature, and there are numerous real-world and experimental examples of learning by show-how rather than verbal instruction. Indeed, it appears that wherever human knowledge of a task is domain-specific and complex, expertise is likely to be inarticulate, at least in part. In the late 1970s, in the burgeoning field of Artificial Intelligence, of which we have already spoken, this was found to striking effect. Computer scientists were setting about building Expert Systems, which were to be computers that could emulate and indeed exceed the abilities of human experts in various fields, including medical diagnosis, business management, product design, and education. The idea was to extract the expertise from a human expert, put the knowledge in a database, code the rules into a reasoning engine, give it a nice user interface, sell it as a product, and then gaze down at night from the dizzy height of the mattress raised by the cash thereunder. The trouble was that the experts often could not articulate their knowledge. This problem came to be known as the *Feigenbaum Bottleneck* after one of the prominent Artificial Intelligence experts of the day.

The bottleneck was not that experts had no insight at all into their expertise, but rather that when they were interviewed what they said was imprecise and sometimes incongruous. Rather than logical stepwise descriptions of their skill, what surfaced instead were loosely formulated rules of thumb, and even intuitions. How could this be? How could we be trusting professionals who seemed to be acting upon instinct rather than fact and reason? Surely expertise cannot be classed as such unless it has been vetted in some way by a higher authority, i.e. by the thinking mind? Surely any system that learns and behaves according to rules that have not been vetted is essentially out of control? If such scrutiny has taken place, then surely it is reasonable to expect that its results should be available for inspection at any time? Of course, such questions come from deep within the everyday model of mind.

The immense natural resistance of the everyday model of mind meant that although it was adapted somewhat to try to accommodate this situation, consideration was not generally given to abandoning it as a theory of how we learn in all situations. According to the everyday model, as knowledge is applied repeatedly to tasks, its locus of control progressively shifts from deliberate conscious procedures to autonomous unconscious procedures. It shifts from a declarative to a procedural knowledge, or to use the popular computational metaphor of the day, it is *compiled*. Knowledge becomes ability. Essentially, the Feigenbaum Bottleneck was explained as knowledge having been incorporated into skills and, in a certain sense, forgotten.

However, there is still a substantial weight of evidence that some expert knowledge is actually acquired without it ever being verbal, in which case no amount of skill in probing for this knowledge could ever elicit it. Indeed, any knowledge elicited in this way would have to be regarded as "made up" or "after the fact". As any of us who have learnt a complex motor skill can confirm, there can be no argument with this for some tasks. This sort of learning was documented as far back as 1890 in William James' huge and influential work *The Principles of Psychology*. However, the "comfort zone" of this explanation has always been tasks of a perceptual-motor nature, such as a golf swing, rather than a mental task that might be said to involve some sort of intelligence. Put another way, the tasks that are considered out of bounds for learning without thinking are those where it is the *decision to carry out* a particular action, rather than the action itself, that is of interest.

Learning Without Thinking

Nevertheless, it seems clear that we can learn to make "intelligent" decisions without the intervention of the thinking mind, with its slow dependence on verbalisation and rehearsal in learning, and its inability to take in all the detail of the present moment. In support of such a view there is a vast body of psychological research showing that subjects can achieve mastery of tasks before being able to report verbally on how the task is done. A lot of this research has its roots in the work of the American psychologist Clark Hull in the 1920s, and many of the experiments since can be described, without too much fear of insult, as variations and refinements of Hull's original method. Hull devised stimulus materials that consisted of complex geometrical forms embedded in a display of other multifaceted representations. These forms were generated from a set of rules. Subjects were presented with a series of them in the guise of a simple memory experiment. Although they were unaware of the rule-governed nature of the shapes, subjects became adept at sorting them in accordance with the rules before being able to report on what the rules actually were. Hull observed that his subjects acquired what he termed a *functional concept,* i.e. an understanding sufficient to guide their behaviour correctly, at a stage of learning prior to a verbal concept, i.e. an explanation.

It is an interesting coincidence that Hull's work was being done at precisely the same time as the establishment and rapid expansion of the Zen-Nippon Chick Sexing School in Japan. In that school in Nagoya, aspirant chick sexers were facing the same challenge, i.e. learning to react in a predictable way to a complex pattern of cues that they could neither describe nor categorise. This is not the first coincidence of Eastern and Western insight that has been mentioned in this book, and it certainly will not be the last.

Many, many experiments support Hull's basic conclusions, although it seems that for every one of these experiments there is another one seeking to offer an alternative view that verbal knowledge may not have been adequately assessed. This is the thinking mind fighting back, but it is nonetheless reasonable to assert that the weight of evidence and the variety of sources argue strongly for a much more parsimonious conclusion, i.e. that we can learn a complex task before we can explain how we do it. There are three common conditions for learning of this type: firstly, that the task is in some way complex; secondly, that the features relevant to learning are not salient; and thirdly, that the subject has not been directed to look for rules and relationships, or for some other reason is not minded to do so.

For the everyday model of mind, the abstraction of structure from complex stimuli may be an unwieldy computation that it is not capable of doing in any evolutionarily appropriate period of time. Herein may lie the key to explaining the ability of our minds to assimilate and intuit knowledge successfully and build meaningful patterns of behaviour without thought – our environment demands it. We could not have survived as a species by weighing everything in a conscious, verbal manner before acting, and later we will discuss the time in our evolutionary past when we did not have this ability anyway. Of course, the evolutionary imperative was not to distinguish a female chick's backside from a male one, or one complex shape from another, but to identify in a reliable manner friend from foe, food from poison, and danger from safety. In other words, there was a pressing need to decide instantly whether to approach or avoid. The ability to act rapidly and intuitively is likely to have been highly adaptive in the evolution of our species, and a mechanism that could make decisions in the moment will have been favoured, even at the expense of a little accuracy. It is this source of intuitive awareness, of action without thought, that we are accessing when the thinking mind is disengaged.

There is another branch of psychological research that is equally illuminating from the point of view of unconscious learning, and fits in well with the evolutionary perspective of making rapid assessments in complex situations. This concerns our ability to absorb statistical information from our surroundings. Although our thinking minds present us with an enormously powerful tool for learning and investigation of our environment, there is another way of learning that requires only our awareness. Our minds can learn by absorption of large quantities of statistical inputs from all around us, and show a remarkable facility in organising this information into patterns that can guide our behaviour effectively and without thought. We can access knowledge learnt in this way in a startlingly short amount of time that the thinking mind simply could not match, although our decisions have a qualitatively different feel – they surface as strong intuitions.

Let us consider a mode of learning in which we learn that things that happen together are related – if *B* happens after *A*, then *A* causes *B*. In individual cases, such a mode of learning is mostly useless; if we look out of the window and it starts to rain we do not conclude that our curiosity causes the precipitation. However, if our minds could accumulate statistical information from much larger samples, then in general it would be able to learn the things that are genuinely related or likely to be so. So, if most of the time *B* happens after *A*, then *A* probably causes *B*, or at least can be used to predict *B*. There is abundant evidence that our minds are capable of doing just this, which we can simply demonstrate by asking ourselves questions about the relative frequency of words, letters and letter combinations in our language. In general, we will be right.

Thinking Without Learning

An interesting and illuminating twist in this tale is that there is also ample evidence that in some cases the thinking mind actually *interferes with* certain types of learning, and that in these cases learning proceeds better if the thinking mind is otherwise engaged. Clark Hull's technique was to deceive the thinking mind by telling it that there was no work for it to do, or directing it to focus on an irrelevant part of his experiments. Similarly, chick sexers are taught how to observe and learn without analysing. However, these techniques only show that the thinking mind is not needed for learning – they do not directly show that it can be an impediment. Other psychologists have adopted a sterner line with the thinking mind, trying to take it out of the game by giving it something else to do whilst learning is taking place. This is where the study of the thinking mind takes a fascinating turn.

Various experimental techniques have been devised for keeping the thinking mind busy. Although they lack the comedy value of the earlier example of Botoxing the faces of experimental subjects, they share its ingenuity. A common technique is requiring that subjects count backwards or perform simple mental arithmetic to the rhythm of a metronome. In this way, it has been shown in some experiments that learning of complex tasks can actually be improved whilst the thinking mind is busy elsewhere. In such scenarios, it has been proposed that even when verbal knowledge can be shown to be valid, it is likely that it has been acquired by the thinking mind *spectating* on our behaviour and thereby drawing conclusions from learning that has already taken place outside of its control.

Similarly, when a task is learnt and subjects are getting along quite nicely with its performance, experiments have shown that when performance starts to dip, subjects will fall back on their thinking minds to work out what the problem is, at which point their performance will deteriorate even further. It is likely that we have all experienced this phenomenon in our own lives, and indeed observed it in children when they suddenly realise they have acquired a competency and then try to figure out how they are doing it. Since we have started talking about learning in children, it is also worth noting a fundamental difference in the approaches to studying learning in adults and children. In the investigation of adult cognition, there is clear bias towards the everyday model of mind, promoting a sequence of learning from conscious and verbal to unconscious and inscrutable. However, this bias seems absent in studies of infant learning, where we much more readily accept that there is a developmental lag between learning and being able to explain what has been learnt.

The study of unconscious or "implicit" learning is a field that attracts much debate amongst psychologists. There is something about this subject that is somehow at arm's length from the more established psychological research. Maybe this is the legacy of Descartes, maybe it is the defence mechanism of the thinking mind, or maybe it is just that there is still much more to be learnt in this area before it is properly accepted. Probably, all three are true. However, regardless of differences in interpretation of these phenomena, both the weight of research evidence and the presence of a strong evolutionary motive for unconscious learning would strongly suggest that the thinking mind is not involved in all successful learning and action.

Selection and Attention

Since the middle of the last century, a central question for psychology has consistently been what causes individuals to select information from the complexity that surrounds them in the way that they do. At all times, there is a literally inconceivable amount of input available to all of our senses simultaneously, and clearly we cannot attend to it all. Nevertheless, somehow we select the features from our surroundings that are salient to us, and seem to get along acceptably well as a result. Or do we?

Usually, we will be unaware of the choices we are making about what we attend to, but meditation and other contemplative practices show us that these choices are nevertheless being made, and this is our next major topic. The Buddha was very clear that we create the world at our senses from the delusions and passions that guide our attention, and this is fundamental to the concept of *kamma*, or *karma* to use the more popular Sanskrit word. He described how delusion and desire condition the very beginnings of what we perceive, i.e. where our senses are attracted, and from there what we actually register in consciousness from the myriad richness of possibility. This ruthless reduction then further nourishes our delusion. We will, of course, develop the concept of *kamma* more as we go along, as it is a central tenet of the Buddha's teaching, and has acquired a limiting and unsatisfactory popular meaning.

The thinking mind of the everyday model is by its nature selective, because its slow processing and limited working memory make it so: it is selective because it is constrained. It has to proceed by picking a manageable number of variables from its environment (both external and internal) in order to make associations between these variables, or to put it another way, to learn and to reason. Despite its restricted capacity and ponderous lack of speed, the thinking mind enables highly effective learning and problem-solving in rapidly changing circumstances, and may account for a fair amount of human evolutionary success. However, the focus of the thinking mind shuts out much of our experience of the present moment, and if it is being misdirected this can be acutely harmful to us.

There is an experiment that has achieved immense popularity on the Internet, where many millions of hits have been recorded on a clip that shows an amusing experiment in the field of cognitive science. In this experiment, two teams are passing a basketball around, and subjects are directed to focus on one team and count the number of passes made. When subjects are allowed later to watch the film clip without having to analyse it in any way, they are shocked to notice that a person in a gorilla suit wanders through the game. This is a remake by the cognitive scientists Dan Simons and Chris Chabris of a 1970s experiment by Ulric Neisser, in which the gorilla was played by a woman carrying an umbrella. In the original experiment, the result was just the same, except of course that the research did not go viral. This experiment shows clearly just how unaware we are when our thinking mind is fully engaged.

The mind of awareness, in contrast, is unselective, and works with all variables in play. It does not have to focus on any particular thing, it is just aware. It is not subject to delusion or pollution. It is not trying to solve any particular problem, and therefore it does not need to discriminate between aspects of its environs that are relevant or irrelevant to its purpose. However, this is not to say that the mind of awareness cannot be focused, or that focused attention always calls for the thinking mind. In meditation, we learn to direct our awareness towards a particular meditation object, such as the breath in sitting meditation or the soles of the feet in walking meditation. We do this with a specific intention, which is to train ourselves to abide in awareness, and thereby to be free of the thinking mind so that our true unsullied nature can awaken and guide our behaviour.

The Contracted Mind

The Buddha's psychological model describes both the mind as it is when still subject to suffering, and also when it has gone beyond. The mind before enlightenment is often referred to as the *contracted mind*. It is named in this way because when the mind follows the thoughts in our heads and forms an identity around the idea of a self, it contracts in on itself and becomes distorted and deluded. Understanding of the contracted mind at a deep and experiential level is a necessary precursor for even the briefest discussion of enlightenment. Suffering can only be extinguished by a profound understanding of its cause, and this cause lies in the limited and deluded perspective of the contracted mind. Realisation of this is something that is experienced, not taught.

The psychology of the contracted mind is built up from simple components starting with the four that we have already discussed: the body and its sensations, and the mind and its contents. Developing awareness of the nature of each of these four elements is referred to in the Buddha's teachings as the *four foundations of mindfulness*, and will lead to the proper understanding of our own nature and our relationship with the world we inhabit. It sounds so simple, but actually seeing into the real nature of these four factors is strangely challenging.

Before describing the details of the Buddha's model of mind, it must be emphasised again that the Buddha's psychology is based on a *process* model of mind, in that it describes how the mind moves between contact and action, in constant change. Here, "contact" does not just refer to our experiences with objects in the outside world, but also includes encounters with the feelings in our bodies and the thoughts in our minds. Another fundamental principle to stress is that there is no need for a concept of self, personality, or anything else that exists separately from these processes, or independently within them. One can use such terms, but fundamentally they are static concepts that have no real substance or explanatory use within the dynamic model of mind expounded by the Buddha.

The everyday model of mind contains processes too, but there the similarity ends. The everyday model is essentially a *computational* model. The processes in the everyday model are predictable, mundane, and functional. They carry out transformations on data, shunt data along the bus from processor to store, and send instructions from processor to effectors. The everyday model is also *architectural* or *structural*, in that there is a place for each of its elements, and well-defined communication pathways between them. However, the key difference between the everyday model of mind and the Buddha's model is that the everyday version has a place for self, and not just any old place – it is the captain's seat on the bridge.

The key message of the Buddha's psychology is that the processes of the contracted mind can be *changed* if we are able to penetrate their nature with our awareness. In this way, we find that we have a choice in aspects of mind that we may have previously seen as automatic or inevitable. Truly understanding this is a critical step on the journey to letting go of the burden of suffering. The essence of the concept of the contracted mind that the Buddha taught is nothing more than a constant stream of cause and effect; if we can change the cause, we can change the effect. More importantly, when we change an effect, we change the cause that leads to the following effect, and so on throughout the whole chain of conditioned becoming. This is fundamentally what is meant by *kamma*.

At the highest level, the Buddha's psychology of the contracted mind is summarised in the five process elements described below. To the untrained mind, all of these happen in a flash, without us being aware of anything but the outcome, and for much of the time we may not even be particularly aware of even that much.

1. We come into contact with the outside world through our bodies, or more specifically through our "sense-doors" – the traditional five senses of sight, smell, taste, touch and hearing, plus the sense of mind. Forms in the external world impinge on our bodily senses, and thoughts and impressions appear in our minds.
2. Following contact, we become aware of the sense object. This awareness is not judgemental, it is just awareness. The impression is just as it is at this point. It is just so. Nothing has been added.
3. On becoming conscious of objects in the outside world or in the mind, there is a mental reaction that evaluates the object on the basis of like or dislike, pleasure or displeasure. This is an instinctive response formed before we have developed any ideas about the object, and it provides an underlying energy to the processes that follow.
4. Still operating in a timescale close to instantaneous, we

then come to form a concept of the object based on how it appears to our senses, and on the feelings that have arisen in response to those sensations. The object is now a construct in the mind and its pleasantness or otherwise is bound to it. It has gained an identity, and this identity entails a judgement. The object is no longer just so in the mind; it now carries additional weight.

5. Again in an instant, our behaviour with respect to the object is determined, for example to prolong our contact with it if we like it, or to avoid it if we do not. By this point, we have *become* the judgement we have made and the action we are taking, and we do not see it as a separate thing from ourselves.

The mental reactions in these processes are effortless and appear to happen automatically. Whenever there is an experience of an object, at that very moment there appears a simultaneous awareness of a judgement, a conceptualisation, a thought, and a reaction. The Buddha once described the senses as being like an empty village, and contact with sense objects as being like an invasion of bandits. However, these bandit attacks are not capricious, but rather are invited in by our lack of understanding of the nature of the contracted mind.

There is also an associated perception that this chain of mental processes is essentially and unavoidably "me" and "mine". The Buddha taught that this is one of the primary delusions of mind, and he showed how these are not the uncontrollable reflexes that they first appear to be. His insight was that actually we have much more choice in how we attend, evaluate, discern, conceptualise, think and react than we realise. Certainly, we have more choice than is offered by the everyday model of mind, in which our judgements and reactions are presented to us whole, and even as the whole of us. What the Buddha's teaching shows us is how to break down the experience of the world and see how our choices actually condition and create the sense of self, moment by moment. The earlier in this process that we can bring our awareness to bear, the freer of the cycle we can become. This is a critical aspect of the teaching, and stands in stark contrast to the everyday model of mind, in which the self is static, and in some sense "already there", seeking to control and direct our interaction with a world that it believes can be made stable and satisfactory.

The Buddha's mind teachings show us that through understanding the true nature of our responses to worldly and mental events, we have the means to liberate ourselves. To achieve the requisite insight, a good starting point is to consider the Buddha's analysis of each of the five constituent process elements summarised above. The rather colourless term *aggregate* is the most common translation of the original Pali word used to describe each of these five process elements. The Pali word is *khandha*, and it is literally translated as "heap" or "pile", or even "tree trunk". So, although "aggregate" is clumsy and does not convey any obvious meaning, the alternative literal translations do not improve the situation. The Buddha did not explain why he chose this particular word, but it is commonly held that he selected it because it implies a burden, as in carrying around a heap of bricks.

If the Buddha had given an explanation for his selection of the word *khandha*, which at the time had no psychological connotations, it would surely have made ε. However, the popular interpretation is somewhat ɔleading. The aggregates are not static burdens like a pile of heavy books, but are burdensome for a different reason, which is that without understanding they can seem to be *unavoidable*. Their effects are with us almost at once, and unless we train our minds, they have taken us over before we can react. Even when we feel we have a good grasp of the whole process in action, we are still prey to it. The term *aggregation* is used in this book because it conveys more of an act of doing than "aggregate", which is more like an inert pile. Whatever word is used for these processes, and personally I find *khandha* the most evocative, the important point is that the self cannot be found in any of them.

The Buddha taught that, unless we have attained enlightenment, these five aggregations function together as the way in which we experience the world, binding us to suffering within it. In his book *What the Buddha Thought*, Richard Gombrich suggests a translation of *khandha* along the lines of "fuel for burning". He relates this to the literal translation of the Pali word *nibbana,* which of course is commonly translated as "enlightenment". The literal meaning of *nibbana* is "going out", in the sense of a flame ceasing to burn. Gombrich´s compelling view of the Buddha´s meaning is therefore that the fuel of the *khandhas* must be exhausted before the mind can see the world as it really is.

We have spoken earlier about how we create our world, and the five *khandhas* are a fundamental part of that process. The way they interoperate is so strongly conditioned within us that being mindful of their ebb and flow does not come naturally. They happen so quickly and so habitually, and are often so familiar, that they give an illusion that they are something we *are* rather than something we *do*, much less something we *choose to do*. The Buddha taught that we need to use meditation and wise reflection to see the aggregations for what they are, and in this way become free of the clinging and grasping that they perpetuate. He spoke frequently of "self-conquest", and what he meant by this was training our minds in precisely this way. Like all our concepts and judgements, self is a conditioned thing, and the conquest we seek is to be free of relating to the world through self-view.

The five aggregations are the basis of our perception of ourselves in each moment, and their persistence and continuous nature contribute to the feeling of a personal and stable concept of *I*. This sense of self is an illusion, and is perhaps the most difficult aspect of the Buddha's teaching for many to grasp. When approaching the teachings for the first time, we may fear a loss of identity because the ultimate destination does not contain self. Although there is a sense in which loss of identity is indeed the goal, this is an unhelpful way to look at the practice. Endless debate and discussion is contained in literature that discusses Buddhism regarding what is the nature of self, but the Buddha himself regarded it as a question that did not need to be answered. He saw it as just another mess of mental activity that takes us away from, not nearer to, the understanding of the present moment that will lead to our liberation. This is exemplified beautifully in one of the Pali *suttas*, in which the Buddha is speaking to the renowned ascetic, Bahiya of the Bark Garment. He says to Bahiya words along the lines of "In the seen, let there be only the seen. In the heard, let there be only the heard. In thought, let there be only thought. There is no self in any of this, and where there is no self, there is no suffering."

It is the loss of *attachment to identity* that we seek, rather than loss of identity itself. As we overcome this attachment, our experience of life is enriched, not diminished. We still have a "self" and a "personality", but we acknowledge that they are changing processes that we can purify and enhance through choice. When the familiar processes of the aggregations fill our minds, we can learn to see them for what they are – causes and effects, mere habitual responses. We learn that these conditions arise *and cease* in the mind. How can we *be* angry or sad? How can we *be* an angry or sad person? It makes no sense when we reflect upon it.

The Three Characteristics of All Things

One of the fascinating things about the Buddha's teachings is that they are essentially a collection of different routes to the same place. In this sense, they do not form an additive series, or logical progression, but any can be picked up and followed depending on where we find ourselves. That said, before we look in detail at the nature of the five aggregations, it is useful to consider first one of the most salient waypoints in the Buddha's map of the routes to awareness. Specifically, we will now examine what the Buddha called the *three characteristics* of all things. This teaching may well become our "go-to" message in those moments in which we find ourselves lost or lacking direction. If we understand and internalise the three characteristics, we will always find our way back home to wisdom.

"Characteristics" is another rather unsatisfactory translation of a Pali term, although by no means in the league of "aggregates", which is up there with "crescent-shaped roll" in my view. Sadly, the source Pali word, *lakkhana*, does not help us here, because, unlike *khandha*, it is not very memorable or evocative, even in its Sanskrit form. Other English translations are "marks" or "signs", but we will stick with "characteristics" because "marks" or "signs" may feel like attributes that worldly things may superficially have, whereas "characteristics" gives a better cue that these properties are *within the nature* of all worldly things. The three characteristics have been discussed many times already in this book, although not as a list of three, and they are that all worldly things are:

Impermanent – whatever is subject to arising is also subject to change and to ceasing.

Unsatisfactory – lasting satisfaction cannot be gained through things that arise, change and cease.

Not self – the difficult one: no matter what our senses and minds perceive, and no matter how strong the sense of self in these perceptions is, none of this is self. All perceptions, views, emotions, or whatever states of mind, are conditions of mind subject to cause and effect, to arising, change, and ceasing.

The Buddha taught that the three characteristics together form a universal and immutable truth that is within the nature of all things. He taught that this truth is applicable "whether buddhas come into the world or whether buddhas do not come into the world", and he referred to all things being "aflame" with these characteristics. When we start to consider the five aggregations closely, it is useful to do so whilst bearing in mind the three characteristics of all things. We see how the aggregations cause us to seek freedom from suffering in permanence that cannot be found, and to continue to intensify our suffering through creating a self that clings to impermanent things. We see how we suffer through attempting to control the uncontrollable, and through striving to find the one thing in this universe that is not subject to change. We see how whenever the sense of self is strong, we create a discordant relationship with the world around us.

When approaching the somewhat elusive concept of *not self*, it is essential to understand that detachment from the concept of self is not nihilism, i.e. the annihilation of self, but actually something entirely positive. When there is no attachment to self and self-view, what arises in its place is a revelation of the dramatic potential of our natural awareness. Although we have let go of self, we feel no loss. We have left self-view behind in the same way that a butterfly emerges from a chrysalis.

The Five Aggregations

We will now look closely at the five aggregations. To set the stage for these five, we first considered a list of four – the four foundations of mindfulness – and then a list of three – the three characteristics of all things – but now we are ready. We will employ the four foundations of mindfulness as our investigative tools: the body and its sensations, and the mind and its contents. When we investigate the five aggregations, it is important to understand that the goal is not simply to break down our experience, or ourselves, into components. We are not merely trying to put everything into a category for the purposes of analysis, as such static concepts would be of limited use. Although our thinking minds may enjoy such an activity, and our scientific literature is peppered with such fascination, this is not the endpoint we seek.

Rather, the purpose of our analysis is to understand the mind *in motion*, and thereby enable us ultimately to choose not to get caught up in it all. We are not trying to *do* anything with the aggregations, we are just learning to recognise and understand them. In doing this, we will come to see that thoughts, opinions, prejudices, likes, dislikes, fears, whatever, are all just so, and we do not need to get involved. When we do not get ensnared within the thoughts that arise within our minds, we can stop identifying with them, and painting them the colour "me". This is the concept of *not self* in operation; if these things were truly us, we would not be able to see them because we could never achieve separation from them. *Not self* can be a tricky notion to grasp, but that is it in a nutshell – if we can consider something objectively, then it is not self, and if it is not self, we can let it be on its way. The aggregations are the excess baggage of the present moment.

As the aggregations and their relationships are explained below, it is important to pause to reflect on

141

them from time to time. This reflection should always be interleaved with our meditation and mindfulness practice, as the Buddha's teaching needs to be understood on more than an intellectual level. As we come to understand the aggregations more, realisation arises that actually there is nothing in our conditioned experience that lies outside them. This is a very profound insight when it is fully grasped because it leads to a view of mental life in which we naturally take responsibility for our thoughts, views and actions. This is not a burdensome sense of responsibility – it is the liberation of choice. If we are in a negative state of mind and we understand the processes by which we allowed this state to arise, then we have the wisdom to choose differently, and simply to put down the means of suffering that we have picked up.

Material Form

Material form is the easiest of the five aggregations to understand – unless of course you are a particle physicist, in which case it is a whole world of weirdness. This aggregation refers to that which is gross and physical, i.e. to objects in the world. It is relatively straightforward to relate to because forms are substantial and slow-moving and therefore can be contemplated directly. Physical forms are not fleeting and hard to distinguish like the mental events we will come to next. We perceive material form through our senses, or "spheres of contact" as they are often called in Buddhist psychology. So, our experience of matter is distinguished through the body – which is also matter; physical form being consumed by physical form.

The Buddha's teachings actually have quite a lot to say about the nature of material form, and as always there are some very satisfying lists to learn if we are so inclined. Little of this will be expounded here because it seems reasonable to assert that we all think we understand the concept of material form well enough already. However, although it is the nature of mind that concerns us in this book, it is nevertheless necessary to go into a few salient aspects of the Buddha's view of matter, because even if we are not particle physicists it is still likely that our view may not be entirely sane.

The aggregation of form includes our own bodies, which of course are physical things themselves. Although it may seem obvious that our bodies are physical matter, we are not naturally inclined to consider them that way. A meditation used by Buddhist monks has the rather memorable chanted introduction that our bodies are "a sealed bag of skin full of unattractive things". The chant then goes on to list these unattractive things, pulling no punches – mucus, pus, bile, undigested food, excrement. It all sounds rather better chanted in Pali! The teaching here is not so much that the body is unattractive, but rather that the body is as it is, and we should not identify with it and thus become attached to it looking attractive, feeling comfortable, or staying youthful and vigorous. Monks also remind themselves in their chanting that they are of the nature to sicken, to age, and to die. Again, this is not intended to focus on the negative, but to focus on how things are.

Understanding the nature of the body is actually fundamental to understanding the nature of the mind. All troublesome thoughts, views and attachments originate in the body, and through understanding the nature of the relationship between mind and body, we equip ourselves to be liberated from misconceptions and suffering. It is easiest to start by considering basic sensations such as heat, cold, and pain, because here it is most obvious that these start as functions of the body. More challenging, but just as accurate, is the insight that emotions too start this way. At the precise point that sensations are experienced by the body, there is no evaluation of their quality – they are just a pattern of activity across our nervous systems. There is an important sense in which a thought is no different. To focus only on the sensations of the body as they are in the moment, and without our judgements and views on top, is to start to free ourselves from the clinging that the other aggregations bring.

All physical form is just physical form, but we have very strong reactions and preferences in relation to such forms, and we spend much of our lives in strife based on these inclinations. At a superficial level, we know which forms please us and which do not. At a deeper level, we ignore the folly of our struggle to surround ourselves always with forms that please us, and we ignore too the hopelessness of the fight to hold on to things that are not part of us but we nevertheless regard as "ours". It is in the nature of the three characteristics of all things (not some things, *all* things) that we cannot get what we want.

And so we come to death. The thinking mind is fundamentally averse to considering that our bodies are of the nature to age, die and decay, but nevertheless they all are. Indeed, when we consider our behaviour, we see that much of it is more consistent with a view that we are immortal than that we are not. We set ourselves goals and we entertain ambitions, as if endlessly to distract ourselves from the fundamental issue of our own mortality. The human realm is a tiny fraction of the life on earth, which in turn is a fraction of all the life that has ever been, and this astoundingly larger proportion of life just *is*. It does not appear to set itself any purpose other than to be and to continue to be. It seems to be a uniquely human activity to attribute a purpose to life other than to live and to generate more life. We do not willingly consider our own deaths, or those of our loved ones. This is strange because clearly death is the opposite of birth; we are all born and we will all die. There has never been anybody yet born for whom this is not true, and yet we habitually ignore our material nature, and death remains something of a taboo subject in most societies, including Buddhist ones.

Matter is as it is, and it is not really such a challenge to come to an appropriate relationship with it. In contrast, the four fleeting, interdependent and interchanging aggregations of mind present us with a much greater challenge, and to these we will now turn our attention.

Consciousness

Consciousness is the base on which the four mental aggregations rest. It is the light of awareness that underlies all our experience and makes it possible. It is what Descartes and Wundt did not consider, and a phenomenon that science still cannot explain. It is something that the everyday model of mind marginalises as passive and powerless, and it is what makes our experience continuous. As conditions arise and we react to them, conscious awareness is always there in the background, and here begins the feeling of an enduring self. Like material form, it is a naturally arising condition, and as such is not something we create.

Consciousness is the point of contact with the aggregation of form, in that it is the means by which we become aware of an object impinging upon one of our senses. In the Buddha's model of mind, there are six types of conscious awareness, with one corresponding to each sense. So, there is sight consciousness, hearing consciousness, smell consciousness, taste consciousness, touch consciousness, and thought consciousness. It is important to emphasise that this "conscious awareness" refers only to the fleeting act of becoming aware, not to the content or consequence of that experience. Consciousness is the initial passive part of the chain of rapid processes that leads to habitual action, for example to turn away from a grotesque sight. It is essential to recognise that this swift sequence of events starts with the awareness of, say, the sight object in the physical world just as it is at that moment, with nothing added. If our minds did not proceed rapidly through the other mental aggregations, we would see sight objects precisely as they are, or more accurately, precisely as our senses perceive them. The Buddha's purpose in drawing our attention to the aggregations is that we rarely see things as they truly are and to do so requires commitment and practice.

The important message here is that, with practice, we can come to separate sensations and awareness from the habits that follow. We learnt earlier how to use our sensation store to help us understand sensations for what they are, as being *like this, this way, just so, just this much.*

This is an important technique in cultivating an understanding of the aggregations in action, in that it helps us dissociate sense contact from what happens next, and in this way we may *change* what habitually happens next. The understanding that this entails is no mere theoretical construct, but can deliver enormous practical benefits. These benefits will be discussed in detail later, and range from managing our mental health to improving our sporting prowess.

Judging

Whilst material form and conscious awareness are naturally arising conditions, this cannot be said of the next three aggregations, which are of our own making, even though they may not feel so. Like their counterparts in horror films, our creations can run amok and ultimately destroy us. What is more disturbing than the classic fabricated creatures of a horror film is that the monsters we create within us are powerful enough to subsume our very identities. The eyes of these beasts stare out through ours, their thoughts overrun our minds, and their actions take control of our speech and bodies.

The aggregation of *judging* is the beginning of the chain reaction. Form is already "out there", and consciousness makes it alive to the aggregations that follow, of which judging is the prime mover. The common translations of the Pali name for this aggregation centre around "feeling", but in selecting the alternative translation "judging" my intention is to convey a more active and personal process. The process of judging places all awareness into three broad categories: pleasant, unpleasant, or neither pleasant nor unpleasant. Another beneficial translation of the Pali may be "evaluating", and the evaluations we make are specific to which of the six sensory modalities presents the object to us; so, there may be a pleasant sound, an unpleasant smell, a taste that is neither pleasant nor unpleasant, and so on. Of course, the fact that there are three possible judgements in six different modalities means – you guessed it – an unmissable opportunity for a list! The *suttas* do not disappoint here, and there is a list and explanation of all eighteen sense components, and unsurprisingly this is not the only list of eighteen things we encounter in the ancient texts.

However, we will resist again the pull of the lists and stay with the essence of the teaching. The role of feeling or judging in the Buddha's psychology is pivotal. Contained in a feeling is a judgement, and contained within the judgement is a delusion. The delusion is that the feeling of pleasantness or otherwise is *a quality of the object itself*, i.e. something separate from us and associated with the object. This delusion persists because it is not instinctive for us to recognise the choice contained within the judgement. Whether or not a feeling is judged to be pleasant, for instance, can depend on our circumstances, or, in other words, on the complex interplay of the other aggregations at work. Being warm in a warm climate, for instance, is not always judged to be pleasant. We may evaluate the same sensations on our skin differently depending on whether we are relaxing by the seashore with a cool drink, standing on a crowded railway platform waiting for a train that is late, or lying in bed being denied sleep. Such judgements cannot therefore be an inherent property of warmth, and we do not naturally pause to reflect on what they are actually like. It is important to work on our understanding of our choices so we can see how much choice we actually do have in the evaluation of the world that arrives at our physical senses and the thoughts that arrive in our minds.

When we explored the use of the sensation store, we learnt how to look closely at the very sensations we are feeling and experience them just as they are. If we are so inclined, we can do this for all of the eighteen types of sense components. As our judgements are not self, we are able to look at them as objects to be considered, held in our gaze at metaphorical arm's length. This scrutiny will serve us well, because it will start to inform our judgements and give us the "feeling wisdom" to enable us to react more wisely when habitual responses arise in our minds. Our natural response will shift from, say, "I am cold", to "This is coldness", and from there we can proceed to much more adaptive recognition such as "This is anger", "This is jealousy", and so on.

An example from the present moment is this: as I type these words I am in a hot country and sharing my space with a very persistent fly, who is enjoying landing on my flesh and on the cup that contains the tea that I am drinking. My natural judgement is that the sensation of him landing on my flesh is unpleasant, and therefore my initial reaction is to put an end to it. But what is the sensation *really like*? When I examine it as a raw feeling, it is nothing more than a light tickle, which as a bare impression could actually be judged to be pleasant. Why this inconsistency, when, after all, the sensation is just as it is? The sensation itself contains neither pleasantness nor unpleasantness, so this is something I have added. The fly does not know that the hand and the ankle he settles on are both me, and nor does he know that I regard the cup as mine. For him, there is no me. I suspect that if he were imbued with enough human intelligence to understand the concept of ownership, he would be prepared to accept my claim regarding the hand and ankle, but the cup may take some persuasion.

When I feel the gentle tickling of his legs on my arm as I concentrate only on the sensation, there is actually plenty less "me" for me as well. This is a key concept in the Buddha's teaching – the stronger the sense of self, the greater the suffering. When the sense of "me" is strongest, I am also creating a very strong sense of a separate "him", and thoughts of doing him harm arise. At a raw level of sensation, the sensations are just as they are, so where does all this other stuff come from? These are my judgements.

It is important to get into the habit of considering the raw sensations that we are feeling, especially when we experience them as being unpleasant. We need to learn to know them as they truly are before we start taking sides against them or trying to get rid of them. For example, the raw sensation of immersing oneself in cold water can actually be perceived as pleasant when considered at the level of the impressions on our skin alone. What makes it unpleasant for us is largely *anticipated* suffering, and that is added by thought rather than contained in the actual sensations in the moment. We should also learn to look at the feelings that come from our emotional reactions, such as jealousy, embarrassment, or social isolation. In this way we can recognise them early, before unhelpful thinking has started. Often, this may be sufficient to allow them to pass, or at least to prevent them from escalating into thought through our resistance to them. If we wait until thinking has seized the feeling, we may then make the mistake of believing the thinking mind's deception that the emotion has arisen *because of* the negative thoughts that are now in our minds.

These judgements that we make are the initial impetus in the Buddha's process model of mind. They are the energy at the beginning of a sequence that could lead us into all sorts of unhelpful and debilitating states. This might include such things as addiction, compulsion, and heedless action to the detriment of ourselves, a fly, other beings, or even all of creation. These evaluations, whether positive, negative or neutral, take on an independence in our minds, as if they are somehow "out there", rather than something in which we have a say. We feel that they happen to us, rather than that they are something that we do, and this is where wisdom needs to be developed to show us otherwise.

Our intellectual history is littered with philosophical arguments about whether we have a choice in our actions, and whether we can truly be said to be free. Interesting as such debate may be for some, this is surely a philosophical and ethical dead end that does not need to be over-elaborated. We do have options, even when the strength of our feelings seems to overwhelm us. We have all felt overpowering feelings of rapture, rage, disgust and emotional pain, but we still have a choice even when standing small and seemingly powerless in front of the tsunami of these feelings. If we can isolate the causes of these feelings then there is no tsunami, or maybe there is still a wave, but it passes under us and we are still on our surfboard.

Attribution

Attribution is the process element in which we recognise and label the sense and mind objects that have firstly arrived at our six senses, then been brought into our awareness through the aggregation of consciousness, and then have stirred a reaction of pleasant, unpleasant or neutral judgement. Whereas the judgement gives a reaction to an object at a raw emotional level, now a concept is added, an idea about the object, or an attribution. The object has been separated out from the stream of input to our minds and given name, form, and boundaries. It no longer exists only in the moment, because the concept we have added allows it to persist as an independent and timeless entity.

To name an object is not a neutral activity, and the Buddha clearly saw that carving up the flow of reality into names is a process to be explored as part of the whole wheel of becoming and suffering. Again, here we have choices that the speed and automaticity of the aggregations may otherwise obscure. A more common translation for this aggregation is "perception", which conveys very well the fact that the process happens at the moment we become aware of an object and that it influences how we experience the world around us. However it does not do as well as "attribution" in getting across the idea that something has been added to that which is perceived. In this regard, "designation" is another excellent translation.

The Buddha's insight was the forerunner of a huge and productive corpus of research in psychology, which shows some persistent biases in the way that we perceive our world. We experience this, for example, when we feel negativity towards somebody who reminds us of a person we dislike, or when we judge favourably the personality or intentions of somebody we find attractive. Evaluations and attributions spread across the web of associations within our minds, each pattern activating another with which a link has previously been formed. The massive parallelism within our brains allows for near-instantaneous activation of multiple related constructs, which in turn causes our perception to be selective as our brains filter out true experience based on the ideas that have been activated. It is not just people dressed in gorilla suits that we do not perceive; our learned biases blind us to a whole host of experience. An excellent summary of a lifetime of this research is contained in Daniel Kahneman's book *Thinking, Fast and Slow*, and we will return to it again.

Just as the judgement of feeling gives something an external quality ("This is pleasant", as opposed to "I am right now judging this to be pleasant"), this is solidified through labelling that object or thought. We give the sense object further independent life by attributing to it a concept, a definition, and a name. The concept we form is likely to have our preferences intimately bound to it, embellishing the object with choices that belong to us rather than to it. It is rare that we consider our part in the way "reality" appears to us, and how natural it is for our concepts of things and people to contain an inextricable judgement of like or dislike, approach or avoid, possess or eradicate, and so on.

A Pali word that the Buddha used to describe the reality that he taught is *sanditthiko*, which means "apparent here and now". Here, he was referring to the experience of the present moment as it truly is, unadulterated by the additions and subtractions of mind that distort our perception. His teaching shows us that consciousness, judging and attribution are all processes subject to cause and effect, and as such can all be investigated and cultivated independently. Superficially these three may feel like one process, but consciousness is only a general awareness of objects and judging is only a raw sense of pleasure or displeasure; it is attribution that grasps at the qualities of that object and forms an opinion. This is essentially a process of belief.

This belief endows the object or thought with a perceived characteristic of permanence that is not really there – "This fly is irritating." Well no, the fly is actually what it is, and the thing that is doing the irritating is my mind. If I operate from the perspective that the fly is irritating then the chain reaction that now begins could turn out very badly for both of us – a random dealing out of death on my part, and a gruesome execution for him. Here is *kamma*; here is me about to be born into the next moment based on the conditions of the current one, and about to inherit the result of my action. Looking at the fly as he sits on my cup right now, actually he is a rather sweet little chap. This judgement is the same process; his appearance arrives in my sight consciousness and I become aware, I feel his form to be pleasing, I give it a name, and he is reborn in my mind with new characteristics. I note as I think all this that he has also acquired a supposed gender, and in this we now have something in common.

We have dwelt upon on the example of the Spanish fly because it shows how *kamma* is a matter of life and death. As one moment gives life to the next, our choices seed this birth. When a moment is born, countless alternative moments are simultaneously unborn. Our choices decide which moment is given life, and our influence on the moment is our responsibility. Through awareness we can ensure that each moment is born pure and wholesome, and we can avoid mindless acts that may lead to the death of such purity, or perhaps an innocent insect.

Mental Formations

Mental formations are the sequence of mental events that happen after the judgement of feeling and the discrimination of attribution have been applied to the sense object or mind object in our conscious awareness. They are the final fulfilment of the processes by which our fly's fate is sealed – will I look upon him with kindness and allow him to go about his business, or will I swat him with a towel?

Although the most widely used translation of the Pali for this aggregation is "mental formations", other translations include "fabrications", "volitions" and "habitual responses". The limitations of our language are such that it is difficult to convey an ever-changing stream of activity through the use of static words, and here in particular, translations are somewhat unsatisfactory. The term "mental formations" goes some way to explaining what is meant by the Pali word *sankhara*, but does not do well in putting across how strong the habits of these thought patterns can become, how fluid and rapidly mutating is their nature, and how dysfunctional their content can be. "Fabrications" is less satisfactory in some ways, but does convey better the complexity of the thought processes we may construct to underlie our intentions, and how little grounding in reality they may contain. Between and behind our mental formations is a seething tangle of fabrications that we have constructed. These fabrications may be about anything at all, such as our relationships, our abilities, our failures, our fears, or our desires. Also writhing about in this lively jumble are all the impressions of our past pain, coiled and ready to spring, adding additional weight to an already burdensome load.

Mental formations are so persistent and continuous that we do not see them for what they are. Rather, we take these habitual reactions to be "givens", i.e. we believe in them and identify with them as parts of ourselves. By identifying with these formations, we give them more life force and nourish them with our being. However, when we investigate them, we see that they are not us at all, and indeed they are not even very much. They are just cause and effect, and as such are subject to change if we will it. When we look at them skilfully, they become what they are – just patterns of ephemeral thought. How strange that something so ruinous can at the same time be nothing at all. If we do not supply them with energy, they just dissipate and pass on their way before they develop into a full story in our minds. Unfortunately, we are rarely mindful enough to act in this way, unless we have cultivated the necessary vigilance. Fortunately, that is now our task.

We draw on all these formations habitually and unquestioningly in responding to events in the external realm. They also underlie our interpretations of the sensations and urges in our bodies that we call our emotions. In responding through our mental formations, we lose the chance to see anything as if for the first time, which means that we react more to the baggage that we have added than to the moment that has just arrived. As the additional encumbrances will tend to be the same stuff each time they come up, so too our reactions will usually be similar. Hereby continues the illusion that responses, emotions, and so on are quintessentially "us", even if we do not like them. This aggregation underlies the whole gamut of complex mental life and may result in action that is wholesome or unwholesome, skilful or unskilful, or none of these. Unless and until we gain insight into the nature of our mental formations, we will relive them again and again whenever the relevant stimuli are present in our environment. This is *kamma*. We will also confuse them with our own identity, and this is delusion.

The aggregation of mental formations is another very fertile source of lists in the Buddha's teachings. In one part of the teaching, there are fifty types of mental formation listed, but, as usual, we will resist expounding the list and hold to the essence of the teaching. The aggregation of mental formations has a much more fluid scope than the other four, in that it encompasses a wide grouping of activities of mind, and underlies our observable behaviour. At the most basic level, our behaviours with respect to objects in the world and objects in our minds are twofold; firstly to approach and prolong that which we like, and secondly to diminish or extinguish that which we do not. Often, our behaviours are much more complex than simple approach/avoid, but the same principles are there.

Let's look at a *kammic* chain of events that is all too common in so-called "developed" cultures today, although it is far from being a standard to which "undeveloped" cultures should aspire. The example is the bizarre phenomenon of road rage, where normally responsible people find themselves overcome by the most incredible surge of fury as a result of an infringement of traffic protocol. This chain reaction starts with an incident that comes to conscious awareness via the eyes, but at this point the episode is as it is; it is just a series of visual events involving the changing positions of some simple mechanical forms. So where does this intense feeling of rage, injustice and hatred come from? Surely it cannot arise simply from contact with the visual forms before us?

The most salient point here is that when our passions are aroused, the sense of a separate self is intensified. This is no doubt fuelled by the fact that we are in an enclosed metal box and our supposed assailant is in another, heightening and emphasising the separation of self and other. In this situation, we fly from sense contact to action in an instant, although it is interesting to reflect for a while on what we feel in the process. We may experience a surging sensation in the solar plexus and a quickening in the limbs if we have to react quickly to avoid danger, but more often than not there is not much of a feeling at all associated with the actual incident, nor any actual danger. Certainly, there may be strong reactions a split second after the incident, but the experience in the moment itself is likely to be somewhat ordinary.

Essentially, the mental formation that we ultimately apply is along the lines of "That person cut me up, and they did it because they are ignorant and disrespectful towards me." We experience this as our ground zero, the origin of the storm, but how on earth do we arrive at a judgement like this that is so out of proportion to the original incident? Our increased identity with self at these times seems to endow us with the power to pass judgement on the supposed aggressor's intentions, and as a result vitriol surges from our past and endows our foe with the summed evil of all others that have crossed us. In a flash, we have travelled a very long road from the initial and unremarkable visual scene of mechanical objects in motion.

When we are seized by road rage, we do not habitually question our mental state, even if for an instant we are able to see it for what it is. Instead, we justify it – "Damn right I'm angry, I have every right to be!" – and we are thereby consumed by it. It is no longer a series of occurrences, a chain of changeable cause and effect. Instead, the anger is what we *are*. There are of course several choices that we make in a sequence of events such as this, no matter how inevitable it may feel. Our behaviour would almost certainly have been different had we known that the other driver was distracted through learning that their child had just been rushed to hospital. Or, more simply, perhaps that the driver made an honest mistake and is now bitterly regretting the inconvenience they have caused us. Things would certainly be different if the driver were somebody we love.

We do not consider such possibilities because we do not want to. They do not fit the pattern of self-view and ill will that we have created. The fundamental part of the process of mental formations is the volitional aspect, and here the translation of *sankhara* as "volitions" is close to the mark. Through volition we form an intention to behave and then follow that intention to produce the behaviour. The input to this outcome may be a simple feeling of pleasure or pain, or a complex web of emotion and thought. In the case of road rage, our sense of self is so strong that we are completely out of touch with any concept that there may be a volitional aspect at all. The entire incident is autopiloted by our mental formations, and our bodies are just a vessel for allowing the whole unnecessary scene to play out.

The volitional aspect of the aggregation of mental formations grasps at our intentions as they form, as if these intentions were some sort of truth that must be obeyed, not something we might question. The consequence is that before we are aware, we have acted. It would only require the insertion of a tiny space in between the processes of instinctive and habitual action to allow wisdom to enter in and influence the outcome. Even the most minuscule adjournment may lead to a weakening of the intention, and perhaps an openness to the fact that others are suffering too. It is this space that we cultivate in meditation, and the wisdom that may arise in this space is what we strive for in our practice.

Washing about somewhere in between the Buddha's concepts of judging, attribution and mental formations are the psychologist's concepts of *associative memory* and *spreading activation*. The view of contemporary psychology, which is consistent with extensive experimental evidence, is that each elemental idea that is stored in the mind, whether it be the concept of a tree, a particular tree, a gesture, a sound, or whatever, is like a node in a vast and multiply-connected network. We have already touched on this whilst discussing biases in the judging process. Each connection between nodes can be thought of as having learned properties that define how one node links to another, how causes are connected to effects, how objects and ideas are associated with their properties and categories to which they belong, and so on.

When we come into contact with something in the outside world or within our own minds, even subliminally, there is a rapid spread of activation across this network, activating many nodes simultaneously. Each activated node in turn activates another with which it has become linked through learning, and the strength of these associations that we have formed will determine what comes into our consciousness and how we respond. In the case of road rage, it is reasonable to suppose that the particular experience of being in an armoured container has already warmed up a network of links associated with heightened self-view. Another commonly used translation of the Pali word *sankhara* is "conceptual proliferation", which fits in very well with this model of mind. This rapid activation of a network of related memories and biases is thought to be the baseline from which a surprising event is determined. As we have already discussed, this spreading activation of learnt associations also affects what we attend to in our environment, and importantly what we do and do not perceive. All this established psychological theory has much in common with the Buddha's view of the aggregations, and certainly supports that view, but the Buddha's original version is much more potent because it directly addresses how we may address unhelpful learned relationships.

No matter how ingrained the habitual action, nor how powerful the urge, we always have a choice regarding our behaviour, and that choice will determine our future. It is our responsibility to connect ourselves with our choices, which may be to spare a fly from the end of a towel arriving at terminal velocity, or to spare a fellow human being from intimidating and disproportionate retribution for a breach of roadway etiquette. As the Buddha said, we are born of our *kamma,* and of that *kamma* we will be the heirs. We are not talking here about any spiritual or physical rebirth, but simply of conditions and their responses. This is often referred to as "dependent origination" in Buddhist texts, rather than the more loaded translation of "rebirth", and we will come to an explanation of it in due course.

Worldly Winds

We have already observed that the Buddha´s teachings approach the same truths from multiple directions, and there is another teaching relevant to the mental formations that is helpful to consider at this point. It is one of the more simple and practical teachings, and concerns what the Buddha called the *worldly winds.* "Worldly winds" is a perfectly evocative translation of the original Pali word, conveying beautifully the idea that there are conditions in the worldly realm that can blow us off course. In the realm of pure awareness these conditions are remote and insubstantial things, but when the mind is caught up in worldly affairs they can be gale force. Of course, the Buddha's intent here was not to refer to the world outside, but rather to the worldly influences within the mind.

The worldly winds come in four pairs of opposites, which are:

Pleasure and Pain
Praise and Blame
Fame and Disrepute
Gain and Loss

In each case, the pressure system that causes the winds to blow is our desire to attain one of these opposites and avoid the other. Until we can detach our minds from striving to obtain one thing and escape another, there will always be a pressure difference and the storms will continue to form. Meditation will enable us to become detached, but we also need wisdom to understand that pleasure, praise, fame and gain are suffering in just the same way as are pain, blame, disrepute and loss. This is an aspect of the teachings that is easy to neglect, particularly when the things are going "our way".

The worldly winds are particularly perilous when blowing around the mental formations. Their energy and direction can get hold of a passing thought and carry it rapidly away from its origin, picking up other mental debris and whipping up a whirlwind laden with destruction. Familiarity with the worldly winds is therefore a skilful means of watching our minds and enabling the mental formations to dissipate. They are worldly tendencies that we must guard against, and they affect all of us alike.

The Mind of Awareness

The Buddha's teachings on the contracted mind point clearly to what lies beyond – the mind of awareness. This is one of the wonderful aspects of his psychology; whilst it explains very effectively how the mind operates when it is still prey to delusion, it also shows equally well the way to emancipation from this contracted state, and maps out the terrain of pure awareness. As meditation practice deepens and we start to free ourselves from the five hindrances, we come to a deeper understanding of the five aggregations that serve to limit our experience. At the same time, we penetrate more and more the truth of the three characteristics of all worldly things, which results in a life-altering shift in perspective. In this way, we avoid the buffeting from the worldly winds and learn the fundamental key to moving between the contracted state of mind and the limitless gift of pure awareness – to *let go*.

When we connect fully with our awareness, no matter how briefly, suddenly we see something beyond the aggregations. Here, I am not using the word "beyond" in the sense of "further on than", but rather in the sense of "other than". When we encounter this boundless state, it is clear that it is something that is not subject to cause and effect, in that it is *already there*. This insight is fundamental, and quite remarkable whenever it is encountered. This awareness is something we contact, not something we create. The experience of pure awareness has no use for concepts such as past and future, or cause and effect, because it just *is*. Although we can consult descriptions of this natural and authentic mind state, in the original teachings of the Buddha or elsewhere, really it is only our own experience that matters. The words we read and hear are at best signposts, and are generally only of use to us as such, if at all. The Buddha's way is primarily one of doing, with thinking only as supporting cast.

Figure 2 is an attempted depiction of the mind of awareness that the Buddha taught, and is offered to emphasise the contrast with the everyday model of mind.

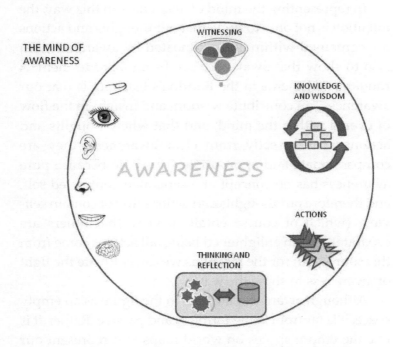

Figure 2 – The Mind of Awareness

A diagram is a very efficient way to communicate a multifaceted theme, but of course it has its limitations. Some features of the model are immediately apparent in the figure, whilst others need a little unpacking. It can clearly be seen that awareness surrounds sensation, action, and all mental events. Less obvious perhaps is the fact that awareness also pervades them, providing that the mind is properly trained. All mental phenomena are permeable to awareness. It is also evident that there are no set relationships or pathways between elements of mind, and that only awareness lies in between. Significantly, the thinking mind is demoted to a resource of mind, rather being the controller or indeed the mind itself as it is in the everyday model.

In representing the mind of awareness in this way, the intention is not only to show that our thoughts and actions are contained within and permeated by awareness, but also to show that awareness can be an *input* to them. A fundamental theme in the Buddha's teaching is that our awareness can contribute wisdom and insight to the flow of events within the mind, and that when thoughts and actions arise directly from clear awareness, they are compassionate and appropriate. This is so because pure awareness has no concept of a separated contracted self, and therefore our thoughts and actions do not contain self-view (which of course entails a view that others are separate). For an enlightened being, all actions come from this source, but for the rest of us we can cultivate the light of awareness to show the way.

Although awareness appears in the figure as an empty space, it is far from being formless and passive. Rather, it is like the empty spaces on world maps that represent our oceans, an energised and powerful force of nature. Like the oceans, it is a bountiful source of unsullied life, and without it our species has no future. There will be more on this latter point later, but for now let's stick with the explanation of the mind of awareness. Continuing the potent analogy with the planet's oceans, our awareness is also prone to cataclysmic vortices and currents. The five aggregations are like whirlpools that draw energy away from our awareness and into themselves. When this happens, it is as if they cast a shadow across our awareness that prevents us from seeing their true nature. We are drawn inside them and we become lost, swept along on a course that we struggle to resist, and which leads nowhere but downwards. Unless we train our minds in the right way, we spin around and around inside the aggregations and are drawn deeper and deeper into the shadows. Sometimes, the disturbances in our awareness can cause certain patterns of destructive thought to become over-energised, and when this happens we become overwhelmed and unable to cope. This is mental illness, a topic we will cover in a later part of the book, along with its remedies.

Nine key features of the everyday model of mind were drawn out earlier, and for symmetry here are nine key features of the mind of awareness:

1. Awareness surrounds sensation, thinking, and action, but can also flow within them.
2. Untrained awareness is subject to vortices that create blind spots within it, in which the five aggregations churn and the worldly winds blow.
3. There are no set pathways between any aspects of mind, although habits of the untrained mind create an illusion that there are.

4. Wisdom is not a static store of knowledge, but an active process of discernment.
5. Wisdom, insight, and wise action can arise naturally.
6. Experience can lead directly to learning.
7. The thinking mind is a resource to be used for reflection and problem-solving, but is not the mind itself.
8. The thinking mind does not have access to all of the mind's knowledge.
9. There is no self.

Earlier, we discussed the everyday model of mind and its origins. It is instructive now to revisit that model based on what we now know of the Buddha's alternative.

The Joy of Being Out of Control

We have already noted the fundamental difference between our two perspectives of mind: that the everyday model is a computational view whilst the Buddha's psychology is a process view. This has important implications for the meaning we attach to the concept of being "in control" of our minds. According to the everyday model, changes in state are initiated and controlled by the master processor, and this central role is carried out by the rational thinking "I". If we do not feel in control of the contents of our minds, we regard this as an aberration, a disorderly state that can usually be rectified by resetting the controller with new instructions. In other words, we try to think ourselves out of any perceived problem. As our experience with meditation deepens, one of the changes in our outlook is the idea that we have a lasting "problem" at all when the winds blow in our minds. We notice, sometimes with an inner smile, that our first reaction to any temporary disturbance in our mood is to start thinking. The breakthrough is that when this happens, we let the thoughts go.

In the Buddha's psychology, the concept of control is merely a means to an end, employed as a method of training the mind. Whilst we are learning how to manage our minds, we practise controlling and directing the beam of our awareness to keep it fully engaged with our meditation object. In doing this, the goal is not merely to develop enhanced powers of concentration, as this would of course just be more striving and therefore more suffering. We have already discussed how experienced meditators warn of the dangers of becoming caught up in the bliss of "absorption", which can actually hinder our progress. It is a step on the path, not the journey's end. Rather, the goal is simply to watch. By learning to hold our awareness in one place, we are able to see the aggregations in operation from a safe position. Once we are in our place of sanctity, we can observe them coming and going and see them for what they are – mere conditions, bundles of cause and effect. In this way, the aggregations and the seeds of the hindrances and worldly winds can pass through the mind without taking up residence.

When we have penetrated the nature of the movements within the mind in this way, we are able to start to free ourselves of their burden. For most of us, this will be a gradual experience rather than a sudden revelation, so patience is wise and so is gratitude for small signs of progress. Until such insight starts to grow within us, the conditioned mind is in a very real sense "out of control", because it is pulled hither and yonder by habitual feelings, judgements, thoughts and actions. However, the way out of suffering is not a matter of increasing control. It is a matter of increasing awareness. Being out of control is not a bad thing at all; it is fundamentally how things are.

Choiceless Witnessing

At the beginning of the book, I disclosed that not all the ideas herein derive from my own thinking or that of others, but rather that some are directly experienced, arising through the stillness of the mind of awareness. I described the thrill that initially accompanies such moments of clarity, which is a feeling of intense pleasure deriving from connectedness to the present moment, as opposed to the solitary and empty pleasure that comes from satisfying the desires of self. I also forewarned you that there will be times when this stillness can seem to be out of reach, when the rip tides in our awareness merge together and become strong enough to carry us away. As with a real rip tide, to resist the current by battling against it is dangerous, and the correct action is to turn away. We need to remind ourselves of our resolve to watch the hindrance of doubt as it arises, not to follow or resist it. It also helps to move our awareness into the body to withdraw energy from the currents that have arisen. More of this later.

When wisdom naturally appears in the mind, awareness is directly feeding thought and action. The Buddha taught that this is the highest goal for our minds, and that it is a natural state to discover, not a new state to attain. Such occurrences may be rare on our path, at least initially, but when they happen it is very apparent to us, and satisfying in a way that no worldly pleasure can equal. In Figure 2, a mental process is shown labelled "Witnessing", which is intended to include this facility of mind, through which we observe insight springing up fully formed, rather than being created in thought. Here, wisdom becomes thought, not the other way around as is conventionally perceived. Wisdom also becomes action, and through witnessing this wise action we gain understanding, again the opposite of the conventionally held flow. Of course, in the Buddha's psychology, speech is a form of action.

This part of the figure also represents the learning that our minds can do, without, or indeed in spite of, thinking. We have already discussed this at length when considering the limitations of the everyday model of mind. Here too, any understanding we are able to articulate and communicate is necessarily after the fact. The feats of learning that can be achieved outside of the control of the thinking mind are of course remarkable, but they only hint at the true capability of the mind of awareness. The wisdom that arises naturally is beyond remarkable. It is understanding in the most fundamental and life-enhancing sense. It is the truth of the way things are.

A Sandbox for the Thinking Mind

The mind of awareness still has a place for the thinking element of mind. Of course it does, because thinking is a very important resource of mind. However, unlike the everyday model, the mind of awareness does not overvalue thinking as the central controlling function, and nor does it give thinking access to all areas. So, the figure simply shows thinking as a process within the mind of awareness. In the figure it is termed "thinking and reflection" to give emphasis to its two important roles: firstly to solve problems as they present themselves to us, and secondly to contemplate the wisdom of our thoughts, speech, and actions.

When we are fully aware, we are seeing things as they really are, both within our own minds and bodies, and outside of them. We are able to see the true nature of our thoughts and deeds as they arise in the moment, and we can perceive the world around us independently of our desires about how it should or should not be. There is an essential separation between our awareness and the contents of our minds. We may notice the thinking mind doing its rounds now and again, trying to make us take an interest in things that it alleges are important to us. It may ask us to plan, to worry, to lust, to plot, to despair, to fantasise, or anything just to make us approach the margins of the whirlpool. As we see and know these patterns, we become wise in the moment, and we let go. We are aware that thinking is not needed at this time and so we let it pass. We have learnt a safe way to relate to thinking, and this is based on *not self*, or *anatta* as it is in Pali. To use an expression frequently employed by Eckhart Tolle, we learn not to "make a self" out of our thoughts.

We have all experienced the surging power of unsafe thought, when the thinking mind overwhelms us with cascading thoughts that can lead us to worry, anger or despair. At the extreme of this harmful spectrum is the all too common phenomenon of the anxiety attack. Although we may develop effective ways to deal with situations when excessive thought is present, we do not habitually consider whether there may be a safer way to live inside our heads during times that are calmer. A crucial step towards the remedy is for us to acknowledge the awesome power of the mind of awareness, not just in learning, but in simply *being*. It is extraordinary, but true, that learning to be is harder than learning to do. It takes almost no depth of insight to realise that we do not need to be thinking all the time, but nevertheless it seems impossible to stop getting involved in the internal babble. When we learn simply to be, we come to understand how thinking selects from our environment at the expense of full awareness of the richness that surrounds us. As we will learn in later sections of this book, it also has a larger influence on our moods than we may know.

Earlier, we discussed how the everyday model of mind has enjoyed a long and intimate relationship with the design of the computer, and is to a large extent still trapped within that metaphor. Although I find similes and metaphors somewhat trite and unnecessary, and habitually pass judgement on those who use them, modern computing provides an irresistible metaphor for the place of the thinking mind within the mind of awareness. The relevant concept in computing is the *sandbox*. A sandbox is a safe place within a computer where untrusted software can execute without being able to control the host's behaviour or alter any of its vital resources. The sandbox construct also underlies our ability to download multiple apps to our various smart gadgets without affecting their essential behaviour.

Following this compelling metaphor, the purpose of

our meditation practice is to create a sandbox for the thinking mind. It is our awareness that provides the sandbox, ensuring that thinking cannot take control of our behaviour without us first granting it the right to do so. Sandboxes are also used by computer security specialists to analyse the behaviour of malware, and here again the metaphor is fertile; when thoughts and intentions are sandboxed (and in computing, there ain't no noun that can't be verbed!) we are able to reflect wisely upon them before we allow them to influence our behaviour.

PART FOUR

THE PATH AND
THE WHEEL

An Ancient Path

We have already learnt that the Buddha claimed only to teach about two things – suffering and the way out of suffering. He was a way-shower and he taught a path that we can all follow to experience the benefits of his teaching. In the ancient texts, he is reported to have referred to himself frequently as *tathagata*, which means "thus come", or "thus gone". Through following the path he described, we too have the opportunity to transcend our contracted natures, and come – or go – to the same place of serenity and liberation.

The Buddha described a path that leads to the end of suffering, and this is commonly referred to as the *eightfold path*. This is one of the fundamentals in Buddhist teaching, and was described by the Buddha in his very first sermon, in which he described the insights that he had discovered. Despite being the bedrock of one of the world's major religions, there is nothing religious or spiritual about this essential instruction. Rather, it is a simple and practical guide to mental training, and it is refreshingly straightforward to describe and understand. Certainly, it entails belief, but that belief comes from our own experience of trying out the path, and is therefore based on personal and direct comprehension rather than blind faith. Even naming it as a path is inspirational, because this emphasises that it is not a theory, it is something we do, somewhere we go.

The universal symbol of the eightfold path is a wheel with eight spokes, and this symbol has existed since the Buddha's time. There are other uses of the wheel symbol in Buddhism, and there are various wheels with different numbers of spokes, each with distinct meanings. However, the eight-spoke wheel represents the fundamentals of the path, and with this symbol we will stay. There is great perceptiveness in the use of the wheel symbol to represent the path, because like the Buddha's path, a wheel has neither beginning nor end. The path begins with wisdom and leads to wisdom. Also, the form of a wheel is conducive to it staying in motion, unless slowed by friction or impeded by an obstacle. In our practice on the path, we encounter both friction that slows us and obstacles that obstruct us, but the Buddha's teachings help us to overcome these retarding factors. The communicative power of the wheel symbol seems boundless at times.

One of the amazing aspects of the path is that it delivers benefit immediately, and continues to do so in increasing measure as our practice deepens. This is what the Buddha meant when he initially described his teaching, or *dhamma* as it is called in Pali, as "beautiful in the beginning, beautiful in the middle, and beautiful in the end". He once told a story of a man who had been shot with a poisoned arrow, and would not allow it to be withdrawn until he knew all the details of the person who fired it, and the composition of the arrow itself. Here the Buddha was pointing to the fact that there is no need to understand the end of the path before setting out upon it and immediately experiencing some release.

The eight steps on the path, or the spokes in the wheel, are traditionally described in three broad categories –

Wisdom, Mental Development, and Ethical Conduct, as follows:

Wisdom – Wisdom is the beginning and the end of the path, and is also contained in every step. The wisdom of sufficient understanding is needed to provide the impetus to start out on the path, and the fruit of the path is wisdom. As wisdom increases along the path, it provides further impetus to keep us developing, and this leads to a perpetual motion that naturally sustains us in our practice.

Mental development – This is the essential fuel for the practice; the training of the mind, together with cultivating the effort required to sustain the training. As we progress, the energy to continue on the path starts to arise naturally, i.e. without the need for us to summon it. It becomes instinctive and welcome.

Ethical conduct – This is the behavioural aspect of the path, which in general consists of indulging in wise and skilful behaviour and refraining from their opposites. This is not any sort of moral absolute, and the choice of standard is personal, but the commitment to a code of behaviour is an essential aid to mindfulness. Such commitment comes not from dogma, but from wisdom.

We will now move on to describe each individual element of the eightfold path. The Pali word *anga* is traditionally translated as "step" when relating to the eightfold path, as this translation fits in well with the concept of a path that is travelled. Actually, the word more literally means "limb" or "member", which works better with the wheel symbol. The eight elements of the eightfold path are neither separate nor ordered, but are interdependent and, like the spokes of a wheel, are all in motion at the same time. In this explanation we won't stick to any particular translation of *anga*, now that the sense of the word has been described.

There may well be a better analogy out there than the wheel, and now and again I try to find it. My particular concerns are firstly to find a way to represent the fact that once the wheel is set in motion its propensity towards movement is self-sustaining; and secondly that some elements of the path play more of a part in this perpetual motion than others. In the preparation of this book I spent several hours with blank page and coloured pens trying to show how elements of the path turn the wheel and how the motion continues under its own impetus. There were diagrams of wheels within wheels, even a flywheel – the whole Heath Robinson panoply. However, that turned out to be just some more thinking, so let's get down to an explanation along more conventional lines.

In the eightfold path, there are eight things that need to be done "right" to turn and keep in motion the wheel that takes us to the end of suffering. By implication, there is also a "wrong" way to do these things, and the teachings are clear on the criteria for the behaviour being right or wrong. Of course, the concepts of "right" and "wrong" here are not intended to imply any sort of moral evaluation – what "right" means in this context is "appropriate to the purpose of progress on the path", and conversely "wrong" means "inappropriate to this purpose, and therefore leading away from progress on the path". The Pali word *samma* that is usually translated as "right" actually means "whole", "integrated", or even "perfect", which gives an insight into the concept that the Buddha was aiming at here.

The eight elements of the path will now be described, using the three categories of Wisdom, Mental Development, and Ethical Conduct outlined above.

Wisdom

Right View

Right view is often said to be the beginning of the path, although it has equal claim to be the end. It is the beginning of the path in the sense that without some understanding of the perspective underlying the Buddha's teaching, there would be no impetus to start or continue. It is the end of the path in that if we truly have right view, then we are wise and awakened and understand things as they really are. To have right view is also to abandon self-view, or at least to know it for what it is. Ultimately, right view is to understand fully the impermanence of things, the lack of stable satisfaction in things that are subject to change, and the path to liberation from attachment to passing conditions. At the beginning of the path, the view is more of a glimpse, but it is still sufficient to see that the Buddha's message has meaning and that the path will lead to the liberation that the teaching promises.

Right view is not a property of the thinking mind, although the trained thinking mind has its part to play. It is something that arises from cultivated awareness, where the release of our grip on thought and a separated self allows wisdom to arise naturally, along with other natural states such as compassion. It is a much more intuitive quality than intellectual understanding. It is to be expected that at the beginning of the path our right view will be more rooted in the thinking mind and its inner voice, but as the three path elements of mental development become more established, wisdom will arise naturally from our awakening mind and it will feel more like "right intuition".

Right view is a good example of the turning of the wheel – if we have right view, then it straightforwardly follows that we will have right intention, as a result of which we will then cultivate the mental development and ethical conduct parts of the path as well. In addition to the three major elements of wisdom, mental development, and ethical conduct, the eightfold path is often described as having two divisions – *vision* and *transformation*. Right view stands alone in the vision category, as it is the impetus to the transformation that takes places through the remaining seven limbs.

Right Intention

Like right view, right intention exists at the start of the path, and is also an outcome of following the path. Right intention is the volitional aspect of our wisdom i.e. the mental impetus to move forward in line with the teaching. It is our resolution to start and continue and to resist the hindrances that will pull us away from the path. It is the commitment to resist sense desire, ill will, worry, doubt, and lassitude, and to stir up energy to do so. So, the term "intention" includes a wide range of positive attitudes, including inspiration, aspiration, resolve, tenacity and will.

Our right intention needs to apply to everything that we do, and in order to achieve this there are some fundamental areas that require our focus. Firstly, and most obviously, there is our intention to let go of the controlling nature of the thinking mind. In doing this, we have to learn to be both kind and gentle with ourselves, because we will frequently be unsuccessful in our efforts. Such self-directed leniency can be quite difficult, because we may naturally apply standards of gentleness and compassion to others that we do not apply to ourselves. We will return to this point later, but for now it is sufficient to say that a helpful guide is to view ourselves in the way that a close friend would view us, which allows for a measure of trust and forgiveness and a willingness to wipe the slate clean.

There will be persistent mental formations that visit us, and it may require months or years of meditation before they no longer arise, so we need to be patient in the meantime and not exert excessive effort in a struggle to annihilate them. There is an important and subtle point here: it is our *resistance* to these formations that we are letting go of, not the formations themselves. The formations will leave of their own accord once we have stopped fighting. If we go on the attack against our unwanted mental states, we exercise all the wrong mental muscles in the process, and create a *kammic* chain of resistance and attachment. Right intention must include being kind to ourselves and to our thoughts.

Mental Development

Right Effort

At its simplest, right effort is the stirring up of energy to progress on the path. We need effort to abandon that which we do not need on the path, namely the hindrances and our clinging nature, and we need effort to cultivate and sustain what we do need, i.e. the mindfulness that lies within us. At the start of the path, our minds are deluded and leading us astray, whereas when we are advanced we are awake and wise. In between these two states we require an abundant supply of energy, both to inspire us initially and then to keep that motivation as we progress. We will spend quite a lot of time discussing right effort, because its opposite comes in so many guises that we need to learn to recognise.

Once the wheel is in motion, we have to deal with friction and obstruction, which derive in large part from the five hindrances. The first two hindrances of sense desire and ill will are described in the ancient texts as being the strongest and therefore the hardest to overcome. In the Buddha's teaching he refers to a state of advancement on the path where much has been achieved, but only three hindrances have been defeated, which are worry, doubt, and sloth. Although sense desire and ill will have been weakened at this point, they are only vanquished by significantly more profound insight. For these two most obstinate hindrances, even when we are overwhelmed by them and we are mindful enough to know we are lost, we may carry on dwelling in them anyway. Knowing we are lost is actually the start of the process of liberating ourselves, and it shows that we have made at least some progress on the path.

Although the Buddha did not seat the hindrance of worry at the top table of difficult hindrances, a personal view is that this hindrance may be more prevalent and obstinate today than it was in his time, and had he lived today he may have emphasised it more. Or, maybe I am just choosing not to let go of my own most troublesome hindrance by externalising it and endowing it with properties it does not possess, such as increased difficulty, or indeed worthiness of reconsideration by the Buddha himself!

When we get lost in the hindrances, particularly when our passions are aroused, our thinking minds are likely to invent stories to justify why we should stay with the hindrances rather than spend our time more wisely. Such tales usually become self-fulfilling, feeding the intensity of the hindrances and so perpetuating them. The most obvious examples of this tendency relate to ill will, where verbal concepts such as "revenge" and "justice" may be invoked to justify some of the most unskilful acts imaginable. As we discussed earlier, the triggers and outcomes of road rage show just how much the hindrance can be fed and amplified in the storm of the aggregations. In the arena of sense desire, we may simply tell ourselves that there is "nothing wrong with a little bit of what we fancy" or that we are "past the point of no return". Fat-enclosed vital organs, and partners lamenting the breaking of a bond of trust would tell a different story about the need to summon up the effort of restraint when sense desire arises. With worry, our minds simply tell us that we are solving a problem, when actually we are pointlessly brooding.

The point here is that it takes effort to choose to countermand choices that our thinking minds have made. When we have chosen to follow our passions, we find that there is an implicit justification for our thoughts and actions that serves to occlude our initial choices. We need to apply significant effort to learn to see all of this start to happen, first at the point of contact, then as the feeling arises and the judgement is made, then as the concept is formed and the thought chains begin, and finally at the point at which we choose to act. Right effort is to learn to recognise habitually the role of the five aggregations in our behaviour, and to learn to let go at progressively earlier points in the process.

The Buddha also taught of "unarisen" hindrances. Where a hindrance has not yet arisen in the mind, he described how we use the right effort of mindfulness to hold it in check. Taking sense desire as an example, whenever the sense organs perceive a form that is judged to be either attractive or disagreeable, if the sense doors are not guarded we become vulnerable. Right effort is not about cutting ourselves off altogether from sense stimulation, although of course this would help at times. Rather, it is an endeavour to dwell for a short time in the space between the constituent elements of the aggregations such that sense desire does not arise, or at least does not take hold.

Sometimes we may succeed in being mindful at the point that a feeling arises and avoid reacting to it, only later to succumb to it when it returns as a thought, drawing on our memory of the event. For example, the memory of a sexual urge may later give rise to thoughts, intentions, and then unwholesome behaviour that may ultimately betray somebody's trust. Or, a feeling of anger may return to stimulate brooding that could then lead to us harming another, even if we dealt skilfully with the original scenario that we now allege caused us hurt. As ever, the four foundations are our guide and the focus of our right effort; sensations in the body are as they are, and the same is true of the thoughts in the mind.

Of course, a major part of right effort is making the commitment to meditate regularly. This may involve getting out of bed a little earlier to accommodate this new aspect of our daily routine, or sacrificing another regular pursuit to allow meditation to take its place. However, even when we are underway with our meditation routine and are seeing the benefits, we may still procrastinate. Procrastination is a special case of the hindrance of sloth, and sometimes it attracts other hindrances to it, in that often we procrastinate by spending our time feeding sense desires, worrying, plotting, or fantasising.

Although we cannot hide from the fact that energy is required for the application of right effort, we will learn to transform the generation of this energy into a joyful anticipation, rather than a wearisome burden. We will not be able to do this consistently in the early stages of the path, and we may even doubt that such joyous effort can arise at all, but we will learn to recognise the hindrance of doubt here and let it go. All we need is sufficient right view and right intention to provide us with that initial energy, and the wheel will start to turn. A simple but effective method of inspiring right effort is to visualise the Buddha's example of resolutely sitting for forty-nine days until achieving enlightenment, and then spending the remaining forty-five years of his life teaching for the sole benefit of others. That certainly places into context the twenty minutes or so that we may be procrastinating about! For my own part, I frequently sit and contemplate, "What would I do if I met the Buddha?", and this provides an injection of energy into my own practice.

An important realisation is that the energy underlying right effort is the very same energy that underlies unskilful behaviour. That is not to say that we should regard our energy as having a fixed budget at any one time, but more simply that we need to make choices about how and where we spend it in each moment – we cannot be in two places at once. With sense desire, ill will, and worry, the instinct to divert all our energy to these hindrances can be overwhelming, so to stir up sufficient energy to counter them is a task that could defeat us at times. It is mindfulness of the here and now that is the key to success at such times, in that the first waves of energy of unwholesome thought and action may be quite small and manageable. By being mindful of these early indications and reacting appropriately, we can remove energy from the landfall of thought that would otherwise allow these small waves to combine and form a tsunami.

So far we have considered the right effort required to deal only with the main requisites: to meditate, to be watchful of the hindrances, and to reflect wisely. However, the full range of right effort we need to embrace is much wider than this, and is subtle and multifaceted. It takes effort to care for ourselves, and to forgive ourselves. It takes even more effort to love ourselves, but all these things we must nurture. When we deal with our loved ones, or our children if we have them, we habitually favour the carrot over the stick, and we are always ready to forgive. We need to learn to confer the same rights upon ourselves, because otherwise we will impede our own progress on the path.

The word "rights" was carefully chosen, because it is important to recognise that we have the same right to good treatment as anybody else. We sometimes drive ourselves too hard, denying ourselves rest and nourishment, and crucially the awareness we need to keep the wheel in motion. Kindness, respect and forgiveness towards ourselves all require effort because they are not generally habitual inclinations, and of course awareness is seen by the thinking mind as a threat to its power base. A good place to start is to forgive ourselves for lapses in our mindfulness practice. Certainly, we need to learn from our errors, but to dwell in self-reproach is not helpful. The other side of the same priceless metaphorical coin is to take a moment to thank and respect ourselves for having sufficient awareness to spot the slip. The modern pressure to earn money to provide for self and dependent others, or just to "be successful", can also lead to us making some harsh pronouncements about our own limitations and therefore self-worth. Such judgements can ultimately be very damaging, and yet it seems to take more effort to refrain from them than it does to sustain them. Nevertheless, it is important that we cultivate the effort of restraint in this regard.

Of course, we may not always feel like being mindful. The obvious case is when we are overwhelmed by our thinking minds, for example when we are highly anxious. Or, we may just be daydreaming or idly flicking through pictures in a magazine and not realise we have lost focus. It is, of course, no crime to be doing these things, but we need to know we are doing them and guard against them taking us to unwholesome states. Sometimes our thinking minds may try to seduce us by telling us that five minutes off from mindfulness won't do us any harm. At other times we may just be physically tired and unable to focus our minds. In all cases, there is something we can do: we can remind ourselves of our resolve, we can call to mind an impression of the joy we feel when in meditation, and we can simply get on with being in the present moment. Even physical tiredness may not be as debilitating as it first seems when one reflects on it wisely without judging, as we have already discussed when considering the hindrance of sloth and torpor. I have learnt of monks who can be alert and mindful even after long periods of sleeplessness. Indeed, it is common in some monastic traditions for monks regularly to stay up all night meditating.

"Right" effort does not necessarily mean sustained maximum effort, and nor does it even mean a large amount of effort. It means effort of the right kind, in the right measure, and at the right time. The path is not about exertion. We can apply too much effort, and we can apply effort of the wrong kind. For example, we can engage in too much formal sitting, when perhaps wise reflection may be more suitable. In the Buddha's time, the monk Sona carried on with his walking meditation despite the fact that his delicate feet were already bleeding profusely, and this earned him a teaching from the Buddha in right effort. Another common misdirection of effort is to put too much into study of books and listening to talks, rather than experiencing the path directly for ourselves. We can withdraw excessively from the world whilst engaged in our "important" meditation (or maybe important book-writing whilst a loved one is working hard on cleaning the kitchen floor, to take a real world example from this present moment!). We can also talk too much about our practice, or just talk too much. The Buddha called his teaching the "middle way", and we need to learn to find this middle way for ourselves.

It is important to understand that the right effort of mindfulness should apply to happy states as well as unhappy ones. Joy in getting what we want is just as much a cause of suffering as sadness in getting what we do not want, although we may not recognise this at the time. As we have already discussed, it is a pervasive delusion of the thinking mind that we will achieve sustained happiness by getting what we want and avoiding that which we do not. All things change, or to use the phrase that has achieved bumper sticker ubiquity – this too shall pass. We must always seek to know the truth of the moment, regardless of whether we react to that moment with pleasure, displeasure, or neither.

Finally, and very importantly, effort is required because actually *our thinking minds do not want us to succeed on the path*, at least not until we have convinced them of the benefit of the practice. Our mindfulness practice has an ever-present adversary, in other words. In following the path, we are asking the thinking mind to surrender control, which is counter-cultural for it. The voice in our head does not see itself as a mere resource of the mind, it sees itself as mind itself, and therefore to surrender control is akin to suicide from its perspective. The contracted mind is initially unaware that there are capabilities of mind to which it does not have access, and it has a fundamental mistrust and fear of letting go, or, more accurately, perhaps being let go of.

Right Concentration

This element of the mental development part of the path relates to our ability to engage in sustained concentration, which is a facility necessary for the arising of insight and wisdom. Unless we can learn to gather and concentrate our awareness, we will be thwarted by the hindrances, driven by the aggregations, and blown by the worldly winds. The Buddha's method to develop right concentration is the practice of meditation, where the mind is focused on a particular object. The energy of right effort is needed to sustain right concentration, and of course right view and right intention are the motivating factors in the generation of this energy. The meditating mind inclines towards its object, acquires it, and then sustains concentration on it. The practice of meditation is to develop and refine this ability to hold the mind in concentration, and thereby learn to let go of thinking and reacting. Actually, with deepening experience, the mind is held by awareness rather than the other way around, and although this is a topic for later, it is useful to internalise such an image at this point.

There are two main effects of working with our ability to concentrate. The first and most direct consequence is that our ability to be mindful in everyday situations will improve, and we will find ourselves more at ease and more *present*. At such times, our responses come from a place further away from self, and are reassuringly more wholesome as a consequence. The second effect is less direct, but in many ways more liberating: when the mind is concentrated, wisdom and compassionate action arise naturally through the quietening of self. The joy of the insight that arises through the mind of awareness can appear unbounded, and provides further impetus to the turning of the wheel. This is one of the key differences between the mind of awareness and the contracted mind, as we discussed earlier.

We have already talked about the beauty in the beginning of the path as being sufficient reason for us to withdraw the poison arrow from our heart and start healing. What of the more advanced stages along the path? Right concentration is not just about learning to meditate on the breath and be mindful in daily life; it also applies to the transcendent mental states that lie beyond this initial experience. Indeed, it is about enlightenment itself, for those of us who may reach that sublime point. There can be no greater reward for right concentration than *nirvana*, to use the popular Sanskrit word for enlightenment.

Right Mindfulness

Right mindfulness is perhaps the most difficult limb of the wheel, particularly in the early stages of our practice, as then we are poorly placed to judge whether we are being mindful or not. Right mindfulness is the awareness that enables right effort and right concentration to work together to develop wisdom.

Mindfulness is the stabilising factor on the path, in that it leads to the mind that is aware, the mind that sees things as they really are, right here and right now. It is the mind that knows when our effort and concentration are properly directed, and when our view and intention are also aligned. When we set out on the path, any measure at all of mindfulness can seem to be out of our reach, but in time the resolutions that we make will bear fruit and the sunlight will emerge from behind the clouds.

Right mindfulness sees through the aggregations as they do their swift work from contact to deluded action. Once mindfulness has started to penetrate this process, we begin to understand ourselves better, even if we are still responding unskilfully. Progressively, we are able to detach more and more, and ultimately our diligence may reward us with being completely free of the aggregations that bind us to our suffering. Mindfulness is developed and supported by the three mighty pillars of our practice – meditation, contemplation, and restraint – which in turn sustain the continued turning of the wheel. It is to restraint that we will now turn.

Ethical Conduct

Fortunately, we do not necessarily have to be very wise to behave ethically, and behaving well can lead to significant progress on the path even when understanding is not present. So, there is a sense in which the three path elements of ethical conduct are the easiest, providing that we have sufficient in the way of right view and right intention to make a start. The wisdom of ethical behaviour does not need to be there at the outset, and it is perfectly suitable for us to wait for it to follow later, as it inevitably will. It is not essential for us to see or comprehend the true value of a behavioural code as such, providing that we are open-hearted enough to follow it for a while to see where it leads. Of course, comprehending is better, but *kamma* is all about intention and the most important point is that we have to start somewhere. This is a persistent theme in the Buddha's teaching – modify the behaviour first and let the wisdom arise naturally. A key aspect of right view is to trust that this will happen. Trust is a key concept here; we are not following rules, we are following our hearts. Of course, we have already learnt that making positive facial expressions and gestures have a beneficial effect on our behaviour, so if empirical support is needed for the Buddha's view, there it is.

A correct interpretation of the concept of *kamma* is fundamental to an appropriate mindset for ethical conduct. It is all too common to interpret *kamma* in a fatalistic way, i.e. to look at any unhappy state as being the result of our *kamma* and therefore in some way deserved or inevitable. However, this is to look at *kamma* from the wrong direction, and the Buddha very clearly discouraged such analysis, or indeed any analysis at all of how *kamma* operates. *Kamma* should be looked at *forwards*, not backwards, and therefore should be merely an impetus to behave in a skilful way. That is all the definition we need, and fundamentally what the Buddha encouraged.

There are two broad aspects to any code of conduct – those activities that are to be encouraged, and those from which we should refrain. The Buddha's teaching of ethical conduct follows this essential formula, but it is not a teaching of moral absolutes or immutable doctrine. Rather, the ethical guidance is aimed at creating conditions that will lead to favourable outcomes for our own progress on the path and for the welfare of others. It is very much rooted in the concept of *kamma*, and although the ancient texts do talk of rebirth into future lives, the important message is about rebirth from one moment to the next. In this sense, it may be more helpful to translate *kamma* as "becoming" rather than "rebirth".

The Buddha did not teach a code of conduct in which actions are inherently "right" or "wrong", but rather that they should be wisely chosen. The emphasis is very much on the *intention* to act, rather than on the action itself. A code of conduct can provide a useful framework for our choices, but no more than that. It is unnecessary and inappropriate to invoke any use of terms such as "morality" here, nor any concept of religious judgement. The ethical code by which we decide whether to refrain from an activity, or embrace it, is *our own standard*. It is a personal regime that we follow because it is beneficial in our practice and we can see its merit.

Although it is wise and appropriate to develop a code of restraint that suits our own circumstances, it is important to emphasise that exercising no self-discipline at all will certainly hinder us on our path. The Buddha was very clear on this point, and it is worth considering his teaching carefully as it is both illuminating and inspiring. To take a specific example, when explaining why one should refrain from indulging in intoxicating liquors, he referred to the fear and harm that our behaviour whilst intoxicated may cause *to others*. In doing this, rather than dictate a behavioural absolute he provided us with a yardstick by which to apply restraint in our behaviour, together with a practical measure of our success. Similarly, the Buddhist "precepts" that are observed by laypeople were described by the Buddha not as rules as such, but as *gifts* that we give to others to enable them to live free from fear, hostility and oppression. These gifts are also given to self, so that we may live free from remorse and cause no harm to ourselves through actions of body, speech or mind. All religions have precepts in some form or another, but the Buddha's explanation of why they should be adopted is surely amongst the most inspiring.

We will not dwell on the five precepts themselves, but for information, they are to abstain from each of the following:

Taking life
Taking that which is not given
Sexual misconduct
False speech
Intoxication

Right Speech

The Buddha's teachings distinguish speech as a form of action. Speech can harm others in all sorts of ways, and this can be intended or it can be unintended. If we contemplate this then we will see that in developing restraint in harmful speech, we are letting go of a little of self and considering more the perspective of another. Such blurring of the boundary of self and other is the basis of more harmonious relationships. Idle chatter and gossip can be unskilful, particularly if we are seeking to enhance the view people have of us by showing our critical talent for mocking others. It is straightforward to experience that there is a stronger self/other division when pointing out the apparent deficiencies in others and a weakening of that boundary in refraining from doing so.

We should set a standard for our use of speech and

then resolve to adhere to that standard. The contents of this standard are less important than the resolution itself, so, for example, we could resolve to refrain from deceiving, insulting, slandering, gossiping, or using harsh language. To desist from gossiping is a particularly easy and effective starting point for the inexperienced traveller on this path. In the other direction, we could resolve to use our speech positively, perhaps to wish people a good day, take an interest in their lives, or praise and encourage where it is due. Whatever our resolution, if it is supported by right effort and right intention, we will live with more compassion and wisdom, and we will improve the harmony in our relationships with others.

It is often said in the context of the Buddhist teachings, "If you cannot improve on the silence, then don't speak." To follow this would of course be another absolute, but it is useful to contemplate. Such a reflection will help us to determine whether we are gossiping unskilfully, and whether our speech is harmful to others. In doing this, it is wisest to make no distinction between situations where the target of the harmful speech is present, and situations where they are not.

Right Action

Right action refers to the actions of the body. Again the teaching has two primary emphases – action from which we are advised to refrain, and action that we should cultivate. Undesirable actions that the Buddha described are those that cause harm, those that involve taking that which is not given, and sexual misconduct. By expressing these guidelines in a positive way, i.e. in terms of cultivation rather than restraint, right action means to act with compassion, to be honest, to respect the belongings of others, and to engage only in sexual activity that does not harm others.

Once more, moral and behavioural absolutes do not need to be invoked. For example, for a layperson living a family life there will be a different standard of sexual misconduct from a monk living in a monastery. A monk will take vows to refrain from any type of sexual activity, and any action that may lead to it in thought or deed. Equally, a person living simply on a remote island may require a different code of conduct regarding the killing and eating of living beings from someone living in a city.

Of course, we cannot know the consequences of all our actions. When we buy clothes or food, we do not always know their means of production, whether any workers were treated badly, or whether the profits of the purchase are being channelled in a way that might harm others. Our personal standards should guide us here, and if we consider these important questions to consider, then we should investigate them to a level of effort that feels appropriate. There needs to be balance, because there will come a point at which the energy we spend in investigation could have been better spent. The more time we spend in meditation and wise reflection, the more likely it is that the right wisdom will arise. Obsessively pursuing the supply chain of a set of new shoes is unlikely to have an impact as great as spending more time in mindfulness practice.

Right Livelihood

The way people earn their livelihood in most parts of the world is now greatly changed from how it was in the Buddha's time. Although one may expect to apply a certain amount of interpretation to the ancient teaching on this subject, actually we discover that the principles are timeless. The Buddha stated that one should earn one's living in the most ethical and harmless way possible, avoiding deceitfulness and undue pressure in our commercial transactions. He listed five specific business pursuits that are harmful and therefore should be avoided: animal slaughter, human trafficking and prostitution, weapons, intoxicants, and poisons.

Many of us spend a large portion of our waking lives at work, and work-related issues can dominate our thoughts outside the workplace. It is therefore important to consider how our work is integrated with our values, and with our practice on the path. To reflect thus is beneficial, and it may lead to a positive change in our lives if we discover an inconsistency. It is also useful to examine our work relationships; how they accord with our journey towards liberation, and how well we are behaving within them. Here again, we may find that we are diverging from our values, or allowing unskilful mental formations to influence our treatment of others. Some mindfulness practice during the working day, no matter how short, will help with this.

A Wheel That Won't Stop Turning

Although the path is challenging and requires constant application of effort and continuous reassertion of resolve, there is some joyous news – once the wheel has started to turn, its natural state is perpetual motion. Like a physical wheel, the wheel of *dhamma* needs an initial impetus to move, and this impulse generally comes from right view leading to right intention. These two prime movers may arise through an initial contact with the Buddha's teaching, then some reflection, and perhaps some meditation, leading to the insight that this is a path that is valid and has meaning. Whether this introduction to *dhamma* occurs through intellectual curiosity, or a desire to improve ourselves in some way, does not matter. The outcome is the same – the wheel has started to turn.

Once this initial motive force has taken effect, the wheel will keep turning as our right view and right intention feed right effort and right concentration. In other words, our resolution grows and gives rise to further energy to pursue the path. Right mindfulness now starts to develop and be nourished, and the perpetual motion machine comes to life. Even a modicum of appropriately directed mindfulness will simultaneously energise all other facets of the path, including the two facets that gave the initial impetus. So, the wisdom and mental development factors of the path form a chain reaction, a self-amplifying sequence of events. At certain times, there will be increased resistance to the turning of the wheel, and often it will be slowed by the need to go around or roll over obstacles, but once it has started to turn and the benefit of the path is known, it will not stop.

The ethical conduct factors of the path contribute further momentum to this perpetual motion, because they too wrap around the movement to meet their own beginning. Once more the initial impetus is right view and right intention, which create the conditions for us to begin to consider applying a certain standard to our action, speech or livelihood. Each time we engage in or refrain from an action as a result of this developing standard, there will be a growing of wisdom as the consequences of our more skilful behaviour are experienced and understood. Even if we have only resolved not to drop litter, a positive reflection may be that we have desisted from the expectation that others will clear up after us. Thereby, in a small way we have reached out to those others and shown compassion through a point of view that is not based entirely on self. True, there are those whose job it is to pick up litter, but this does not confer on others the right to be heedless. Such small acts become self-perpetuating as we come to realise that there are more skilful and wholesome ways to live. Mindfulness increases as a result, which in turn encourages further virtuous action.

As the wheel turns, the hindrances are gradually transformed, weakened and left behind. The hindrances can be seen as the friction that would slow the wheel, and so as they are reduced the wheel can turn more freely. The worldly winds are calmed, and no longer blow us towards obstacles. A wheel that has an initial motive force and that encounters no friction or obstruction is a wheel that is perpetually in motion, and here the Buddha invented something unique that transcends worldly physical limitations.

PART FIVE

CARING FOR OUR MINDS

The Everyday Model of Mental Health

Drug treatment for psychological issues started to become common in the 1950s, together with an underlying and unexpressed message that sufferers had too much or too little of something in their brains, which the drug would put right. Here we find a pervasive and highly resistant belief about the mind – that problematic mental states *happen to us*, and are therefore in no sense *created by us*. Everyday language shows this bias clearly; for example, we say that we are "under" stress, not that we are "doing" stress. The everyday model of mind has an equivalent in the domain of mental disorders – the *everyday model of mental health*.

In the mind of awareness that we have discussed so far, our mental states are of our own making, and the degree to which we believe in them is within our control. It follows, therefore, that our mental wellbeing is our own responsibility. This may sound like a harsh message for those who find themselves in emotional difficulty at the moment, but that is certainly not the intention. In fact, it is quite the reverse. It is a message of hope that by accepting this responsibility not only can there be an improvement, but there can be a lasting recovery. It is not a matter of pulling oneself together; it is a matter of forming a different relationship with one's thoughts and feelings. The prime mover in this new relationship is the belief that we can change ourselves, and that we deserve the kind effort that this requires. Right view is essentially the antithesis of, and the antidote to, the everyday model of mental health. In the paragraphs that follow, we will use depression and anxiety to focus the discussion, as these are the most common forms of mental distress, but the principles that are explained are equally applicable to a wide range of mental health issues.

Some people may need additional help from medication at certain times, whether to help with their mood, their physical anxiety symptoms, or simply to get them some sleep. A personal opinion is that if the medical profession were less obsessive about people becoming "psychologically dependent" (whatever that means) on sleeping pills, they would end up prescribing a whole lot fewer drugs that are much more damaging to minds and bodies. Some minds worry more than others, and some minds have more of a tendency than others towards low mood. I myself am prey to both of these challenges, and have come to learn well my triggers in life. We are all different, and so the development of right view and the application of right effort are more of a challenge for some than others. However, we are also all the same, and so we all have the same capacity to change and treat ourselves with kindness. Therefore, we all have the same opportunity to set ourselves free.

When we have reached what John Bunyan so evocatively termed "the slough of despond", we may feel that we do not have enough strength to apply ourselves to finding some stillness and perspective on how our thinking mind is hurting us. At such points in our lives, a personal recommendation from experience is to meditate for much shorter periods, but more frequently if it feels right. That said, we must be on our guard against applying excessive effort at such times, as this tends to provoke thinking. If our thinking mind has conquered us, then a half-hour of sitting may just give it thirty minutes to torture us some more, whereas a ten-minute session may be enough to achieve some stillness and let some of the thoughts go by. Even if we find no serenity at such times, we can at least identify the persistent thought patterns that are visiting us. Regular returns to these short sessions will sustain the awareness of how our thoughts are affecting our feelings, and will have the precious benefit of creating gaps in thinking that will prevent further deterioration of our mental state. Even if we feel that we have not benefited from the meditation, we should at least acknowledge that we have tried to be kind to ourselves.

Back to the 1950s. Although there were antidepressant drugs available then, the number of diagnosed cases of depression was a fraction of today's numbers, and treating it with medication was not commonplace outside of a hospital setting. In contrast, prescriptions of tranquilising tablets for "the nerves" were common, and their use increased to become widespread until the mid-1970s. Those of us of the right age (or who are fans of the Rolling Stones) may recognise the phrase "mother's little helper", which referred to tranquilisers such as Miltown and Valium. These were used in bewildering quantities in this period, often by stressed mothers at home with young children. Use of sleeping pills was also widespread. The underlying medical view was clearly based on the everyday model of mental health: looking after young children was causing stress to happen to young mothers, and they needed a drug to reduce this stress. There is no doubt that the constant attention demanded by young children is immensely challenging, but still it is curious that no question was raised that stress may have been something these mothers were doing, rather than something being done to them. The use of these drugs fell away quite sharply after this period, as they became stigmatised owing to problems with addiction and recreational use, but the bias remained and the search for "happy pills" intensified.

In the 1970s, research started on less addictive and more targeted drugs to help with psychological issues. During the 1980s, significant advances were made in understanding how antidepressants work on brain chemistry, and specific drugs were developed to target these chemical processes within the brain. The breakthrough drug was the notorious fluoxetine, or Prozac to give it the more positive and punchy name used by the drug company marketeers. This drug achieved meteoric fame and fortune from its first introduction in 1988, accompanied by extensive media coverage and even a film starring a Hollywood actress. Prozac was the first drug of its type and the darling of the popular press, but there are several other drugs in the same "class", i.e. *Selective Serotonin Reuptake Inhibitors*, or SSRIs. Other common names in bathroom cabinets are Zoloft, Celexa and Lexapro.

Serotonin is a brain chemical that is popularly associated with happiness, and simply put, Prozac and its other family members prevent the reabsorption of this chemical and thereby work according to the following unstated equations:

Lack of serotonin = depression
More serotonin = happiness

Again, we return to the important point concerning the role of our own minds in how we feel. Whilst sufferers of depression may be heartened that their problems are being attributed to a lack of a certain brain chemical that can be straightforwardly replaced, there is a need for a deeper perspective on this. To think that mental wellness depends *solely* on increasing the level of a substance that for some unexplained reason depressed people lack is fundamentally to look at things through the wrong end of the metaphorical telescope. This is not to deny that for some of us such treatment may be appropriate at a particular time, but the point is that we need to understand the contributions of our own thinking and behaviour, else we will merely enter a cycle of recovery and relapse. It is also worth noting that there are nutritional and other natural approaches to boosting the "happy chemicals" in our brains, and these may be a much better starting point than the cash cows of the pharmaceutical industry. I am a believer in the efficacy of the herb St. John's Wort in helping with low mood, and find that it works very well for me. It is not suitable for all bodies in all states, and therefore of course the reader should seek guidance from a medical professional before taking it, or indeed any other medicine.

All human behaviour can be explained at a chemical level. Of course it can, because our minds are made out of the stuff that chemists study. However, it does not necessarily follow that this is a useful way to consider our minds. Certainly, such analysis can take us to some interesting, amusing, and baffling places, but ultimately it is impotent. At the most fundamental level of description we are just atoms, and at this level too there are some mind-bending concepts to distract us from the real issue of the search for truth. For instance, there can be no concept more astonishing than the fact that there is physically nothing more to us than atoms, and these atoms are exactly the same whether we are alive or dead. Once we are gone, they will just go and find somebody or something else to be part of, like they did before us, and like they will carry on doing until the end of creation. Let's stop this now, and follow the Buddha's example in accepting that some questions do not need answers, and the only worthwhile explanations come from that which we truly experience through our own awareness.

The point here is that in seeking a reductionist explanation such as a chemical one, the essential element is being missed (no pun intended). Our thoughts affect our feelings, which is something we can directly experience to be true, and therefore our moods are our responsibility. The amount of serotonin washing about in our brains is a related matter, but it is a sideshow until we have accepted some ownership of our mental states. Antidepressants work by trying to simulate the chemical balance of a happy brain, but we can learn to maintain this state naturally in a way that is safer and more lasting. As we have already noted, this is not to say that some minds do not have more of a tendency towards a low emotional tone than others, or that some brains don´t have lower serotonin levels, but the key point is that, for most of us, our thoughts fundamentally determine *what happens next* on detecting low mood.

In my opinion, the drug companies are being somewhat nefarious in promoting the idea that a chemical imbalance in our brain is something that just happens to us, and something that only taking medication can address. Despite the positive results achieved by drugs such as Prozac, people who have not experienced the drug before may be unaware that their symptoms are likely to worsen significantly in the first month or more of taking the drug. This exacerbation of symptoms happens as the brain gets used to this new invader changing the way it works. There is an ethical question here, or at least a serious question of social conscience: a patient who has been assessed as in need of a drug like Prozac is in a vulnerable state, and a period of four to six weeks of feeling worse could put that person at serious risk. Here, I do not seek to court controversy or enter into moralising debate, but would make the emphatic point that mindfulness practice may be a better first line of defence than a cabinet full of two-tone capsules. It may also be that a herbal serotonin boost such as St. John's Wort may be an effective supplement to a diligent routine of mindfulness practice for those who need additional help for a while.

Ancient Light, New Perspective

Over the last few decades, there has been a growing connection between the Buddha's teachings and Western theories of mind. The results of this convergence range from coffee table guides for more satisfying personal relationships, through books and CDs teaching meditation, to clinical methods of treating dysfunctional behaviour and mental disorder. With the benefit of hindsight, it is a joy to look through the history of this union, witnessing the initially disparate parts coming closer and closer together before meeting and becoming whole. It is fascinating to see how these diverse elements have been attracted towards each other, like a loose formation of birds that suddenly starts to wheel and dart as if with a single mind. We feel an exhilarating sense of wonder when we observe this behaviour in flocks of birds and shoals of fish, and there is similar inspiration in the turning point that has recently occurred in the relationship between ancient Eastern thought and modern Western clinical psychology.

Figure 3 represents the journey of the essential elements coming together.

A Light From the East

The prime mover for this convergence was the growing awareness of the Buddha's teachings in the West, shown at the beginning of the upper arrow in the figure. In the

214

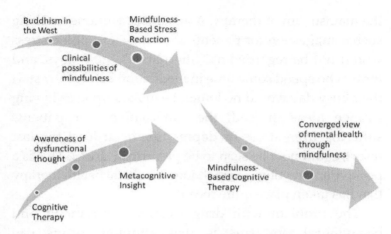

Figure 3 – Buddhist Influence on Western Mental Health View

middle of the 19th century, even though Buddhism was the dominant religion in the world, accounting for around a third of the human race, very little was known about it in the West. Much of the popular knowledge before this time was apocryphal and inaccurate. Buddhism was generally regarded in the West as some sort of primeval worship, or even as an inferior imitation of Christianity, such was the strength of the belief that it could not be older than Christianity. We are lucky to know so much about it now thanks initially to the great French scholar Eugène Burnouf, who in 1844 published the comprehensive, accurate and sensitive book *Introduction à l'Histoire du Bouddhisme Indien*. This book may have been the first accurate account of Buddhism in the Western world.

The interest in the Buddha's teachings has been steadily growing in the West, such that now the use of meditation techniques for relaxation and stress reduction has entered the mainstream of therapy. A general practitioner making such a suggestion for patients showing signs of life stress would not be regarded as "alternative" these days, and those who spend some time in meditation before they start their busy day would no longer be looked upon as having strange ideas. Indeed, the "alternative" for patients suffering from stress or depression, or at least the last resort, could now be seen to be prescribed drugs. This is a positive and revolutionary change in mental health therapy that has taken place quite recently.

The problem with drug treatment for mood and behavioural problems is that although drugs can sometimes treat symptoms quite effectively, they will not prevent relapse. It is generally accepted amongst mental health workers that when drug treatment is ceased, the reoccurrence of the original problem becomes likely. In contrast, mindfulness practice is beneficial when relapse is possible, because it allows a natural stability to arise in our minds, levelling our responses to disturbing thoughts and feelings and thus avoiding escalating patterns of harmful thought.

As we move along the top arrow in Figure 3, we see the growing acknowledgement in medical science that mindfulness has clinical possibilities. Since the early 1980s, Jon Kabat-Zinn's Mindfulness Based Stress Reduction (MBSR) programmes have been adopted around the globe, following Kabat-Zinn's initial insight that meditation could be employed in a clinical context. The method involves a structured eight-week course in which a number of different meditation and mindfulness techniques are taught. Patients are encouraged to develop a new relationship with their stress, based on observing it rather than identifying with it or taking sides against it. Kabat-Zinn's book *Full Catastrophe Living* summarises the results of extensive experience with the MBSR programme in dealing with headaches, high blood pressure, and back pain related to stress. The book also gives excellent practical advice on meditation and yoga. By the way, the rather alarming title is derived from a reference to family life as "the full catastrophe" in the film *Zorba the Greek*, so essentially it refers to mindfulness practice in everyday life.

A Conundrum in the West

Now let's move to the other converging strand, the lower arrow in the figure. In parallel with Kabat-Zinn's work, psychologists were making advances in the treatment of disorders of the mind, deriving from the new cognitive science, and without any direct connection with Eastern thought. Often, psychology's status as a "proper science" has been questioned, and a frequent criticism has been the lack of cumulative theoretical progress compared to the more established sciences. Could cognitive science provide a base for this elusive phenomenon of "real" progressive science, or would it be yet another "bandwagon", to use the derisory term of one of the leading thinkers of the day?

Experimental psychology has always provided a very fertile ground for published research papers and lively debate, and one can pick more or less any period in recent history and see intense and forthright intellectual sparring between highly capable scholars. These debates may swing one way or another for a while, but they often do not seem to build in any way towards an additive and convergent view of the operation of the mind, or even of the matter being discussed. Sometimes the arguments seem to be carried on a wave of psychological fashion that eventually loses energy and collapses, leaving it beached and exhausted. I remember whilst still a psychology student in the 1980s happening across the great debates in "mathematical psychology" from the 1950s and staring with wide-eyed wonder at the intricate and incomprehensible (to me) mathematical modelling that had been so painstakingly assembled, and wondering why this just seemed to have fizzled out. Surely such intensity and intellectual agility should *take us somewhere*? Such is the frustration of experimental psychology. However, there are times when it is not like this, and fortunately there are some satisfying turning points at which knowledge starts to become established and cumulative, and debate falls away. This has happened in the area of cognitive therapy for illnesses such as depression, although Arthur Koestler's analogy of the sleepwalker is quite appropriate for how some of the protagonists arrived at their conclusions.

It started in the 1970s with some pioneering work by the renowned American psychiatrist Aaron Beck and his associates. Beck developed a therapeutic technique that he called *Cognitive Behaviour Therapy (CBT)*. He established clearly that there is a relationship between the way people think and the way that they feel. By changing the way his patients thought about themselves and their life situations, Beck found that he could change the way that his patients felt, and thereby reduce the likelihood of relapse and reoccurrence of depression. CBT has been shown to be effective both with therapy administered alongside drug treatment and also on its own. Following his initial work with depression, Beck successfully applied CBT to other so-called "disorders" of the mind, or to put it in a way more appropriate to CBT, to other dysfunctional patterns of thinking. Indeed, the Beck Institute's website today lists around a hundred different conditions that can be treated with CBT. In addition to depression, the site lists such conditions as phobias, eating disorders, various types of anxiety, panic attacks, compulsions, and personality disorders.

In his initial work on depression, Beck's rationale for CBT was that the therapy worked on some basic dysfunctional beliefs about self-worth, particularly where such beliefs could be shown to depend on approval from others. His therapeutic techniques centred around identifying these problematic views and helping his patients recognise and accept alternative, less harmful perspectives. Although the therapy was effective, its theoretical basis was questionable because patients were reliably shown still to hold dysfunctional beliefs even after apparently successful treatment. So, although CBT became well established, there was no satisfactory explanation of why it was effective, and this left it in a somewhat vulnerable state as both a therapy and a theory of the dysfunctional mind.

The Turning Point

The breakthrough came in the 1990s in research done by the Cambridge psychologist John Teasdale and his associates, drawing on some theoretical work that Teasdale had done with his Cambridge colleague Phil

Barnard. Barnard and Teasdale theorised that an individual's vulnerability to mental disorders such as depression is related to their reliance on a particular mode of mind, a *doing* mode, in which they identify with the thoughts in their mind as "self". The Cambridge pair identified an alternative mode of mind, a *being* mode, in which thoughts are just seen as mental events passing through the mind. The theory was that individuals who can move flexibly between these two modes will be less vulnerable to depression. Those able to do this were identified as having high *metacognitive awareness*, which is the ability to be aware of thoughts as just thoughts. In contrast, those with low metacognitive awareness would get caught up in the contents of their minds, and would regard their thoughts and mental states as inevitable consequences of their life situations. These people who tended to be locked in the doing mode were likely to be more vulnerable to disorders of the mind.

In other words, Barnard and Teasdale's theory was that the thinking mind is the source of the problem here, and the mind of awareness is the solution. According to the model of mind developed by these two scientists, the thinking mind presents us with a very specific obstacle, in that it is constantly *measuring the gap between how things are and how it desires them to be*. Their essential argument was that people suffer according to the extent to which they live their lives experiencing this gap. The convergence with the Buddha's teaching is now directly apparent, and it is enthralling to read the two bodies of work side by side – here in a book of theoretical psychology is the Buddha's exact definition of suffering being used as a potential explanation for clinical depression. Indeed, the parallel continues: the alternative mode of mind that leads the sufferer out of depression and away from relapse is a being mode, where the mind accepts the present moment just as it is, without any associated need to make a change. The motive force for mental health is *sanditthiko* – apparent here and now.

Teasdale and his colleagues took this work further, and through a series of experiments firmly established the validity of their theory. This ingenious and inspired body of work was a true turning point, and disposed of the lurking criticism that psychological science could not deliver cumulative progress. As we move along the lower arrow in the figure, research is shifting from one paradigm to another. The earlier approach is to identify patterns of problematic thought and belief that are stable over time in patients with psychological issues, whereas the newer methodology seeks to examine the thoughts that become active at the start of a depressive interlude or other mental health issue. This fresh, more dynamic approach was the catalyst for much deeper insight, and provided the eventual explanation for the effectiveness of Beck's CBT.

Teasdale and his associates went on to develop measurement techniques that attempted to calibrate individual differences in metacognitive awareness, and thereby predict a person's susceptibility to relapse into pathological mental states. The measure that was developed was called the *Measure of Awareness and Coping in Autobiographical Memory (MACAM)*. In the MACAM, participants are asked to imagine themselves in a number of mildly depressing situations, after which a structured interview is conducted to elicit the specific memories from their lives that these situations provoked, together with the feelings they stimulated. Trained assessors are then able to rate quantitatively the degree of metacognitive awareness present. At the low end of the metacognitive awareness continuum, subjects describe their feelings in undifferentiated and generally bad terms, and as being caused by external events. Moving higher up the continuum, subjects are able to differentiate the various elements of their feelings, identify their own role in generating them, and ultimately recognise their choice not to follow these feelings.

Experiments using the MACAM show that individuals with high metacognitive awareness are able to avoid depression and negative thought patterns more easily during stressful life situations, when compared with individuals with low metacognitive awareness. Teasdale went on to distinguish a specific form of metacognitive awareness, which he termed *metacognitive insight*, which is essentially the high end of the scale of metacognitive awareness. The distinction here is that while somebody who has high metacognitive awareness is more aware of their thinking, somebody who has metacognitive insight is aware of their thinking as just thinking. For sufferers of chronic worry or depression, metacognitive awareness is a step forward in their therapy, but it is, of course, just more thinking at a time when thought is so intimately related with the debilitating states that are being experienced. It is the concept of metacognitive insight that provides the therapeutic breakthrough and the turning point in uniting psychological research and the Buddha's teachings.

Although in the 1970s pioneers of cognitive therapy

such as Aaron Beck were aware that this "stepping back from thought" played a role in recovery, the later insight of researchers such as John Teasdale was that this is actually the primary therapeutic factor. It is the detachment from the thoughts that delivers the restorative payload, not the replacement of one thought pattern with another. So, here we have the explanation of the effectiveness of CBT – it is not the *content* of the thoughts being worked on that makes the difference, it is the patient's *relationship* with thought. The main clinical benefit derives from inserting a gap of awareness between dysfunctional thought patterns and patients' habitual responses to them. Indeed, if thought is approached in this way, the thoughts are no longer dysfunctional, because they are just thoughts and are not acted upon.

Although CBT still sought to offer its patients alternative patterns of thought to access at their most vulnerable times, the opportunity now was to help patients establish a new relationship with their habitual ways of thinking and therefore with their emotional tone. Teasdale's work shows that patients do best when they relate to their thoughts in a wider, more "decentred" way.

The stage was now set. More and more people throughout the West were finding truth in the Buddha's teachings and adopting them as a practical way of life, or as a religion. Therapists were starting to exploit the insights in the teachings and getting positive results. There was empirical evidence showing that awareness of thought, or a "being mode", could play a positive therapeutic role in reducing the chance of relapse for patients with debilitating psychological conditions. Theoretical and experimental psychology had arrived at a model of mind that was entirely consistent with the Buddha's psychological teachings described earlier. The seeds of a dramatic congruence had been sewn, and now mental health therapy was ready for a major coming of age. We have now arrived at the meeting point of the arrows in the diagram.

When all of this came together at the meeting point of the arrows in Figure 3, a highly productive union was formed, leading to what is now referred to as *Mindfulness Based Cognitive Therapy (MBCT)*. Kabat-Zinn and Teasdale were joined by two other pioneering psychologists, Mark Williams from Oxford, and Zindel Segal from Toronto. A book by these four authors, *The Mindful Way Through Depression*, is a landmark publication and a personal recommendation. MBCT is based on a similar eight-week programme to MBSR, but the scope is expanded to encompass a wider terrain of mental health. The clinical results of MBCT in preventing recurrence of depression are both positive and compelling.

Although the breakthrough work has been with depression, the approach is also being considered and used for a range of physical and psychological issues. The Oxford Mindfulness Centre at the Oxford University Department of Psychiatry lists a wide spectrum of physical and psychological issues where mindfulness techniques may help. These include chronic pain, psoriasis, cancer, health anxiety, chronic fatigue syndrome, stress, generalised anxiety disorder, bipolar disorder, and psychosis. In this section, we will mainly discuss the work with depression, because this gives the full flavour of how the mind creates its own problems, and how mindfulness leads us out of them. Reading (and acting upon) the book by Williams, Teasdale, Segal and Kabat-Zinn is likely to bring enormous benefit to all who read it, not just those who suffer from depression.

Guard Well Your Thoughts

Psychologists have identified that "rumination" is a major factor in depression. Rumination, or "brooding" to use a popular term, occurs when the thinking mind becomes trapped in thought. It cuts off the sufferer from normal living and clear perspective, and leads to chains of destructive thinking that become prolonged and self-perpetuating. Essentially, the thinking mind is trying to "solve the problem" of depression, through intense and restless reflection on life events that have formed the trigger to the current episode, and on possible future outcomes, all without much in the way of a sense of proportion. As our mood starts to sink, the mind may dwell (also unhealthily) on what is wrong with us that makes us feel this way. It tries to take control of the depression and get rid of it through all this additional thinking. However, incessantly elaborating the problem in this way actually grows the burden, bringing in related but unhelpful feelings, such as fear and self-reproach. These additional feelings feed the original mood, and a progressive escalation of low mood is perpetuated.

Even when it is clear to us that the rumination is doing no good, or indeed quite the reverse, we still find it very difficult to resist. We fear that if we let go of this rampant thought then we are casting ourselves into the abyss and abandoning all hope of a "solution". Actually, this cannot happen because the abyss only exists in the thoughts that we are refusing to let go. Our negative thought patterns are highly resistant to being evicted once they have acquired tenancy in our minds, because they make their cover story of being our saviour all too believable. As time moves on, the thinking mind adds more and more problems that were not present at the start of the rumination, but even so we are still believers.

We have already acknowledged that it is an awkward truth to face that when we are brooding, we are suffering because we want to. We talk to others about our problems to validate and nourish them, not to solve them. We may find that righteous indignation occurs in our minds when somebody tries to coax us out of our bad mood by lightening the moment. "Stop trying to placate me, I am too busy with my important suffering," we say. Or rather we don't say that, but perhaps things would be clearer if we did. One of the most influential monks in bringing Buddhism to the West, Ajahn Sumedho, has frequently said that during his training in Thailand his teacher Ajahn Chah would mock him for being a monk who "enjoyed suffering" when he felt the need to talk or complain about his problems. Most of us could probably identify somebody we know who enjoys suffering, and so it is odd that we struggle to recognise this quality in ourselves. It is a valuable lesson, and one acknowledged by psychologists, that we can learn much about the limitations and biases of our own minds by observing the behaviour of others. We really are all not so very different, and indeed how could we be?

It is no coincidence that another common translation of the hindrance we termed "worry and flurry" earlier is "restlessness and brooding". Brooding is a mental habit, and it brings with it other mental habits that are similarly destructive. The title of this section "Guard well your thoughts" is taken from the Buddha's own words, and is a key message in Buddhist practice. It is adaptive to turn to the Buddha's four foundations of mindfulness and the five aggregations to see the truth of this habit. The process may start with a single thought that arises in the mind, or with a sensation felt within the body. Or, it may start with daydreaming, which is the nursery slope of rumination. A time when we are particularly vulnerable to feelings of low mood leading to spiralling negative thought is immediately on waking. Whatever the condition of mind, the significant factor is what happens directly thereafter. If we allow habitual patterns of harmful thought to kick in, then unless we are on our guard, these will in turn lead to further formations, which will trigger emotional responses. We may then label these as deeper sadness, or even fear or panic. These formations keep on coming, attracting others, and driving us on to still more desperate states. Using the Buddha's model, it is straightforward to see why depression tends to return in sufferers, because the formations are already there, fully formed and ready to respond to their triggers.

Of course, it is not only depressed people who ruminate, and doubtless we can all recall episodes in our recent lives when we have become lost in a maze of negative thought energy. The problems start when we are unable to extricate ourselves from this mental quicksand. When we start sinking down, our thoughts preoccupy us and take us over, and before we know it we are living almost entirely inside our own heads. We withdraw from other people and from activities that we previously enjoyed, and the ensuing isolation allows further harmful thought patterns to enter in. A very common example of such negative thinking is to regard everybody else as leading charmed and carefree lives, and then resent them for being the person that our minds have created. Our thoughts fatigue us, and so the spiral continues. We learnt earlier that one of the translations of the Pali word *khandha* is "heap". When we think about all the things we have to do not just right now, but soon, today, this week, this year, and so on, the heap weighs us down and fatigues us, even though we haven't started on a single one of the things that we have placed on our list. If we focus only on the present moment and the task at hand, our energy is preserved, but when we ruminate we are unable to do this.

In books on this subject, a popular diagrammatic image is a funnel, which is supposed to represent the sufferer spiralling downwards and becoming more and more isolated and bound to the feeling of depression. An example is shown in Figure 4. The descending motion in this image is consistent with the popular language of depression, where we say we feel "low" or "down". There are several versions of the model, only really differing in the labels that are added to the spiral as it descends. Even without labels, the image is highly evocative. The funnel is wide at the top, reflecting a broad and adaptive experience of life, but it narrows towards the bottom where only depression itself holds sway. To escape, the sufferer needs to climb, but the funnel has increased gravity to prevent this. So, he or she languishes at the bottom, incapacitated and lacking the strength, and ultimately the will, to ascend.

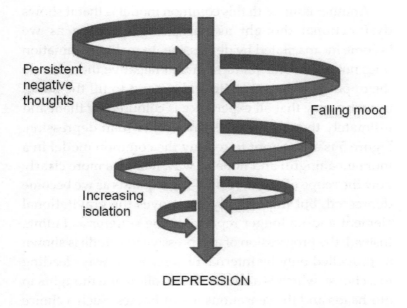

Figure 4 – An Unhelpful Image: Sinking Into Depression

Although this is a popular and potent representation of depression, it is very misleading, and offers no apparent hope for a remedy. This view of depression implies that we fall passively into the spiral, and the gravitational pull of the vortex provides the downward momentum. In other words, when we "fall" into depression we are helpless victims. In reality, we have not so much sunk down, but rather we have imprisoned ourselves in our own thoughts. It may be hard for us to accept at first, but "falling" into depression is not entirely passive, and we are able to make choices that can prevent it. The momentum is not at all a gravitational pull, but rather a *push* from our own mental habits. We are not *sinking* down, we are *thinking* down.

Another issue with this common model is that it shows dysfunctional thought as narrowing in scope as we become incapacitated by depression. In reality, rumination does not follow this pattern, in that negative thoughts do the opposite – they escalate and expand to fill the mind, in such a way that all experience is coloured by them and ultimately there is no experience other than depression. Figure 5 is an attempt to redraw the common model in a more meaningful and hopeful way. It shows more clearly how the scope of negative thinking expands as we become depressed, but importantly it removes the gravitational element and no longer represents the sufferer as falling. Instead, the progression of a depressive interlude is shown as propelled only by internal factors, and always leading to a choice, which is a choice not to follow the thoughts in our heads and the sensations in our bodies. Such a choice may often be overrun by a torrent of thinking and judging, but each time we choose not to follow a thought or sensation, we create a space between strong aggregations that may be just enough to allow in the light of awareness that will ultimately save us. Another advantage of the revised model is that it applies to all debilitating mental states, not just depression. We do not "fall", for instance, into anxiety or compulsion.

Although pharmacological approaches to treatment of depression can be effective, specifically treatment using antidepressant drugs, these treatments work on the physiological effect rather than the psychological cause. For patients treated with antidepressants, it has been shown that depression is likely to return in more than half of cases, and this likelihood increases sharply if the sufferer has suffered two or more episodes. Encouragingly,

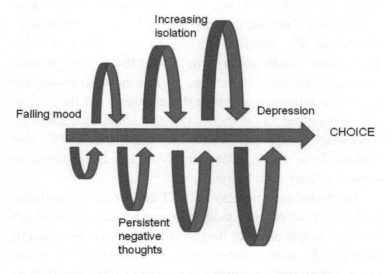

Figure 5 – A Better Image: Thinking Into Depression

evidence shows that MBCT has a significantly beneficial effect in reducing the probability of a relapse. MBCT patients will still experience unhelpful thoughts and low mood, and may oscillate on the brink of a relapse, but they are better equipped to allow the potential episode to dissipate.

The initial stimulus for depression is likely to be a significant event in the sufferer's life, usually one associated with a loss. Such a loss can take many forms; common ones are the loss of a loved one, and a reverse in financial or other status. The nature of the thinking mind's role in depression is such that the depressive interlude leaves a deep and wide set of mental formations behind, multiply connected to other formations, and which then take a much lesser initial stimulus to activate. Not only might the initial trigger for a relapse be much less emotionally charged, but also it may be only tangentially related to the original perceived loss. This is why depression tends to return, and MBCT has proved successful because it teaches people how to recognise these injurious formations at the moment that they arise, and choose not to let them start the avalanche that can otherwise completely obliterate mindfulness. To use Eckhart Tolle's potent imagery, MBCT helps patients to recognise their pain bodies.

The broad techniques of MBCT are consistent with the Buddha's teaching in meditation and reflection, although the third major pillar of Buddhist practice, i.e. restraint in speech and action, is not contained within them. There are some differences in emphasis relating to the specifics of the mental states that are being addressed, but there is no essential inconsistency in the approach. The increased emphasis in MBCT tends to be on the cultivation of compassion and gentleness towards self, although of course this too is present in the Buddha's teaching.

We have noted throughout this book that a key difference between the mind of awareness and the thinking mind is the ability to be present in the moment. The thinking mind cannot work well with the present moment because of its highly selective nature, and as a result its comfort zones are the past and the future, which it seeks to control. We have also discussed how the thinking mind's tendency is to judge and try to change the present moment, i.e. to close the gap between the state it desires and the state it is in. It is the perception of this gap that is the root of our suffering, and when we are in a debilitating mental state, it is this perception that starts and sustains the destructive rumination. With the mind of awareness, in contrast, there is no judgement and no gap. The mind of awareness is content with the present moment, and indeed when only the present moment is perceived, the bliss of sufficiency arises. MBCT seeks to help people access the mind of awareness and thereby avoid the thinking mind seizing control whenever a trigger condition arises that might otherwise allow ruminative thought to set in.

The ultimate goal is to be able to look straight at our destructive patterns of thought, to recognise them and to know them well. This may take some courage and strength at first, because the thought patterns can appear overwhelming. At our most vulnerable times, it may be more appropriate just to notice them but go no further in investigating them. As we develop more skill in relating to our thoughts and feelings, we may find the fortitude and resolve to be able to consider them directly. In so doing, as well as learning better the sensations that accompany these thought patterns, we may be able to ascertain something more of their true nature. In this way, we will regain intentional control of our attention and no longer be tempted into these habitual quicksands of thought. The patterns will still be there, and we will still feel them being triggered, but we will learn to be compassionate to ourselves at such times, and we will understand the folly of trying to get rid of them. As ever, the goal is non-judgemental mind-body awareness, not annihilation of that which does not please us.

So, here we see that psychology has made a genuine breakthrough, and attained the cumulative theoretical knowledge that it has frequently been accused of lacking.

Indeed, psychology has gone one step further in establishing cumulative theoretical insight: it has gained the backing of an ancient model of mind that is both theory and therapy, and unquestionably the greatest system of psychological thought ever expounded.

Your Mind, Your Choices

There is a wealth of literature available to help us live harmoniously within our own minds, although as noted previously it is strange that it targets only adults. A personal favourite is *Manage Your Mind* by the two Oxford cognitive therapists Gillian Butler and Tony Hope. Mind management techniques are broadly based on the underlying principle of cognitive therapy that we have already touched upon in the work of Aaron Beck. Their essential tenet is that mood and thought are linked; identify errant thought patterns, seek another perspective. In general, these methods do not embrace the Buddha's teaching directly, but there is a clear convergence there for one who is looking. For example, the Buddha also taught of cultivating opposite states to weaken unhelpful mind habits.

A key principle expressed in self-help sources is to *recognise that we can change*. This is consistent with the Buddha's view of *not self*; through such recognition, we are accepting that the thoughts and behaviours that may be causing problems today do not define us permanently. Looking at ourselves in a different way is also a fundamental theme in these texts, and a common recommendation is that we should look upon ourselves as a parent may look on a child; perhaps sometimes disapproving, but always forgiving and loving. This may come across as somewhat sugary and insubstantial at first, but it is a teaching of immeasurable potency. We have already acknowledged, but it bears repetition, that we are always ready to forgive those we love, but do not confer the same privilege on ourselves. This parental love simile is present in the Buddha's own teachings, and is very frequently used by Buddhist teachers today. Within it, we can see a broad base of the principles of the Buddha's view. For instance, there is awareness of our behaviour as merely a set of actions we can change; there is the hindrance of ill will towards self; and there is the third mark of all things – separation from self-identification.

Mindfulness and the pursuit of the Buddha's path are powerful ways to end the dominion of the thinking mind and the problems that it brings. However, they are not the only means to this end, and to think they are would be to identify with a position and thereby defeat our purpose. In the Buddha's teachings, there is a concept of "fetters" that bind us to the cycle of suffering, and which are essentially a continuation of the list of five hindrances. One of these fetters is "attachment to rigid views", and the implication here is that to assert that the Buddha's teaching is the only way to a true understanding of mind would be an example of such a dogmatic and self-defeating outlook. This fetter, like the others, should be set aside, or "cut through" to use the Buddha's words.

There are various compatible techniques of mind care and management that are available from other sources, and which we can consider to help us along our path. Our good habits do not need to come exclusively from the *suttas* that record the Buddha's teachings, despite their bottomless potency. Likewise, not all of our wisdom needs to arise naturally through mindfulness and meditation, although this is certainly the route to the deepest understanding. Borrowing wisdom from others can also be effective, but because the entry point to consciousness for such guidance is the thinking mind, we still have some work to do to incorporate it into our behaviour. Wisdom that is added through the thinking mind is less powerful and enduring than wisdom that arises directly through awareness, but it can provide a shortcut if used skilfully.

In the sections that follow, we will discuss various effective techniques of mind health and safety. Essentially, we will consider a toolbox approach, in which there will be different tools applicable in different circumstances. We have already lifted the lid of this metaphorical toolbox earlier in this book, when we discussed ten ideas for maintaining our mindfulness outside of formal meditation. We will now go deeper and discuss some other methods, but which of them will be most helpful to us will depend on our own individual circumstances, characteristics, and progress on the path. Some of these methods are taken from the Buddha's teachings, and some are not. Where lessons are taken from non-Buddhist sources, we will see that there is a clear convergence with the ancient wisdom, reflecting how cognitive therapy has benefited from the wondrous convergence between East and West that we have already discussed. We will start this part of our journey with the worst case – the moment when we feel that it has all come apart for us.

Two Refuges When We Are Lost

We all falter, and sometimes we fall. This is as true in the mental realm as it is in the physical. We now understand that the psychological obstacles that cause us to trip are habitual and unhelpful patterns of thinking and doing, and we also now know that these are lying latent, ready to take us over when our guards are down. Of course, there will be events in our lives that are truly difficult to deal with, and at such times we may feel overwhelmed. However, even at such times we can resolve to cultivate steadiness in our understanding that it is our thought habits that drag us under, not the events themselves. If our resolve does not prevail at a time of duress, however, then this is normal enough and no cause for negative views.

Sometimes we hit the metaphorical floor so hard that we cannot get up straight away. We may even find it comfortable lying there and decide to rest there for a while. The thinking mind takes a curious comfort in wallowing in distressing thought patterns, which is something that we may come to recognise through reflection. Our subjective experience at such times is that we are out of control, although really there is not a lack of control; there is too much of it. Our inner voice is filling the mind with thought and the body with tension, to the point that there is no other experience at all. As our skill in meditation and reflection grows, we will start to notice what happens in our minds at times of crisis and witness directly how we habitually add energy to our cascading thoughts and increasing emotional response. A more difficult, but equally important, realisation is that we also feed troublesome mental formations by resisting them. Although resistance is instinctive, it is also futile – if the thoughts and feelings are already here, we cannot get rid of them, so what is needed is simply to let them go.

Fortunately, there are two rock-solid places of refuge

when we arrive at these challenging points in our lives, both equally vital and uplifting. If we fully understand and embrace these two refuges, then we will be able to remain in contact with inner peace and happiness through our difficult times. We will also be able to look upon ourselves with compassion and take comfort in the fact that we know what to do.

Forgiving Ourselves

The first place of refuge is *self-forgiveness*, which means that we should look kindly on our reaction to a situation, no matter what may be the nature of that reaction. This is particularly so for our initial reaction to a perceived problem, because of course without this condition the effects would be different. Dwelling in judgement of ourselves is profoundly unhelpful, and is one of the worst things we can do at this time. For instance, we may choose to think that up to this point we were doing so well in our practice but now we have thrown it all away by going back to bad habits. This is certainly not so, and if we decide to let these thoughts go, we may see that actually although we do feel bad, we are now better equipped to deal with this. We have learnt to recognise our negative thoughts, and the associated patterns of bodily sensations that they provoke and follow. We have therefore added a measure of awareness and removed a measure of self-view. This is actually considerable progress, and may be just enough to stop continuing further into the vortex. If we have learnt, even for a moment, to be able to see our thoughts as thoughts and our bodily sensations as bodily sensations, i.e. the Buddha's four foundations of mindfulness, then the only difference between us and an enlightened being is how consistently we do this!

At our lowest points, we can expect to have trouble with our right effort, as our energy levels may drop. The hindrance of sloth and torpor will visit us loud and long. Our right intention could therefore stay as mere intention rather than inspiring action. We may also encounter the hindrance of doubt, about the path itself and about our ability to stay on it. Other hindrances will also pay us a visit, such as distraction through sensual stimulation, worry, and anger at self and others. What is vital to recognise is that it is *perfectly natural* for thinking minds to think such thoughts, because this is just what thinking minds do. The way forward is always to forgive ourselves for the habits of mind and then let them pass on their way to extinction. Remember, we are not trying to get rid of thoughts that have already arisen; we are learning to sandbox them and also to reduce the tendency for them to arise in the future.

Retaining our Right View

The second place of refuge is *retaining our right view*. Right view is the prime mover and sustainer of the perpetual motion that will liberate us from our suffering, and we need to nurture it to maintain ourselves on the wise path we have already chosen. The Buddha said, "Open are the doors to the deathless to those who can hear." Here he was referring directly to the need for us to retain our right view. When using the expression "the deathless" he was

240

referring to pure awareness, which is the one thing that is not subject to cause and effect, to arising and ceasing. If we are always open to its presence then we too are not subject to these phenomena, and therefore are beyond suffering. This quotation may be somewhat difficult at first, as the word "deathless" is unfamiliar and therefore has a somewhat mystical quality, but it is a quotation that tends to be a long-term and profoundly helpful companion of travellers on this path, and hence it is offered here.

It is helpful to cultivate feelings of gratitude and love towards our right view, which is something we can do during the *Set* phase of our formal practice, and during frequent contemplation gaps that we insert into our everyday lives. Our right view is amongst the most precious things we will ever own, and here again the parental love simile is relevant – we must always keep it in sight.

As we have already discussed, the natural state of the mind is happiness, and it is essential not to lose sight of the fact that no matter what our mental state, this happiness is always there to be touched. To know that we can still make contact with this happiness in our darkest hour may be the most comforting thing we will ever experience, and this will energise the perpetual motion machine and strengthen our right view. It may only be a glimpse at such times, but this fleeting appearance of joy and the message of hope that it carries will ultimately guide us out of any inner turmoil. Yes, our recovery may be with faltering steps, yes it may take a zig-zag motion, and yes there may be some periods consisting of only backward steps, but *it will happen* if we maintain contact with our right view.

As we have previously noted, meditation is not the only route to this experience, but it is probably the most reliable. Sometimes, this joyous feeling may arise seemingly from nowhere whilst we are going about our daily activities. It is well documented that this happened to the Buddha himself during his childhood, when he spontaneously entered a state of deep *samadhi* whilst watching a ploughing competition. Indeed, it was the memory of this that inspired him towards the "middle way" following his six years of austere practices. At other times, such a feeling may arise as a result of a more tangible inspiration; for example, the behaviour of another person or an aspect of nature. For me, it is dogs and trees.

Often, just to remember the four foundations of mindfulness can be enough to steady ourselves in our right view. If we can learn habitually to view our experience through the four foundations, then the enhanced understanding that this delivers is deeply restorative. Certainly, in my own life I find myself saying frequently to myself, "The mind and its contents, the body and its sensations", particularly when I feel my composure starting to leave me, and often this will be enough to put things back into perspective. We have so far avoided the term "mantra", and we will keep it that way, but in terms of phrases that are worth repeating over and over again, this one is probably amongst the best that could be chosen. There is another that I favour, which is "Housebuilder, I see you", and this refers to the first words that the Buddha spoke on achieving his ultimate enlightenment. He likened the thinking mind to the builder of a house and declared that through many a rebirth into suffering he had sought the builder of this house, but now the housebuilder was seen and the house destroyed. This image is particularly useful when we find that the mind has flown off into intense and unhelpful ruminative thought.

Of course there may be times when we feel that we cannot find our right view, and this is likely to be at times when excessive thought has caused our minds to be overactive. When our minds are in this state, it can be difficult for wisdom and joy to surface, and the effect it has on our sleep patterns can exacerbate the situation. We may at such times be in need of more practical remedies, so here are eight effective ways to respond. In time, we will learn the combination that works best for us, and of course we may discover more of our own.

1. We can try a short meditation to re-establish our presence in the moment. Walking meditation may be best if we are agitated, or focusing on an aspect of an activity in which we are currently engaged, such as driving. Sitting meditation may not be appropriate if we feel that we will have to exert effort to suppress cascading thoughts.

2. There are times when it is best simply to distract the thinking mind, by engaging in an activity that consumes it. If we are unable to do this, for example when we are lying in bed waiting for sleep, we can fill our thinking minds with other less troublesome thoughts, such as remembering the specific details of a scene from our past. There is no shame in distracting our thinking minds like this, because it displays the critical understanding that thinking is unhelpful at this time.

3. We can look at the turmoil in our thinking minds and actively choose not to go along with it all. We remind

ourselves of our right view – all this thinking is not our natural state, it is not the pure awareness that we seek to cultivate and in which we choose to abide. It helps to say to ourselves, out loud if it feels right, something like "I do not live here" or "I do not choose these thoughts", or indeed "Housebuilder, I see you." This can be a remarkably energising technique for turning away from ruminative thought, particularly if combined with the next technique.

4. We can access the sensation store and call to mind the impression of a smile or the joyous sensation that arises in meditation. Or, if our meditation practice has taken us beyond the initially rapturous connection with awareness, there may be deeper states of ease and equanimity that we can summon to mind.

5. Another effective method for calling up our inner peace is simply to ask ourselves, "Is there peace here?" This straightforward question will focus us on the gaps in thought, and we will see that actually our joyful awareness is still present, albeit overrun with thought. Even in our most troubled times, it is rare that our answer to the question will be that there is no peace to be found anywhere.

6. We should nourish our bodies with good food, exercise and rest. We should avoid putting things into our bodies that may agitate our minds or lower our moods. So, we should keep away any sort of excess in stimulating drinks, alcohol and sugar. Alcohol in particular can feed a cycle that leads to anxiety and depression. A certain amount of renunciation can really lift our mood through reaffirming our self-respect, or in other words our right intention. If sleep

is an issue, then a herbal sleep remedy, such as one containing valerian, may be helpful.

7. If we feel we have temporarily lost our right view, we can go looking for it. It is often illuminating to ask ourselves questions such as "In what ways have I changed since I started following this path?" If we have been practising well, it is certain that we will be able to respond to this question in a positive way, no matter how small the progress may appear compared to the end goal of full enlightenment. For example, we may have become more compassionate to other people, stopped swatting flies, started to recognise harmful thinking, or have a more balanced relationship with material possessions, intoxicants, and social status. Whatever the changes, if we are prepared to acknowledge them, then this will be enough to reassure us that we have some right view and will provide a spark to reignite our right intention.

8. Lastly, we can turn to the practical matter of routine. At times of despair, there is a tendency to start behaving differently, particularly with respect to unwholesome distractions of sense desire. Excess of alcohol is an obvious example, as are food, uninspiring television, and unwholesome Internet searches. When we lose our self-restraint then we lose our self-respect and with it the energy sustaining our right view. It is of immeasurable benefit to focus on our daily routine and catch ourselves when we start to make unwise choices. Even when we are in a mental state that meditation would not suit, we can still maintain a routine that will uplift us. It is extraordinary how disproportionately inspiring a simple act of self-restraint can be.

Ten Good Habits of Mind Care

So far, we have discussed only our greatest challenge –
when we "lose it" – and how we can steer ourselves
around such mental storms. The methods described to
face these states of despair are essentially the key
practices to keep us on the path even when our minds
are more centred, and this is why they were considered
first. Although the two sure refuges above are an
effective lifejacket, it would, of course, be better for us if
anguished states did not arise in the first place. By
following the path that the Buddha taught and retaining
our right view, we can make these occurrences less
likely, but we all waver now and again, and it is
therefore helpful to be able to recognise the warning
signs that we may be becoming unsteady, so that we
may make adjustments to our mindfulness to head off
any potential stumble.

The nature of mind is such that we need to nurture a
wide range of good mental habits and to adopt them as a
system of mind care at all times. Without constant
vigilance, most of us will find that our minds will quickly
slip into habits that present a significant challenge to our
contentment and wellbeing. Here are ten good habits of
mind care to supplement the two sure refuges. Some may
be gems that you pick up and carry far on your path, and
some may just be stepping stones that you use once in
crossing over to the further shore, but each will lead to
forward motion for somebody at some time. Ultimately,
in learning to manage our own minds, we come to
measure up better against the yardstick the Buddha left us
with, which was the exhortation to reflect frequently on

the following question: *"The days and nights are relentlessly passing. How well am I spending my time?"*

Understanding the Influence of our Emotions

At times when there is some sort of downturn in our lives, our emotions can ambush us and make things a great deal worse. We learnt earlier that a fundamental principle of cognitive therapy is that thought influences emotion, and emotion influences thought. It is essential that we remember this, as this principle really is the Swiss Army Knife of our mental toolkit. Just knowing how our emotions can influence our thinking is immensely psychologically healing during our most vulnerable episodes, and it is no exaggeration to say that for some it could even be lifesaving. At times when our emotions are running hot, the last thing we need is for the thinking mind to come barrelling in and inflame the situation.

In the history of our species, emotions seem to have once served a purpose in motivating us to action. Our emotional responses evolved to prepare us for behaviours that positively influenced both our own survival and that of our close kin. Then, much later in our evolution, along came the thinking mind, and an unfortunate side effect took hold. The thinking mind instinctively tries to take control and solve all problems that present themselves to us, and therefore when we are in an agitated state, it tries to figure everything out. It is perhaps amusing, but certainly not helpful, that at such times the newer cortex in our brain is deliberating on outcomes, whilst our older midbrain is screaming at the body either to fight or run away. The increased arousal that is around when we are emotional leads to more urgency in the thinking mind's search for solutions, which is undoubtedly an accidental outcome of the interaction between two biological systems that evolved independently. This energy in turn stimulates a greater intensification of the emotion in the midbrain as thinking becomes more and more knotted and distorted. This can be particularly severe if our sleep has been disturbed and we find ourselves in this turmoil in the middle of the night. We will return soon to the topic of nighttime thought-escalation.

The Buddha did not talk about emotion as such, and indeed there is no real equivalent word in Pali or Sanskrit. He talked of passions, and of the roots of our motivation, but a relatively static concept such as emotion does not really figure in his teachings. His more dynamic view would place the energy of emotion across all of the mental aggregations, and in the eye of the storm that causes the worldly winds to blow. However, despite the lack of a specific concept equivalent to emotion in the Buddha's teaching, the lesson is the same – identification with our mental states causes us to suffer, and at times of passion the suffering can be disproportionately intensified.

Today, we use the word "emotion" freely, even indiscriminately, but do not give due consideration to the sensations of our emotions as being distinct from the thoughts that may follow. To the contracted mind, this is all one indivisible mass of thought and feeling. The sensations of our emotions come from arousal of the nervous system, and underlying them are common physiological responses. Such physical responses include increased heart rate, redistribution of blood flow, trembling, crying, sweating, and so on. These physical reactions may have served our ancient ancestors well in flying from or fighting with foes, for instance, but nowadays their beneficial effect is at best marginal.

To understand the influence of our emotions on our thoughts, and vice versa, is an essential step on the way to right mindfulness.

Recognising Triggered Chains of Thought

Sometimes it is necessary to think a lot. When there is a real and complicated problem that must be solved, we need to engage the thinking mind for sustained periods. Sometimes, there may be time pressure associated with determining a solution to our predicament, and the situation may be one in which the challenges come in at a faster rate than we can deal with them. At such times, we are vulnerable to thoughts running wild, even at times when we are trying to rest, and therefore we need to improve our acuity in spotting the initial signs.

At the first sign that we are becoming tense, we should increase our vigilance regarding the sensations in our bodies. We must learn to notice the first physical signals, such as tightness in the chest, headache, or dry mouth. If we fail to catch these immediate indications and let thought enter in, we may become flustered and confused, and our thoughts will begin to run riot, feeding the fire. Even if we have enough mindfulness to notice the beginning of the storm of thought, we may by then be too preoccupied to deal with it. It is unlikely that we will choose to do even five minutes of meditation at these times, but it is difficult to overplay how restorative such a practice can be. If we are able to notice the early physical indicators and be with the sensations just as they are in the moment, then we can head off the tendency to allow them to give energy to the riot of thought that has already started in our minds.

Whilst recognising the influence of feelings in the body, the key thing is to be watchful for thoughts that come into our minds that are not relevant to the task at hand. As we have already discussed, such thoughts can be activated as stored habits by the sensations in our bodies, or by other thoughts in our minds. As both sources are subject to greater arousal at times like these, their ability to set off irrelevant habitual patterns is enhanced. When extraneous thoughts enter our minds, we should just note them, name them if it is helpful to us, and then let them go. In this way, we can avoid the escalating thoughts and feelings that will initiate the expansion of the spiral shown in Figure 5. If there really is a problem to be solved, we flip the spiral over along its open end, retaining the direction of thought, so that now thought narrows towards a problem solved. This is the proper function of the thinking mind.

Knowing our Priorities

Although it is a tired and meaningless cliché to say that the pace of life is now faster than it ever was, living in the modern world is certainly a challenge. The idea that modern living is inherently "hectic" is a common marketing message in the media, evident for example in the fatuous naming of petrol station fast food opportunities and workplace vending machines. These are designed to perpetuate the myth that we do not have time to make rational choices about how to nourish ourselves as we rush from important task to important task, and therefore should unthinkingly ingest the junk that they purvey. Life is probably no more inherently frenzied than it was when *Homo sapiens* first appeared in the fossil record, except that dealing with absurd marketing messages is now an additional burden.

The basic stressors of life for our species have been broadly similar for thousands of years: essentially that we must provide for ourselves and others, and deal with illness, injury, and death. In times gone by, the threat of being eaten by a prehistoric leopard every time we sallied forth from our cave must have been somewhat stressful, but one may nevertheless speculate that our ancient ancestors were happier than we are today. Of course, it is impossible to determine with any certainty that such a conjecture is valid, but it is certainly very plausible. The reason is that without the sophistications of writing and language, our forebears could not create to-do lists that they could never complete. Nor were they constantly bombarded with messages that they were in some way inadequate in comparison to other early humans, or lacking in key possessions to make them whole.

What causes our discomfort is not the stress of modern living, but the associated propensity to create to-do lists that are not matched to our basic life values. Most of us create them habitually, and then we allow their unfinished state to cause us stress. At times they seem to call out to us, reminding us of all the things that we have not done.

For my part, in heedless moments I find myself adding to my list things that I have already done, so that I can then cross them out and make my lack of progress in other areas look less threatening. Our thinking minds love a to-do list, because it is an easy means by which they can seize control. Even if we are not actually engaged in dealing with any item on the list, we can still be worrying about all the things left to do, or getting fearful about more items being added, or considering the dark consequences of failing to complete tasks. If we then start doing things that do not contribute to the list, such as distracting ourselves with television or food, then the thinking mind can also engage in some lively self-criticism.

The lesson we need to learn is that not everything on the list has a right to be there, and that there is a proper order in which to address the list's contents. Moreover, we need to understand that there is a very clear point at which we have done enough to be at peace, and this is when the *important* things are complete. The definition of "important" here is significant and very specific – *important* equates to *consistent with our life values*. Remembering the Buddha's question about how well we are spending our time, we should allow no other measure of importance to be our guide.

To determine our true life values, the trick is to begin with the end in mind, and here the meaning of "end" is literal – death itself. Imagine you could somehow be invisibly present at your own funeral in two years' time, and therefore have the opportunity to hear what people are saying about you. What would you like to hear those people say? What would you wish to hear from your close family? Or your friends? The insight here is that your answers to such questions will quite clearly illustrate the values that you hold dear, and once you understand your core values you can use them to guide you in how you spend your time. It is likely that some of the kind words you would wish to hear would relate to changes in your life that you have not yet made.

Through this simple exercise, we can free ourselves from the tyranny of our lists. Wherever there is a choice about what to do, we can make it simply on the strength of how closely it matches our core values. If there is no match, then the task is not important. Doing this not only helps us deal with our lists, but leads to a sharp increase in self-respect as our actions now acquire an integrity that they previously lacked. When all of our behaviour is consistent with our values, we are most at ease. We come to realise that previously the important things often did not get done because the list did not show them as being urgent, where our definition of "urgent" related to the time in which a task needed to be completed, not its importance. Once we understand our cherished values, we may come to realise that some of the things we previously considered to be urgent really did not need doing at all. Just because a task is approaching its completion deadline does not mean that it is actually urgent in any sense that really matters. Doing the important things should become routine, and in this way the to-do list becomes just a set of "other things" and as such is less threatening because we know we are taking care of the important things.

This is a common technique of mind and time management, and is extraordinarily effective. What makes this exercise so valuable is the time period selected between the present moment and the imagined funeral. The example used above is two years, which is sufficiently long to allow us to make changes in our behaviour to produce the outcome we desire at our funeral, but is also sufficiently short to require that we commence immediately. It is not the precision in the time period that is crucial; it is that procrastination is not an option.

Knowing our Mental Habits

Through meditation and wise reflection, we are able to identify our most persistent habits of mind, which of course will differ from person to person. We can start to recognise how the five aggregations operate within us, and become familiar with our own habitual judgements. In particular, we can start to discover the most troublesome mental formations that we carry around, and what situations are most likely to trigger them. We are also able to consider the five hindrances and not just recognise when they arise within us, but also come to know which ones are our most enduring companions (worry and flurry for me!). It is especially important to notice the patterns that occur when our passions are aroused, or when there is some reversal in our circumstances that casts a shadow across our awareness. In reflecting thus, we can come to experience and relate to the Buddha's teaching in a deeply personal way. Of course, personal understanding of the path is the only way to liberation.

We previously discussed Eckhart Tolle's concept of the pain body, and this idea is particularly evocative in this context, as it gives rise to an image of a close formation of unhelpful thoughts that always travel together, and that arise fully formed whenever we experience some sort of emotional challenge. Recognising our own unique harmful habits of mind, or pain bodies to use Tolle's concept, is an essential initial step in helping us towards our goal of perpetual inner peace. Of course, ultimately we seek to let go of all habits of mind, but to recognise the most troublesome ones is a very useful first priority.

To help us recognise and, more importantly, let go of our most bothersome mental tendencies, there is a tool in our mind care toolbox that is ideally suited to the task. This is simply to enumerate the various persistent formations to which we are prey and give them names. These names should not contain judgements; they should simply be names. Naming the guests we accommodate within our minds allows us to greet them when they call, and this creates a natural distance between us and them that may be just enough to let them go by. For example, and drawing on my own unhelpful proclivities, there may be:

The Mind of Catastrophic Outcomes
The Mind of Too Much to Do
The Mind of Remorse
The Mind of Personal Inadequacy
The Mind of Unresolved Childhood Issues

Some take this idea further and suggest that we adopt light-hearted names for our mind habits, viewing them as constant companions, even like pets. So, for example, the Mind of Catastrophic Outcomes may become "Dr Doomsayer" or something along those lines. The intention here is to lighten our touch, to reduce our resistance to these formations, and thereby to encourage an attitude of peace towards them. They may one day leave us, but as it won't be any time soon, the best we can do is to learn to live harmoniously with them. Following this line, a useful technique may be to view these boiling patterns of negative mind energy as being like puppies, or tiger cubs, rolling around in the mind together, entangling themselves in a joyous ball in their play, and then separating to take a nap when they have had enough fun. This renders it all less personal, and also makes it easier to show the guests in the home of our awareness some compassion.

Accepting the Present Moment

It seems an obvious question, albeit one that our thinking minds would not habitually ask, but could we simply accept each moment and thereby choose not to suffer through resistance? What basis does this idea have that the present moment should be different anyway? If it is clear to us that acceptance will free us from the suffering that we create, why do we persist in measuring the moment against a standard that it cannot attain? These questions do not deny us the right to react if things are not going our way, but challenge the wisdom of suffering in the process of doing so. The Buddha referred to patient forbearance as "the highest practice", and this willingness to be with the moment, without resistance, is exactly what he meant.

We resist the moment because that is what thinking minds do. It is in their nature. They do not live in the present, because they cannot. They evolved and grew powerful because of their ability to solve problems relating to our future, and to learn from the past, but somehow they got control of the whole mind. There is an old joke that somebody visits the doctor and says, "It hurts when I do this", to which the doctor replies, "Well, don't do it then." This old joke has been a constant companion to me for almost as long as I can remember, but not just because of its humour. It also contains deep wisdom when applied to the mind of thinking, attachment, and suffering – don't do it indeed!

When the issues of the moment are stripped of the judgements and thoughts that we have added, we can see them for what they really are – mere conditions. A very powerful option at this point is to choose to accept our situation as it is and divert our life energies away from resistance. Resisting the present moment is much more wearing than we may realise, and we can only know this through the lightness of spirit we feel when we let go of our opposition. It is important to be kind to ourselves when we choose to accept the present moment, as it is easy to slip into a negative pattern of thought by deciding that acceptance is a sign of weakness. On the contrary, mindful and wilful acceptance is not weakness; it can be both strength and wisdom. It draws on the insight that our true happiness does not lie in getting what our thinking minds tell us we want, or indeed in satisfying any other of the thinking mind's ego-driven ruses. We can still choose to act in such a way that gets us something we want, but we do it from a position of acceptance of where we are now.

Eckhart Tolle gives an inspiring perspective on this in recommending that we accept the present moment *as if we had chosen it ourselves*. This may seem a very tall order to us, particularly when we are suffering. It is one thing to accept the present moment in the sense of being accepting of it, but actually to *desire* it is something else entirely. However, the wisdom in Tolle's view is profound – to accept the moment fully can surely be nothing less than to desire it, because anything less implies resistance. Another suggestion that Tolle makes frequently, and which also bears repetition, is to ask ourselves what problem we actually have in the present moment. When we ask this question, we are urged to be careful not to project ourselves into the future or past, but to consider the question as it relates to the very instant of our current experience. This question is most effective, because it points directly at the here and now, casting aside thought that can only dwell in other time zones. Tolle points out that in this very moment, actually, we do not have a problem at all, just the moment. He is absolutely right, of course he is, but sometimes it takes significant resolve, not to mention courage, to accept this.

Both the past and the future need to be handled safely in our thoughts, and to do this requires a wise perspective on both. We have to loosen our grip on the past, because we cannot change it. We may have behaved unskilfully there, but all we should carry forward is what we have learnt. Revisiting the past with our thoughts makes us unable to experience the present moment, in which we could witness the joy of awareness and behave more appropriately. To linger in thoughts about the past is also deeply dangerous from the perspective of mind care: our thinking minds are blind to the obvious truth that they cannot fix the past, and in trying to do so they can take us to extremes of despair.

The future is no safer as a destination for the thinking

mind. The future has not happened yet, and is therefore indeterminate, but this will not stop our thinking minds trying to nail the jelly to the wall. Really, all we can ever know about the future is that it is uncertain, and therefore the only wise option is to accept this willingly and deal with what comes. The future will become the present when its time comes, and we will experience it then. Today is yesterday's tomorrow.

Accepting the present moment can be simply having the presence of mind to *do nothing*. Of course, when there is a real problem to be solved, then we should act. However, when the "problem" is that we have erred in the past or that the future is uncertain then a "solution" from the thinking mind is the last thing that we need. The instinct to solve this type of problem seems natural and appropriate to us, but this is a dangerous delusion. The only outcome will be escalating thought and further suffering. At these times, the best type of thinking is no thinking, backed by the positive decision not to act. We need simply to steady ourselves, choose not to abide in unnecessary thought, let the universe do its work, and be accepting of the next moment that comes our way. As we discussed before, until this becomes our natural response, it may help to remind ourselves out loud of our resolution not to enter into unproductive thought at these times.

Resisting the present moment is certainly an instinctive habit, and it may feel like the addiction is too strong to break. There is a parallel here in the physical realm that may provide a valuable insight. The practice of yoga is undoubtedly a beneficial means of contributing to our mental and physical wellbeing. Even if we only use yogic positions for stretching exercises, this remains so. When we stretch, we encounter physical resistance at the limit of the movement, and it is natural to feel that we can go no further. However, if we take our attention to our breath and then on each outbreath allow ourselves to go a little deeper into the stretch, we will see that more is possible, and then still more. The nature of resistance is not what it first appears to be.

Moment o'clock – Maintaining our Attention in the Present

Of course, if we are to accept the present moment then we need to experience it in the first place. It is important always to try to be in contact with the present moment, no matter what we are doing. It should at all times be moment o'clock in our lives! In formal meditation, we deliberately reduce the stimulation available to the mind, and in this way we can connect more readily to the moment. In meditation, the moment is all there is and it is clear when our minds have lost the connection. However, our everyday activities present much more of a challenge, because everything is in motion and our minds are not inclined just to allow this movement to be as it is, but rather they attach to it and agitate it into a full commotion. In these circumstances, to remain in the moment may seem like an impossible challenge for most of us, and understandably so. This is because the sense of true awareness is subtle and refined, and therefore hard to find within the maelstrom of conditions and responses that are simultaneously in play. What we need is a coarser anchor point that is more readily accessible and identifiable.

The breath and the sensations in the body are most often used as meditation objects, because they have this quality of coarseness that means that they are easily accessed and clearly perceived. So, to anchor ourselves in the present moment, we can return to the breath, or to the sensations elsewhere in the body. The world continues to turn around us, but now we have a part of our attention centred in the here and now, and it is clear to us when we lose this focus. When we concentrate our attention in this way, we do not need to dedicate all of it to the breath or body as we seek to do in formal practice, just a percentage to create a space between the conditions that arise and our responses to those conditions. This is particularly important in those challenging situations where our habitual reactions are lined up like well-drilled soldiers ready to go over the top. If we always keep back some awareness for the breath or the body, then we can catch the emotions and triggered chains of thought before they escalate. Or, if the hair trigger has already set off our mind habits, we can use our awareness to form a firebreak around the resulting formations so they do not spread and merge.

In calmer times, we can use this same guidance to enable us to ensure that our minds do not wander off into harmful patterns of thought and intention. Let's deal with the future first. To hold and pursue life goals is perfectly normal and healthy, providing that we do not pollute them with attachment to outcomes. For instance, it is reasonable to desire to earn more money to make our life circumstances more comfortable, and likewise it is appropriate to work to achieve that goal. What we need to remember in doing this is that we must not postpone our happiness until all is achieved, and we must experience every step of the way to the fullest extent possible. As we strive to achieve something, we should keep our awareness anchored so that errant thoughts and attachments are noted and do not cross the firebreak to acquire self-significance. If our minds are fully in the future, then we are separated from the present, and the nature of that separation is suffering. We experience a gap and thereby make ourselves incomplete. If we are wholly in the present, then there is no lack or suffering, and we remain whole. We therefore need to learn to catch ourselves projecting forward, and bring at least a part of ourselves back into the present moment. The breath and the body are always there as readily accessible touchpoints for us.

Of course, another human tendency is to dwell in the past, and again caution is needed. Travelling into the past for the purposes of judging ourselves and wishing we had done otherwise is very harmful, and here too we need our firebreak. Excessive consideration of the past is brooding, and as we have already learnt, this can be very damaging. Naturally, we need to learn from our mistakes, but this is all we should seek to carry forward from the past. The past is relevant in the sense that its cause and effect have led to the present moment, and this needs to be understood, but in other respects it does not generally deserve our attention.

By dwelling in the future and past, we strengthen the troublesome mental formations, the *sankharas*, and build up their affinity with self-view and the perception that we are incomplete in the moment. If we have lost ourselves and cannot locate the present moment in the chaos unfolding around and within us, we should simply open up to the breathing or the body and locate that which is real and now, and from this safe place we can watch the show. As the Buddha said, the truth is apparent here and now, *sanditthiko*. This is the great gift of the *dhamma*: that the teaching is always accessible; it is what we are experiencing right now, and therefore there is no such thing as a bad time to grow in our practice. We simply meet ourselves where we are in the moment, and work with what is.

Acting Immediately

It is immensely liberating to face problems directly and as soon as they arise, and yet frequently we do not do this. It is also energising to do something we have been putting off for some time. When issues are not faced, our thinking minds will keep reaching out to them, usually worrying them out of proportion, and generally destroying our peace and happiness in the process. Until they are addressed, our problems will enter our minds uncalled for, and even invade our dreams whilst we sleep. The human appetite for procrastination is particularly strange in this context, but is nevertheless sometimes insatiable.

Issues in our lives are, of course, often real rather than imagined, but we need to be careful to regard them as events in our lives, not as life itself. Such events are not us, and they do not define us. We must try to be aware that a "problem" is merely a label we may apply to a particular set of life events, and if we are gentle with ourselves we can see how much we are adding not only through that label, but through further thought, particularly about the unknown and unknowable. That is not to say that the issues we face might not require effort, ingenuity and courage to solve, it is just to say that they are as they are and it is important not to add to them with unhelpful thought.

When we turn to face our perceived problems, then in general they may be much smaller than we initially perceived them to be, or at least easier to deal with. This is because we are looking only at the facts of the matter, rather than the accompanying nonsense that our thinking minds have contributed in the time it took us to decide to act. Our thinking minds are presented with plenty of opportunity to build up our problems if we spend time thinking about them rather than acting, which of course we generally do. Also, in thinking about challenges that we face rather than dealing with them, we stretch the envelope of time that we allocate to them, and a large part of the relief we feel when we have acted is that we have finally ended this self-inflicted suffering.

Before we can act upon our problems, we have to clear out some mental clutter that will just get in the way. This clutter is our unnecessary thinking about the past and the future. We can clearly identify the contribution of thoughts about the past, as these tend to be punctuated with useless self-criticism, and wishing "If only I had done otherwise." In other words, we are thinking, "If only things were other than they are now." Although our thinking minds seem to enjoy this sort of thing, it is clearly absurd, because of course things can only be as they are now. Thoughts about the future are equally easy to spot, as these are characterised by "what-if" scenarios that are not happening now and do not, therefore, need to be dealt with. Again, a preposterous waste of time. The thinking mind can be very cunning and can appear most convincing that it is actually helping by contributing all this disturbing and anxiety-creating thought about the past and the future. However, our task is to set all this aside and identify one simple thing: *the task in the present moment that needs to be done*. This task needs to be a concrete thing – deciding to do some more worrying does not count!

Once this task has been identified then we have one undemanding thing to do, which is to decide whether it can be done right now. When we have decided this, actually there is no "problem" as such, there is just the task that needs to be performed now, or not. If the task cannot be carried out now for some practical reason, then only one thing needs to be done, which is to decide when it will be done. In order to prevent the thinking mind "making itself useful" by worrying that we are going to forget to do it at the allotted time, then it may help to write it down. That is all there is to it; the rest is useless thinking. The thinking mind is very effective at problem-solving, but it should carry a health warning: problem-solving only counts when it is directed at a task that we are actually about to do, and it should not be directed at a hypothetical problem that our minds have thought up and which is not actually happening.

If the task that needs to be done is particularly repellent to us and we do not feel enough strength to face it with mindfulness alone, we can try promising ourselves a reward when it is done. This is a very common therapeutic technique amongst psychologists, drawn from old-fashioned behaviour therapy, but still used to great effect today. There was a time quite recently in my own life where I had got myself into a very challenging situation and I had a series of unpleasant tasks to perform over many months, all of which were highly effective in stimulating my most persistent and damaging mental habits. For each of these tasks, I awarded myself "music points" and I kept a log of my points tally. On every fifth point I bought myself a piece of music that interested me, and in that way I actually started to look forward in some measure to carrying out the task. Interestingly, these problems returned recently on a grand scale, although this time mindfulness and occasional herbal sleeping aids have been sufficient.

Sleeping Well and Waking Well

Falling asleep is an act of letting go. If our thinking minds have been especially active during the day, it is good to have some techniques at our disposal to aid in the disengagement that leads to sleep. One method that is effective whilst lying in bed is to use a meditation technique to focus the mind away from the rampaging thought that may otherwise keep us awake. If we are tired, this way of letting go will allow sleep to take us. It is best to select a meditation object that we do not use in our daily formal practice, because otherwise this may cause us to associate our meditation object with sleepiness when we need to be wakeful. One method that may work is to focus on the sensations in a body part, preferably one nice and far from the origin of the storm, for example the feet. To do this, we move our attention to each toe, feeling the sensation of the sheets against it, any warmth or cold, the sensation on the upper surface of the toe, the sensation underneath, and the space between it and the next toe. When we "move" our attention there, we should take this literally – we try to experience the attention actually in and on the toe as if our consciousness were inside it, rather than contemplating it from afar. We can then progress from toe to toe, then to the top of the foot, around to the underneath and so around the ankle. As we do this, our thinking minds will let go.

Although the body can function adequately with reduced sleep, an appropriate amount does nourish and energise us, and there is no doubt that our moods are affected by a lack of it. It is an excellent and straightforward life skill to observe how much sleep our bodies actually need. On the occasions that meditative concentration is not enough to allow our bodies to let go and drift off, there is no shame in getting some additional help now and then. Some herbal sleeping remedies are actually remarkably effective for those that are able to take them, particularly if we have learnt effective mind management techniques to accompany them.

We also need to understand how to manage our minds on waking, as this is a time when we are particularly vulnerable to unguarded thinking. Here, it is important to distinguish two different types of waking, the first being normal waking following sufficient sleep, and the second being waking unnaturally early, usually accompanied by anxiety. Let's talk about normal waking first. The reasons not to get out of bed are legion, from the seemingly innocuous unwillingness to break the seal of comfort that envelops us, to the more troublesome reluctance to start a busy day and instead to spend time becoming anxious in anticipation. In other words, at this time we are particularly susceptible to the hindrances of sloth and torpor, and worry and flurry, and indeed to the other hindrances as well. I have a strong affinity for the saying that we should get out of our bed as if it were on fire, and although this is something the Buddha did not say I feel he may have agreed. He did give specific guidance to his monks only to take sufficient in the way of rest, and this direction is followed in Buddhist monastic communities to this day. If we are awake, then no useful purpose is served by lingering in bed, unless perhaps it is an act of kindness that we afford ourselves, for example to rest for longer at the end of a long working week in which we have not managed to sleep sufficiently for our body's needs. Another good reason to rise promptly is that this is a good opportunity to meditate, setting the mind for the day ahead.

Now let's turn our attention to a problem that affects most people at some times in their lives, and this is the unwelcome experience of persistent nocturnal waking. Before tackling this issue directly, we will set it in a context that may aid its understanding. There is a phenomenon that has been observed amongst people with damaged visual cortex in their brains, and which has come to be known as *blindsight*. Such patients are able to react to stimuli in their visual fields that they cannot consciously see. An exciting explanation of this phenomenon is that it is the result of activity in sensory structures within our brains that predate the evolution of the mammalian eye and visual cortex. The argument is that the optic nerve passes through evolutionarily older structures on its way to the visual cortex, and that such structures would once have been our primary sensory apparatus. These older structures may once have been part of a cruder and less specialised sensory system that did not make the same distinctions that its modern successor does between, for example, sight and hearing. This explanation leads to a fascinating speculation: the reason we seem to have sharpened visual and aural senses in situations that we fear, such as walking alone through a dark and lonely place, is that our heightened arousal activates these older structures. We then become much more attuned to events in the periphery of our visual field, where predators may once have lurked in the shadows.

In a similar but entirely useless way, there are times when our level of arousal seems to promote in our thinking minds an increased ability to detect imaginary threats to our wellbeing. Even though at other times we would be able to judge that we are losing perspective, for some reason in the small hours of the night the irrational thoughts seem to keep coming in from all sides and seem all too credible. They surge out of our sleeping minds to wake us up and start us brooding when we have the least power to resist. However, in contrast to the plausible and useful explanation of blindsight, there is no explanation for why we worry ourselves into states of desperation, sweat-soaked and sleepless in the middle of the night. Our increased mental vigilance at night may well be a throwback to an ancient protective mechanism to stop us being attacked as we sleep, but the thinking is completely futile, as the light of day will usually reveal. The remedy is simply to understand this and firmly say, "I will not follow" to ourselves if we wake in a ruminative nocturnal frenzy. If problems are swirling around in our minds, it can help to write on a note by the side of the bed any things that need to be considered on waking. Leaving a notepad and pen by the side of the bed can be reassuring, even if it is not used. These are simple but remarkably effective techniques to reassure our thinking minds that we have taken heed of their concerns, and therefore that they can now pipe down. We can then close our eyes and distract the thinking mind with a meditative technique such as moving the attention into the body.

Turning Towards our Demons

There will come a time when we are ready to turn to face some of our most difficult thought patterns, which perhaps we have come to regard as our demons. These tend to be associated with strong emotional feelings, and so are the ultimate challenge for our mindfulness. If our practice on the path is developing, we may have already cast a few sideways glances in their direction, and may now be starting to relate to them in a different way. For example, we may have started to consider the raw sensations they bring and be gently investigating them. Maybe we are calling up sensations from the sensation store either to suppress these impressions, or just for comparison. Or, perhaps we have been able to hold them a while when they have arisen and been able to see more clearly how they operate within us to influence our thinking. When we have some confidence in remaining detached from these feelings, we may be ready to face the associated thoughts more directly, by actually calling them up with the sole purpose of investigating them. Maybe we are already starting to gain some insight into their origin.

We should not rush into this practice, however. We must consider ourselves to be ready first. With practice, and the courage that comes from increasing right view and right intention, we can look hard at our demons as a spectator would, not getting involved with them, just holding them gently in our awareness and considering them. It is important to regard this as a difficult practice and one that should be approached with some care. The rip currents in our minds are strong in places, and they can carry us very far away from where we started very quickly. We need to use our wisdom to spot this happening, and then return ourselves to calmer waters before we exhaust ourselves in the struggle. If we become fearful that we are becoming overwhelmed, we can always send up a flare to light our way; for example, by calling up joy from the sensation store to replace what we are feeling, or just shifting our attention to the breath. If neither of these actions works for us, we can always just distract ourselves. When we look at emotional thought patterns like this, we are breaking the habit of falling into them, and little by little we will come to see them for what they are.

Understanding Other Minds

Identification with the wants and needs of the thinking mind also causes problems in our relationships with others. The simple reason for this is that unless these others are enlightened beings, their thinking minds will share the same delusions as ours. So, when two contracted minds are communicating, they will both be trying to preserve what they have, attain more that brings them pleasure, and avoid things that they do not like. They will both believe that if they are successful they will achieve lasting contentment. The essential outlook of the contracted mind is like a fight for survival: it fears anything that might diminish it, or worse, extinguish it. It sees other minds as attacking forces. As we have already discussed, its most treacherous ploy in this struggle is to convince its host that the stakes are maximally high and that it is *self* that is threatened. If two minds are engaging each other from this standpoint, the experience of at least one of them will be unsatisfying and unproductive, and conflict is always possible.

The contracted mind tends to play what is termed in game theory a *zero sum game*. Such a scenario is a mathematical model in which one participant's gain is matched by another's loss, and therefore the total gains and losses always make zero. This type of game is also called a *strictly competitive, win-lose* or *conflict* game, and each of these terms describes its nature very appropriately. It is fascinating that every time we expose one of the habitual assumptions of the thinking mind, we encounter a view that seems somewhat preposterous, but nonetheless is universally held. This is one of the reasons why the Buddha hesitated before deciding to embark on his teaching ministry – how could one man alone deal with delusion on such a scale?

One of the richest veins in self-help literature concerns relationships between people, although plenty of it is aimed at how to get what we want from others, often assuming a zero sum game. We can consult countless sources about communication, assertiveness, negotiation, conflict resolution, intimate relationships, and many other related subjects. Some of this guidance deals with personal relationships and some of it with business relationships, the difference being quite important to many authors. Throughout this vast literature there runs a common theme that is somewhat familiar to those acquainted with the teachings of the Buddha. This universal message is that when we are relating to another person, we need to try to loosen both parties' island perceptions of self. To do this, we are urged to try to see our interactions through the mind of the other person, and to impart information to them so that they may do the same. Just as we habitually create a self within our own minds, so too do we "create" the person with whom we are interacting. Both delusions are equally unhelpful and need to be set aside.

To reduce the separation between our thinking minds and those of others requires five essential skills. There are variations and refinements of these skills in the vast body of information out there, but probably none that adds substantially to these five. In some we see the Buddha's teaching clearly and directly, and in others we see it more subtly, but in none is it absent. These skills are:

1. Don't automatically follow the story your mind is telling you
2. Make it clear what you want
3. Try to see the interaction from the other person's perspective
4. Don't pursue a zero sum outcome
5. Avoid behaviours that emphasise self and other

We have discussed the first of these skills quite extensively already, and we will return again to the theme of the contracted mind as a storyteller, but this time with something of a science fiction twist. We have learnt of the relationship between emotion and thought, and between thought and emotion. We are now therefore on our guard against the fabrications that the contracted mind can add to a feeling, and are better equipped to see the beginning of an escalating chain of unnecessary thought. There can be no richer source of stimuli to our habitual emotional responses than interacting with another being, so in this domain we need to be particularly mindful of the thinking mind's creations.

A good way to avoid the contracted mind's inventions is always to be aware of how we are reacting physically to the person with whom we are communicating. It is useful continually to scan the parts of the body that give us the best clues to this. The stomach and chest area where our organ tree is located is a very good source of evidence. In doing this, we become aware of the subtle changes in our body as our minds perceive an assault. These bodily signs are cues to look into our minds and ask ourselves whether what we are thinking has any basis of truth in relation to our situation. Within our minds there are also cues to watch out for, which are thoughts that strongly emphasise *I, you, he, she, we,* and *they*.

In situations where there is conflict, so too can there be anger, and anger is one of the main stimuli for the thinking mind's storytelling. Familiar techniques of anger management start with learning to recognise our anger simply as a pattern of sensations within our bodies. Thoughts get added, but these are fabrications – the origin of the storm is within the body, not in the web of righteous views that follow. When we recognise the anger as it arises as a mere pattern of physical impressions, we have the opportunity to let it all pass and not jump into that anger, with all the habitual reactions that would then ensue. Thus, the old saying "count to ten" is appropriate advice, in that it involves an element of delay between feeling and thought, and also an element of distraction, so that the sensation can stay as it is and fade naturally. In psychological terms, it is a technique that promotes the metacognitive awareness that we have already discussed. Thomas Jefferson's much-quoted qualification of this advice to count to a hundred if we are *very* angry also has wisdom, in that if we are particularly determined to allow our anger to take control of our minds, we can quickly get a count to ten out of the way and then really surrender to mindlessness!

We should be particularly vigilant when we are interacting with somebody we do not like. It is not the goal of our mental training that we should like everybody, so we need not get hung up on the idea that disliking somebody is a problem, providing that we understand the nature of our dislike. Our thinking mind may weave a web of deceit around the real reason, which may be, for example, that we dislike that person because they have something that we want. Once we know the truth rather than the story, we can move forward. We should not resist our aversion, but rather just note it and give it a name if we wish. However, we do need to get into the habit of wishing that those we dislike be well and happy, else it is likely that we will get caught up in zero sum thinking.

Turning to the second of our five skills, when

communicating with another person our thinking minds often seem totally averse to stating clearly what we want. This is particularly true if the essence of the communication is a negotiation. The truth of this seems to be that the thinking mind's identification with self results in it seeing any openness as making us weak. In stating what we want to another being we tacitly believe that we make that person less likely to give it to us, or we give them additional bargaining power through knowing what really matters to us. Here we see clearly the zero sum assumption at work within us, but modern research now interprets negotiation and conflict as a system of informed interactions in which the end result maximises the benefit for *both* sides. Communicating what we want is not weakness, but can actually be an assertive behaviour. It allows the other person to understand us better and try to fit in with our needs. It also gives them the opportunity to respond with what they want, which is then the basis for open negotiation.

The third skill to discuss is understanding another person's point of view. Unless we are prepared to do this, we have two problems. Firstly, our range of negotiating techniques is severely limited, and this may cause us to fall back on merely restating what we want. Doing this adds little to the negotiation, and may act as an irritant. In our efforts to re-present the same argument in a fresh way, it is likely that we will be perceived as bullying, cajoling, or using any of several other unwelcome behaviours. Secondly, not understanding the other person's needs puts us in a position where we tend to assume that our needs clash with theirs. This creates an ego-based power struggle that needs a winner and a loser before it can end. There is no basis for negotiation or common ground here, and even if we are the winner, this is likely to discolour our relationship with the other person and therefore in the long term there may be a net loss. In other words, we have won in a negative sum game.

A related point is that putting ourselves inside another mind is a good technique for improving our relationship with ourselves. If we do this, and judge only our outward behaviours, we may well see ourselves in a way that is fundamentally different from our own self-image. For instance, in this way we may perceive ourselves to be successful and confident, whereas inside our own minds we are consumed with doubt. The learning here is that in general when we see somebody else as accomplished and assured, this may be a creation of our own mind and they too may be beset by anxieties. Such an insight will lead to increased compassion both to self and others. We may also come to see that our negotiating style might be regarded as belligerent and inflexible, even if we did not intend it to be so. The Buddha encouraged his monks to have an easy relationship with feedback on their conduct, even when this included criticism or admonishment, and this is good advice for all. We should learn to take criticism well, and consider well our motivation and language when dishing it out.

Our fourth mind skill to reduce the separation between self and other concerns not pursuing a zero sum outcome. Let's look more closely at the alternative to the zero sum game. Assertiveness training is based on the concept of *abundance*, i.e. there is something in any negotiation for both parties. So, instead of a win-lose bargaining strategy, it is win-win; getting what we want from a negotiation does not necessarily entail the other person getting less or nothing. What is meant by abundance is that the territory of the disagreement needs to be seen as having no limits, otherwise the negotiation is about one person getting more and the other less. To use one of the common metaphors of assertiveness professionals, the cake that is being shared does not have finite dimensions, and removing a piece does not affect the amount of cake available for others. This is because each participant will have a different view of the whole cake, and place a different value on each piece of it. A cake is a truly dreadful metaphor here, and so is a pie, but in the field of assertiveness training these seem to be the standard reference metaphors. The key point is that in practice, in any negotiation it will rarely be the case that everything that matters most to one person is also everything that matters most to the other person. So it follows that if we understand the other party's needs better, we can still get what we want, but the negotiation can still give that party something that they want too. This becomes possible only if we have taken the trouble to understand them.

Another common technique in negotiation, which again diminishes the separation between two thinking minds, is to identify the common ground, i.e. the things that we are not negotiating about. This serves to emphasise the similarities between us, and therefore gives a firm ground on which to negotiate the differences. It is useful to reflect frequently that we as humans are all in the same position; we are born and we die, we have the same opportunity to be enlightened, and we face similar challenges along the way. Such are the fundamentals; we are more similar than different, and in negotiation and conflict this reflection will serve us well. If we are not communicating respectfully, compassionately and peacefully, then something is in the way, and that obstacle is identification with self.

Lastly, in conflict or negotiation we are urged to avoid various antagonistic styles of interaction and the essence of what is being taught is the same again – to reduce the sharp edges of self and lessen the separation between self and other. There are some quite obvious hostile behaviours that increase separation, such as name-calling or attempting to persuade the other person by browbeating. We will find that in such circumstances sentences may often begin with the word "You", and this is a cue for us to examine our behaviour. Less confrontationally but still tied up in self, we may make an attribution about another person's motives that is more about projection of our own ego than about genuinely understanding the other's position. Again, the cue might be a communication starting with "You". Although this may seem like fairly obvious stuff, as self-help literature often does, when we investigate our own behaviour we may find that we are not as wise as we like to think we are!

Of course, as usual we can always fall back on the mental knotted handkerchief, which is particularly important when engaging with another person in a situation that could cause our passions to be aroused. We can choose what works best for each of us, but the key characteristic of our chosen device must be that it keeps us in contact with our resolution to behave mindfully. As an example, I will share one of the techniques that I personally have found useful. Earlier, I introduced the *anjali* gesture, and often I have discreetly maintained this posture whilst in a charged negotiation with another person, probably without my potential opponent noticing I was doing it.

PART SIX

STILL TRAINING
OUR MINDS

Body and Mind Again

The Buddha spoke of two sets of five that must be set aside, and these are the five hindrances to meditation practice, and the five aggregations through which our minds habitually create our suffering. He spoke of crossing the river to the further shore, but unless we learn to be mindful at all times, we will succeed only in making short visits to that shore, always to return to the hither shore of our suffering. To take up residence permanently on the yonder side of the river of craving, we need to be able to integrate our formal practice with our everyday lives at all times. As the Buddha said, we need to "empty our boat" of attachment, aversion and ignorance in order to proceed swiftly and lightly to the other side. To do this requires significant vigilance, resolve and understanding. There is no better way to feed the perpetual motion inherent in our path than to experience progress directly, and in this section we will go deeper into the practice and elaborate on these signs of progress. We will also venture further into the nature of those factors that hold us back.

We will follow here the same pattern as we did in the earlier part of the book, by considering two of the three main pillars of our practice: meditation and wise reflection. However, we will not travel straight there, but rather we will take a detour first into an aspect of practice can be more accessible and enjoyable for some people. There is no principle of mindfulness training that says that we cannot seek to develop our minds in arenas that we find attractive and pleasurable. To enjoy our mindfulness practice is no hindrance, providing that we are always ready to let go of the enjoyment, along with everything else. Pleasure can be particularly helpful in the early stages, as it feeds our right effort. Of course, it can also feed the hindrance of desire and thereby lead to attachment, but we can save this as a problem for later. Although attachment is the very fire we are trying to contain with our meditation, it is important that on our way to liberation we are practical – some attachments may actually help us for a while. I have heard one monk describe helpful attachments as being like the rungs of a ladder when climbing upwards – it is perfectly fine to reach out and grasp one as long as we can then let go and reach upwards to the next rung.

Our detour is to explore mindfulness training in learning proficiency in a skill or a sport. This is a highly productive arena, so much so that it has for centuries been a central focus in Zen Buddhist training. I know of one very committed practitioner of *dhamma* for whom it all started with a desire to improve his squash game, and through this he developed a deep interest in right view of the mind-body relationship. Part of the insight here is that in skilful and coordinated bodily action the thinking mind needs to retire to a safe distance in order to *allow* the body to learn and then to execute what it has learnt. The more profound insight is that not only can we trust our actions when our thinking minds are disengaged, but the ensuing natural behaviours that arise can be pure and skilful. What we learn is that all the thinking mind needs to do is to set the strategy and provide the energy to maintain it, and so again it is ready, set, let go.

Meditator's Elbow

After the Second World War, a rather beautiful book was published. *Zen in the Art of Archery* was written by the German philosophy teacher Eugen Herrigel and has remained a popular book ever since. This book is a warm and careful exposition of the acquisition of skill in archery, as taught by a Japanese Zen master. Archery is one of the arts used to teach Zen mastery in Japan, other examples being sword fighting and flower arranging. It is perhaps somewhat surprising to consider that the cultivation of awareness can be taught by both sword fighting and flower arranging, but at a deeper level it is profoundly revealing. The essential theme of Herrigel's provocative book is learning to be completely aware, and the development of skill in archery is merely a framework through which this theme is communicated. Herrigel spent some years in Japan as student and teacher, and this book is his account of the wisdom he gained.

Zen training methods enable the student to acquire skill in archery, or indeed in any of the Zen arts, without the intervention of conscious effort and thinking. A running theme within Herrigel's book is that the self needs to be absent in learning the art. One of the many evocative similes is that the timing of a student's release of the bow string should be like that of a ripe fruit falling from a tree; it happens when it is ready, without conscious intention, and independently of expectation.

It is tempting to pause for a while to delight in the wonderful metaphors and examples in Herrigel's book, but noting thoughts of reluctance, we should press on. After all, Zen is taught by doing, not by thinking, and any analogy is more useful as an image than as a set of thought propositions. Zen instruction involves an intense focus on the present moment, to a degree that actions are performed in an almost ceremonial fashion. This is acknowledged in the naming of the centuries-old Japanese art of preparing tea – the "tea ceremony". The tea ceremony was created by a Zen priest and its purpose is to emphasise the harmony, simplicity and beauty in the otherwise mundane aspects of sharing tea with others. The whole process is closely choreographed for all participants down to the finest detail of the movements that the host and guests make with their hands and even their fingers.

The influence of Herrigel's book grew steadily, and it was certainly a landmark in the introduction of Zen teachings to Europe. However, the mindfulness teaching within it was still very much grounded in its Buddhist origin, and this is likely to have been something of a barrier to its appeal in the West. Furthermore, the Zen Buddhist tradition is especially challenging to Westerners in its austerity and unfamiliarity, which may have further limited the reach of the book. Other schools of Zen that were challenging their students with impenetrable riddles, or *koans*, were similarly unpalatable to Western tastes.

A step change in the popular understanding of mindfulness came in a book published in the early 1970s; this one adopting the much more approachable discipline of the game of tennis as its subject. *The Inner Game of Tennis* was written by an American called Timothy Gallwey, who had an interest in education and was also committed to meditation practice. Its central point is that the thinking mind is the first opponent to deal with in tennis, and how we manage this "inner" opponent will critically affect the game with the "outer" opponent on the other side of the net. Indeed, the thinking mind is described as such a fearsome opponent that it can destroy our game without our real tennis opponent needing to take their racquet out of its cover.

The Inner Game of Tennis created something of a sensation and became a bestseller in a very short time. It was the beginning of a successful series of *Inner Game* publications for Gallwey, and the foundation of a substantial coaching industry using mindfulness methods in sport, life and business. Of course, our interest here is not in the tennis serve or bank balance, but rather in the health of the mind and the universe. Gallwey's book was a major event in the popularisation of an ancient message about the nature of mind, but its inclusion here is because it is a key reference on the subject of concentration meditation practiced through sport.

Gallwey explains that within the mind are born such formidable adversaries as fear, self-doubt, worry, self-reproach, and distractibility. They can assail us one at a time, or can form themselves into groups, but in either case the outcome is the same – they get in the way of the natural flow of our game. Substitute tennis for meditation and indeed life, and here we find Gallwey essentially talking about the hindrances and fetters. Just as the Buddha had done two and a half millennia before, Gallwey explains that to achieve our full potential we have to quieten the interference from the thinking mind and be at one with what the body is doing in the moment. He suggests that the only role for the thinking mind is in setting the goal and direction of the game, and that the body should then be trusted to execute the game naturally. This is right view applied to tennis.

Gallwey goes on to explain that learning is best achieved by directly experiencing how things are, rather than having them carved up and analysed by the thinking mind. Indeed, the best results are obtained when the mind is silenced, and the way to silence the mind is to focus on the body. His teaching methods deliberately set aside the thinking mind by using visualisation of outcomes and recollection of feelings instead of verbal instruction. This accords with the intent of the *Set* phase of meditation described earlier, providing an essential orientation and resolve and then allowing our own natures to find the target. It also essentially restates the method in Herrigel's book, albeit perhaps in more accessible terms.

Intervention from the thinking mind disturbs our awareness by making it selective. Most of us will have performed some sort of activity where we have felt ourselves to be "in the zone". This feeling is not confined to sporting activity, although sport is the domain in which this feeling is perhaps the most salient, apart from meditation of course. For those of us who have learnt to ride a bicycle or a surfboard, we may remember the first thrill of balance, and how it inspired us. Of course, a competent cyclist will never say that they think about how to balance their lumbering frame on two thin wheels. Similarly, a surfer will not look at their feet, because they know that where the eyes go, the body follows. Rather, cyclists and surfers just allow their bodies to do their thing. It is a safe bet that if we ask somebody what they were thinking when they played that great golf or tennis shot, they will say either that they were thinking nothing at all or that they were merely visualising how they wished the shot to turn out. Again, the body is being left to its own nature and the thinking mind has learnt not to intervene. It is an equally safe bet that if you ask somebody that question whilst they are in the zone, they will instantly wobble and fumble their way straight out of it.

Following Gallwey's example, many teachers in sport these days will ask the student to note and fully experience the way the body feels when things are going well, in an effort to try to associate that feeling with the underlying natural movements and thereby allow the body to reproduce them as an unanalysed whole. Instructors are likely to work with the student in the way we did with the sensation store, trying to direct the attention to the essential nature of the feeling, its location and its movement. They will not try to break it down and analyse it, or grasp it in any way, but rather will encourage their student to retain it as a pattern to be matched as learning progresses. When something goes badly, the key thing is for the player to let go of the self-criticism and analysis and try to recreate what is good. Showing somebody a film clip of themselves performing an action well and badly, or allowing them to compare such clips to those of experts, will allow much deeper learning than will verbal instruction. Gallwey found that pointing to a few salient areas of comparison without speaking too much would intensify learning.

Psychologists often use the word *flow* to describe this feeling of being in the zone, after this term was first coined by the Hungarian psychologist Mihaly Csikszentmihalyi. He described it as a state of joyful and effortless concentration, in which there is minimal concept of self or time, and little effort is required to sustain it. In other words, flow just is, and it allows our actions to be imbued and inspired with our full attention without the encumbrance of self and all its complications. He described it as *optimal experience*, following extensive interviews in which people described being in a state of fundamental happiness, and he found examples in such diverse domains as writing poetry and participating in extreme sports. It can also be experienced, I can attest, in writing passages in a book about the teaching of the Buddha. What psychologists have also found, through many studies, is that the workings of the thinking mind are effortful and fatiguing, whilst a mind in flow draws on a resource that is not limited in the same way.

The Inner Lesson

Of course, this journey into bow and racquet sport has not been made to make us better archers or tennis players. Rather, it serves to point to, and better understand, a habit of mind that we need to overcome if we are to make the progress to which our right intention aspires. As is evident in the *suttas*, right mindfulness needs to be approached from multiple directions, and the more routes and waypoints we know, the more likely we are to find our destination. There is an obstacle to our liberation that for some reason is easier to overcome in the arena of skilled physical action than it is in skilled mental action, but it is nevertheless the same obstacle. This is the reluctance of the thinking mind to surrender to being in the zone, or using Csikszentmihalyi's expression, to flow. In contexts that require us to let go and let our bodies be wise, we seem comfortable about being in the zone, and indeed see it as desirable. In contrast, to let go and let our *minds* be wise is much more of a challenge.

In the physical realm, we do not see any problem in the "not self" nature of our letting go. It does not raise any existential or philosophical questions regarding whether we are still ourselves when we let go of thinking in this way. We simply trust the wisdom of our minds and bodies in the present moment. If a thought arises, then it simply arises and ceases, perhaps accompanied by an inner "not now" to help it on its way. We would consider it preposterous that a tennis champion might react to a thought about paying a bill when in the middle of an important match. Certainly, we do not see ourselves as "unconscious" when we lose our fascination with the contents of our thoughts in these circumstances. Indeed, this would appear nonsensical – how could we be unconscious and still play an effective game? We are awake, aware, focused, in the zone, but not thinking about what we are doing, or indeed about anything else. In terms of the present moment, we are not just awake to it but we have a heightened awareness of it. We are ultra-awake, and yet still not thinking about what we are doing. Of course, we are also still recognisably "us".

So, clearly in learning a skill or a sport we can achieve a state of deep concentration and use our thinking minds to direct our purpose whilst at the same time stilling their chatter. We can "lose ourselves" in what we are doing. However, although precisely the same task presents itself in meditation, our willingness to let go is dramatically reduced. In meditation we can observe that the mind seems more fearful of letting go, perhaps because it is staring more directly at the "not self" aspect of mind rather than glimpsing it from the periphery. Meditation is perceived by the thinking mind as being confrontational – a power struggle of sorts. The Buddha referred to this fear and taught that it is to be set aside, and his language was not gentle – he exhorted us to "conquer" it, using the analogy of battle.

The first step in our self-conquest has to be understanding, and for those of us who choose to use mindfulness techniques to learn a skill or a sport, we have a valuable insight into the understanding that is needed. The essential problem is that at the very point that the mind has learnt to let go of thought, the thinking mind will jump in with a judgement. Even if it is only a simple judgement like "Hey, now we are getting somewhere", it will be enough to pull us back from the blissful state of awareness and land us back in the cycle of pointless thought that the thinking mind prefers. As we become more skilled in meditation we learn to deal with this better, in that the non-thinking state is more naturally joyful so it is easier for the mind to find its way back home. With this in mind, we will return to the practice of meditation.

Meditation Again

As we develop our formal meditation practice, the basics do not change, although our approach is likely to adapt itself to the characteristics of each individual mind. We should endeavour to meditate at least once a day, because regular practice helps develop the concentration we need to train our minds to be still outside these periods of formal practice. A routine also gives us the feeling of commitment, which is of immeasurable value. Earlier, we learnt a basic meditation technique, and now we will build on that. It is important to emphasise here that there is no "moving up" to some sort of "advanced" meditation methods, and although there are higher states of mindfulness to attain, it is not necessary to learn any new skills. As we have already determined, meditation on the breath is how the Buddha did it, so there is absolutely no reason to seek an alternative.

What we need now is more of the same, albeit with deeper understanding, and perhaps a little additional guidance on the more refined aspects of technique. Now may be a good time to consult the Buddha's original teaching on the subject, as documented in the *suttas*. This is not a requirement; it is just a suggestion, because the original text is simply a delight. For those who are interested, the relevant *suttas* dealing most directly with meditation are the *Mahasatipatthana Sutta*, and the slightly more compact *Satipatthana Sutta*. Translations of these texts are freely available on the Internet, owing to the quality of generosity that is pervasive amongst fellow seekers of truth. Many other *suttas* are similarly inspiring, and my own view is that their wondrous descriptions and similes can even provoke *samadhi* directly, as the words of the Buddha himself seem to reach out through the centuries to touch us in the deepest way possible. At first, it can be a little off-putting that the *suttas* are rather repetitive, but looked at in another way this has a certain charm, and of course Buddhist practice is all about looking at things in another way. The accepted wisdom is that the frequent repetition in the *suttas* derives from their original verbal form, and the associated need to preserve the messages they contain. In any case, many of the themes in the *suttas* are truly worthy of repetition, and the use of language is beyond inspiring. Of course, our task remains constant – it is not to become erudite in ancient scriptures, but to learn to let go. When we have gained some facility with letting go, all that remains is to learn to do it more often and then learn to do it earlier.

To help us with our practice, we have learnt quite a lot about how minds operate, through what we have learnt of the Buddha's teaching so far, through some consideration of contemporary psychology, and through our own experience. We are now familiar with the hindrances to the practice that the Buddha identified, which work to bind us to our suffering: sensual desire, ill will, worry and flurry, sloth and torpor, and doubt. We have also travelled together along the eightfold path of perpetual inspiration, with its elements of wisdom, mental development and ethical conduct: right view, right intention, right effort, right concentration, right mindfulness, right speech, right action, and right livelihood. We have explored the Buddha's model of mind as a series of cascading and interrelated processes that can carry our thinking minds far away and obscure from us the choices we make in how we feel, think and behave. We have learnt that these mental processes operate within the context of our delusion, which we have referred to as the "contracted mind". Thus, we now have some insight into how the contracted mind creates and relates to a world of impermanent conditions, and how our tendency to attach to such conditions in terms of self leads to suffering.

In addition to describing the Buddha's psychology, we have also looked at the everyday models of mind and mental health, to which our minds incline and which Western culture perpetuates. In doing this, we have exposed a crucial truth in the way the mind operates, a truth that is so counter-intuitive that we must reflect very hard on it before we can see its veracity. This is that the thinking mind's operation is largely *unintentional*, and when it is operating like this it can be highly problematic. The power of the thinking mind is actually in its intentional use, but unfortunately this is not its habitual mode, and its habits can be seriously deleterious to our relationships with ourselves and others. In contrast, our usual relationship with the mind of awareness is an unintentional one, but where we can direct its operation intentionally, a whole new world of positive outcomes opens up to us, along with the promise of lasting peace and happiness, first for ourselves but ultimately for all beings.

This is the framework within which we are now practising, and through which we can look into our minds with true understanding. The path is an experiential one, so we need to keep meditating and bringing more of that meditative experience into our daily lives. Little by little the sheer beauty and penetrative insight of the Buddha's teachings will open up to us, and the astonishing scale of his achievement will be evident. We are now ready to return to the basic guidance offered earlier, in the light of the distance we have covered since then.

Sitting Again

Earlier, we discussed meditation technique under the headings *Ready, Set, Let Go*. This was of course a weak pun, but nevertheless it was a useful device, so we will do it again.

Ready

Again we sit, and again we adopt a stable and dignified position as best suits our bodies. When we are first setting out on the path of formal practice, our experience may be that the position of the body is particularly significant to us, in that we find ourselves becoming uncomfortable and physically restless. We may experience discomfort in our knees, or in our backs, depending on our sitting position. We may also experience numbness or pins and needles. As our sitting practice develops such things seem not to trouble us as much, if at all, and we tend to sit down and concern ourselves less with choices about the fine-tuning of our cushion, position and posture. This is partly because we are experienced in knowing what suit us best, but more because we have developed a different relationship with our physical selves. We have learnt that pains and other discomforts change and pass away without our intervention, and we have realised that feelings in the body are just as they are and as such are not particularly challenging. Of course, it is also because the perpetual motion of the path has set in and consequently the strength of our intention to get down to it has increased.

Again we set our timer, and so we begin in the same way as before. We may now be ready to meditate for longer, and indeed if our practice is developing well then the perpetual motion may cause us to want to do so. As before, there are no rules, and we should not believe any thoughts that tell us that the longer we sit, the more progress we will make. Nor should we give credence to any notions in the mind that wish to tell us that as an experienced meditator we ought to be able to sit for a long time. We may choose to sit for a long time and benefit from it, or we may not. There may be practical considerations that suit a particular length of sitting, or there may not. Such considerations are not places for our minds to dwell; they just are as they are. A monk may meditate all day and all night, and a surgeon in a busy emergency department may only manage a few minutes here and there. The important thing is, of course, how well each is able to watch their minds in formal practice, and then to sustain their mindfulness throughout the day as a result of such a discipline. Each moment is an opportunity for mindfulness, not just the moments that constitute our sitting practice. We must learn to make our choices wisely, and always take a little time to consider the truth of the reasons that the thinking mind gives for these choices.

Although patient endurance is a skill that we need to cultivate to help us along our path, the art of sitting in meditation is not all about endurance. A physical analogy here is helpful: our natural instinct is often to push ourselves to the limit to get the most benefit out of physical exercise, but science does not back this up. We develop our muscles most effectively by lifting weights whilst maintaining proper technique, rather than grabbing and jerking at the heaviest weights we can manage, and we burn the same calories in walking a distance as we would in running it. So too in meditation; the maintenance of good discipline during the sitting is much more important than its duration. There will inevitably be times when we are unable to sit at all because we simply do not find an opportunity. At these times, it is important not to spend time thinking that we should be sitting, lost in remorse and self-criticism because we have failed. This is just the way of the thinking mind, always comparing how things are now to how they "should" be and making us suffer as a result of the perceived gap. If we cannot meditate, then when such a thought occurs to us we should spend a little while just watching our mind and breath. Even if it is just a few moments, this is fine, and we can satisfy ourselves with the thought that a few moments of mindfulness is better than a few moments of worry that we have not been able to be mindful.

Now that we have had some experience of meditation, it is appropriate to offer a few words on technique. Firstly, although there are no absolutes or rules, it is usually best to keep the mind focused on the breath in a single place. We select the point in our bodies that works best for us, and then within our meditation session we stay with it. If we go looking for the breath in different places during our meditation, then our minds are moving and this will obstruct our path towards the one-pointed concentration that pushes open the door to the deeper states of meditation. At the beginning of our practice, the meditation object, i.e. the breath, starts out as a "coarse" meditation object. It is coarse, as opposed to subtle, in the sense that it is physically there and straightforward to acquire. As our meditation progresses and we enter states of tranquillity, the awareness of the breath becomes more refined and less focused on the physical sensations. It is more focused on the "isness" of the breath, or the "whole body of breath" to use the Buddha's words. The mind itself will naturally progress in this way, and so there is no need to make a conscious choice to change the meditation object – we just go with it.

Set

Again we set our mind of gratitude, compassion, forgiveness, and resolution before we focus on the breath and begin letting go. We discussed earlier the power of regular *intentional willing*, and we may now be seeing some of the benefits of this, both within our regular reflections at the start of formal practice and within the way we carry these intentions into our daily lives. The practice is actually very powerful and is one that we should maintain and develop further. Regular repetition of a willed outcome helps strengthen the intention and increase the tendency for the product of our wishes to arise in our awareness at times when it is needed. Sometimes when we practise intentional willing we will really mean it, and sometimes we will really, *really* mean it. Sometimes, we may just be saying the words to ourselves in mindless ritual, perhaps even questioning the practice as we do it. All practice is beneficial.

Amidst the maelstrom of our everyday thoughts, and set against the tremendous motive power of the aggregations of our minds, regular reminders of our basic course and values are essential. This is as true when we are experienced meditators with thousands of "flying hours" as it is when we are just starting out. If we feel resistance to any part of this intentional willing, then we can learn from that resistance and make a mental note to investigate its truth during a time of wise reflection. This is particularly so when willing forgiveness towards others, and even towards self. When we look at the translations of the daily chanting done by Buddhist monks worldwide, we see a great deal of intentional willing. A well-known and widely practised formal meditation involves the projection of loving kindness, and this is derived directly from the Buddha's instruction to his monks. The meditation starts with directing forgiveness and love towards self, and then gradually spreading it out to those close to us, and onwards to include all beings in all realms. Some of the words and imagery in such meditations and chants are truly beautiful and very inspiring, and we will return to this specific meditation soon. Loving kindness is wishing beings to be well and free from suffering, and declaring our own intention to play a part in achieving this outcome. Its spirit may be general and all-encompassing, but its application must be individual by individual, whether human or otherwise.

To help elaborate the concept of intentional willing, and to provide further inspiration for the development of this important part of the practice, here are some examples of intentional willing that can be heard chanted in Buddhist monasteries around the globe, often at daybreak. These relate to the more personal parts of right view, right intention and right effort:

May the cultivation of this practice lead to the end of every kind of suffering.
May the forces of delusion not take hold and weaken my resolve.
In gladness and safety, may all beings be at ease.

It may be that our gratitude for the practice has deepened at this point. Perhaps certain teachers have helped and inspired us, or we have read some translations of the major *suttas* and studied accounts of the Buddha's teachings for ourselves. Our efforts may have already delivered some positive changes in our lives and in our relationships with others. In short, we may have more reason to be grateful now than we did before. If so, we may wish to personalise this part of the reflection some more and direct our gratitude accordingly. For example, in my own practice over the years I have found myself expressing deepening gratitude to the Buddha himself. It is important not to forget to be grateful to ourselves for setting out on the path, for applying the effort to give it momentum, and for having the wisdom to continue. Being grateful and respectful to ourselves is fundamentally important, as it is only by acknowledging our own efforts that we come to understand fully that we can change. At times of despair, it is also the solid rock on which we can steady ourselves.

One of the "perfections" that are described in the Buddha's teachings is generosity. There are ten perfections, but at this stage I am sticking to my earlier promise about resisting the lists, so will just consider this one. The perfection of *dana,* as it is in Pali, is to give without expectation of receiving. Buddhist monks are beggars who depend on laypeople for all their requisites (four of these, or eight if you count each of the ones about the robes!). The requisites include all the food that the monks eat, which must be explicitly offered. If you observe monks receiving food, they do it without giving thanks, as to do so would imply that the giver is expecting something in return. Or at least so it is in Buddhist countries where such behaviour is the norm. Since the Buddha's time, this is how the monastic tradition has been sustained, and generous gifts have enabled the tradition to continue and be communicated in an unbroken line for over two and a half millennia. The giving of the Buddha's teaching, of *dhamma,* is the highest form of generosity. Some of this teaching is now reaching you, and without the perfection of *dana* this would not be the case. Of course, liberation is not the exclusive privilege of monks and nuns – in the act of giving, the giver also benefits through the opportunity to let go of attachment, and to experience the gladness of heart that is unique to giving without expectation to receive. These are reasons to be grateful, and also an inspiration to give.

There is another aspect of gratitude that can be immensely potent, and which is a worthy subject for wise reflection. We discussed earlier the powerful exercise of enumerating our values and using them to guide our behaviour and priorities, starting with a visualisation of our own funeral. This can be a life-changing exercise, and can deliver immense benefit not just for ourselves, but for those around us. Those we love and value are more likely to feel loved and valued, and as a result our relationships will improve some more. If we have chosen our values well, we will be grateful for them in all sorts of ways, not least for the resulting change in how we feel about ourselves. In our opening reflections during our formal practice, we may therefore also give thanks for our values and for our resolve in keeping them.

We may also have developed a closer relationship with our ability to be compassionate and to forgive, and we may now understand better any resistance we feel to these two important elements of our practice. It was noted earlier that when we are cultivating a mind of forgiveness at the start of our formal sitting practice, we may experience some opposition from our thoughts and we should just let that go. After some experience of doing this regularly, we will come to learn more about the nature of this resistance, and using wise reflection we may come to know something of the truth of it, and be grateful for this.

We will certainly now be more familiar with our own mental aggregations, and how our unique mental habits work to bind us to our own personal style of suffering. We must accept that these are habits of a lifetime, and therefore that it will take a long time for them to fade, if indeed they ever entirely leave us. To try to extinguish them is resisting and striving, and as such will just bring more suffering. So, in the meantime when we set ourselves for meditation (and indeed at any other time that seems appropriate) we should consciously forgive ourselves for them. This is a very powerful reflection.

Just as we have stayed with our chosen meditation

object of the breath, continuing with the same reflections as we have used previously is perfectly appropriate. Again, it is in no way a sign that our practice has not "progressed". It is likely that we will wish to refine these reflections, but there is no significance if we do not wish to. As we should frequently recollect, there is nowhere that we are heading with our practice other than towards deeper mindfulness, and whatever takes us towards that end is the right thing. Ultimately, we will leave all of it behind.

The late, great meditation master and Buddhist abbot Ajahn Chah is reported to have frequently said that one should study one's own heart rather than the Abhidhamma. (The Abhidhamma is one of the major components of the canonical Pali texts that document the Buddha's teachings, and is regarded as the most "theoretical" as it deals in detail with the Buddha's psychology.) This is a very relevant point: study of our own hearts and minds is *our path* leading to *our wisdom*, and we need to learn to decide *for ourselves* what is right for us. The way to do this is to feel, see, hear, and discern inwardly, rather than seek too much guidance in the words of others. Our teachers are the world around us, our own minds, and the majesty of the moment itself. Great Buddhist scholars can guide us, but the throne of liberation is our own cushion. In the introduction to this book, we noted that the Buddhist scholar Venerable Narada Maha Thera had described the Abhidhamma as being "dry as dust" to those who read without understanding, and here he is making the same point. Nevertheless, we have reason to be grateful for his translation, which is freely available on the Internet as a result of *dana*.

Actually, staying with the same practice can be quite useful. As our practice develops, we will develop greater understanding of the meaning of our reflections and resolutions. This will in turn enable our determination and intentional willing to flourish, and will shed light on where we are still resisting and where we need to apply some more effort. Just as with the inner game and with Zen training, imagery and projected feelings are much more likely to be useful than verbal affirmations and conscious thought. There is nothing wrong with saying "thank you", or making a gesture of thanks such as the *anjali*, but the generation of the feeling is the more important part. That said, repetitive verbal instruction to self is also useful, because if it becomes habitual it can act as a mental knotted handkerchief to remind us to apply wisdom at times when otherwise it might be lacking. Many of us who practise will have uttered the phrase "let go" to ourselves literally thousands of times.

For example, if we have conflict with a particular person over a sustained period of time then they may have been the subject of our intentional willing on a regular basis (or perhaps they should have been), and we may now be starting to relate to them in a more beneficial way. Sometimes, it may be that we have really searched our minds and cannot find a shred of a reason to regard their behaviour as being motivated by anything other than malice. In such a case, then letting go of our aversion will prevent us from suffering any more because of it. Even then, there is considerable power in wishing that they be free from suffering, as it works on one of the toughest of the hindrances within us: that of ill will.

The perpetual motion of the path will have deepened

our resolve by now, and we may have started also to experience its prime mover – the joy that arises in meditation. So, when we make our resolution, the difference may now be that joy arises. If it does not, or if this happens sporadically, then that is just fine; it is just as it is, and like all things is of the nature to change.

Let Go

This is to be our final detailed discussion of meditative experience, and I left this section completely blank even after finishing all other sections of the book. This was certainly not my intention, but I never felt that I was quite ready, and did not dwell upon my reasons. It occurs to me now that I did this in the hope that my own practice would have deepened sufficiently to allow me the confidence to talk about deep states of meditation in a way that may help others. Or maybe it was that I did not feel qualified. Perhaps there was another reason why I was reluctant to speak on this subject, as it is so difficult to know for sure the truth of one's own behaviour when cascading mental formations are in play. The Buddha knew when he was ready, and I have encountered a few who were also comfortable in this arena, but for most of us there is always a doubt that we are well enough practised to speak on such a subject. I have heard one monk effectively grade other monks by their "meditation hours", in the same way that pilots do with "flying hours", and certainly there are many who have completed more hours on the cushion than I have.

However, this is as it should be, and the famous saying

"If you meet the Buddha on the road, kill him" is relevant here. This is a quotation from the Chinese Buddhist master Linji Yixuan in the 9th century, and of course is not to be taken literally. What it means is that any conceptualisation about our attainments on the path is by its nature an obstacle to further progress, and therefore needs to be set aside. It is better to press on with the practice than to pause to consider one's accomplishments. This is perhaps why even to speak of such matters is considered a gross breach of discipline in Buddhist monastic traditions. It is somewhat incongruous in this context, but nevertheless very fortunate for us all, that the Buddha did not hold back from speaking about his own attainments in practice.

Are We There Yet?

As our concentration improves we will notice our thinking becoming less persistently present during meditation, as our fascination with our thoughts falls away. We will also become less attuned to the outside world impinging upon our senses, and we will be less aware of the passage of time. However, by far the most salient aspect of our experience as we progress with our meditation will be the arising of intense happiness.

As we experience more and more the one-pointedness of mind and the bliss that arises through deep meditative concentration, we will become familiar with the deceits of the thinking mind that cause us to lose this. Fear and doubt are often present when we recoil from blissful states, because we can feel ourselves letting go of thinking and entering a state in which the inner voice is no longer in charge. We sense immediately that this state is different; it is buoyant, it is bright, and, in the deepest sense imaginable, it is thrilling. Then we fear that we are losing our "self", and the alarm is enough to pull us back. Effectively, this is the hindrance of doubt that this is a wise thing to be doing, and again we return to thinking, analysing, and fundamentally *resisting*. As we become more practised and can return to this pivotal point more readily, we will find the mind oscillating between entering into a sublime state of awareness, and withdrawing into mundane thinking. It is our resolve that drives us forward, and the contracted mind's terror of diminution that pulls us back. The thinking mind can be subtle in its deceptions when we are at the point of letting go, and thoughts will frequently come in a helpful guise.

Once we have learnt to let go of the fear and doubt that holds us back, we will enter a blissful and calm state and be able to remain there, at least for a while. Thinking is still present at first, but it is not heeded. There is just awareness of the breath, together with a deep and tranquil joy. The breath is all that there is. There is no reaction to body, to sensation, to sound, or to thought. All these things come and go, but they do not stay. They cause no disturbance or strife. There is just awareness.

The Five Factors

This is a glimpse of the fruit of the path in the distance, brought about through the beginnings of right concentration. We have now stepped onto a stretch of our path in which the possibility of the end of suffering is understood suddenly and more directly, both in terms of our own suffering and that which exists throughout all of existence. Although we should not cling to this as an attainment, we can take great encouragement from it and allow the surge in our right view, effort, and concentration to suffuse our practice.

We have already been introduced to the Pali word for concentration, *samadhi*, and this term is often used to describe a deep state of meditation that is also referred to as *one-pointedness* or *absorption*. As we come to connect with these deeper states, it becomes more natural to use the Pali terms, because they are as they are and can be imbued with the appropriate meaning through the context in which they are used. As we frequently recollect, this is an experiential path, and even if the words used in translations are near the mark of the experience itself, we will only really understand them when we are ready, so it is best just to refer to these states by their Pali names and trust ourselves to recognise them when we arrive there.

Although we may have experienced momentary bliss, the gates of paradise have not been left wide open for us. Indeed, for the modern Western mind they are closely guarded and sprung to shut again when pushed ajar. The threshold to what lies beyond letting go is a precarious point at which our minds will waver, even though during the *Set* phase of our meditation we resolved that this very step would be a joyous leap. The thinking mind recognises that this is a state of mind that is not of its making and indeed one that has no need for it, so it instinctively recoils. At this stage in our practice, the thinking mind is likely to be the stronger in this fascinating battle between it and the awakening and more potent mind of awareness.

Even if our right concentration is strong enough to allow us to take that life-changing stride forward, the thinking mind will hook its metaphorical braces around the metaphorical door handle to cause us to be yanked back and fall on our backsides.

Fortunately, the Buddha's teachings in this area are direct and powerful. The depth of analysis and the descriptive power of his observations regarding the progression of the higher meditative states are simply astounding, and belittle any psychological theory that has come since. He distinguished "five factors" of absorption, which are stirred and gathered together by the energy of our concentration and are essentially five milestones that mark the depth of our *samadhi*. These five factors are by no means purely theoretical, but on the contrary are readily experienced as qualitatively different. They occur as natural antidotes to the five hindrances, which at this stage in our practice are still holding us back. Each factor is opposed to a particular hindrance, and through repeated practice these five factors increase in strength and cohesiveness until we are able to resist the hindrances more effectively and then ultimately set them aside.

The factors are as follows, the first two being causal factors linked to our right effort, and the next three being effects:

Initial application
Sustained application
Rapture
Ease of mind
One-pointedness

Initial application is the engagement of the mind with the meditation object, and in stirring the energy to do this we are countering the hindrance of sloth and torpor. Once we have acquired the meditation object through concentration, then of course the next challenge is to stay with that object. As we steady the mind with the consistent effort of *sustained application*, then the hindrance of doubt is overcome; we gain confidence that this is the path to liberation through understanding and being with the nature of mind at a deep and refined level.

Those were the causal factors, so now on to the effects. The first, most noticeable effect is the arising of *rapture* once sustained application has been mastered. The use of the word "rapture" is no exaggeration here; no sales pitch for meditation, but a commonly observed phenomenon. When the mind is concentrated and calm, the awareness that surges into our minds is accompanied by an experience of bliss. The initial rapture is the natural antidote to the hindrance of anger and ill will. The pursuit of this feeling is not why we meditate, as meditation should not be used as a holiday destination, but it is certainly something that will spur us on. Early in our meditation practice we will glimpse this bliss, but our thinking minds are likely to grasp at it instantly, or start to judge and analyse, at which point it vanishes. This is a very strong learned habit of mind, but it is one that we need to relinquish. Try as they might, our thinking minds cannot penetrate, prolong, or recreate this rapture; they can only push it further away. To regain it, we need to return to the essentials of our practice and let go again.

We talked earlier about the experience of being awestruck; for example, in the presence of some wonder of nature. We discussed how the initial rush of awe will naturally subside and leave behind a lasting ease of mind in the presence of the original stimulus, and this ease is something that never diminishes. The object continues to beguile us and the ensuing serenity is the result of its effect on the thinking mind; the thinking mind retreats into the background, as it seems to accept that it is incapable of adding anything at all to the experience. This mental calm is the next of the five factors, but in meditation there is a crucial difference: although the breath is every bit as captivating and wonderful as any other wonder of nature, this beauty is only apparent if we concentrate on it. It does not demand our attention in the same way. This is the fourth factor of *ease of mind*, which arises as the natural antidote to the hindrance of worry and flurry once we have learnt to let go of rapture.

Of course, ease of mind is a pleasurable experience, and as such we will be inclined to attach to it, thus hindering further progress in our practice. In the fifth factor of *one-pointedness* or *absorption*, we have learnt to let go of this feeling of ease and happiness. It no longer fascinates us, and the mind becomes free to leave it behind. Now we are at one with the meditation object, and this is a state in opposition to the hindrance of sense desire. It is at this point that we relinquish the judgement of pleasure in meditation that could hinder our further progression through craving it. This is a state of satisfaction beyond rapture, as it is the deepest acknowledgement of non-attachment and non-craving – we have all we need to satisfy us in the moment, and yet all we have is our breath. We become recovering *samadhi* junkies, and our substitute drug is the most powerful of all – *the sufficiency of the present moment*.

First Jhana and Beyond

A Pali word that is used frequently in connection with the deep states of meditation is *jhana*. Unlike other Pali terms, *jhana* is not typically translated or rendered as a concept in any other language. It is just *jhana*, or rather *jhanas*, because there are eight of them. The *jhanas* are a sequence of advanced meditative attainments, for which the prime mover is *samadhi*, the state of one-pointed meditative absorption. The Buddha would urge his followers to attain the *jhana* states of meditation, and this encouragement remains to this day in the training given by senior Buddhist monks to juniors in their charge.

Above, we discussed the five factors, although we left unanswered the obvious question – *of what are they factors?* This was a deliberate omission. Although experience in meditation is direct and clear, explanations are often not so, and it seemed appropriate to take small steps when dealing with a subject that is beyond worldly confines. The five factors are the factors of *jhana*, or more specifically of the first *jhana*. Through mastery of the two causal factors of initial and sustained application, and then being able to progress consistently through the three successive effects of rapture, ease of mind, and one-pointedness, we attain first *jhana*. The five factors are all present in this first *jhana*, so we have not yet transcended any of them at this point. As we said earlier, we are recovering, but not recovered. Nevertheless, first *jhana* is a mighty attainment.

And so we find ourselves entering the first *jhana* state. Once we are able to access some *samadhi*, through initial and then sustained concentration on the breath, we will start to experience the familiar surge of rapture that indicates that we are in the zone. All we need to do to make progress on this road is to keep a focus on the breath and keep letting go, and that includes letting go of the rapture. In doing this, we are not trying to get rid of this rapture, or actively striving to move beyond it, but rather we are just setting aside any fascination with it. In this way, we will learn to stay in an absorbed state as intense pleasure subsides and gives way to a contented peace, which in turn settles into one-pointedness and serenity. As we develop familiarity with the two causal factors, and the three successive effects of letting go, we can then become practised at both entering and exiting first *jhana*, all of which is needed for this initial, but nevertheless considerable, attainment.

To reach this point is not a cue for spiritual ambition, however. The Buddha warned of trying to push on too quickly, using the analogy of a foolish cow who sets off to find new pastures without first familiarising herself with her own, and then becomes lost and cannot find her way home. The Buddha was pointing to the fact that before contemplating any higher attainment, we need to become adept at gaining and maintaining the absorption state we have already encountered. Before we bound forward, we should consolidate our learning. There is a difference between being able to stand up on a surfboard and being able to ride the Pipeline.

So, our task now is to become accomplished in all aspects of this state. If our concentration breaks, then we simply return to initial application, then sustained application, and so re-enter *samadhi*. It sounds so simple, but we will frequently slip back, and it is inevitable that life's challenges may cause us to become separated from previous attainments for lengthy periods. That is certainly my own experience. This is all good and helpful, however. When we set out on the path and apply effort to stay on it, we are already improving the world that we inhabit, and if everybody were to do this then few problems would remain. There is no rush, and indeed in pushing on too quickly there is a danger of falling prey to striving. Striving can lead us into unhelpful dead ends of self-view; for example, "I am good at meditation."

In the Buddha's descriptions, there are eight stages to *jhana*, but for now we will discuss only the first four, which are the four so-called "material" *jhanas*, which essentially form the basis of the Buddha's description of right concentration. The material *jhanas* involve meditation on things that are substantial, such as the breath, although there are other techniques too that we will not cover here. In moving through the first four *jhanas*, the meditator progressively overcomes the five factors through increasing stability and confidence in meditative experience, deepening purity of awareness, then a more complete immersion within *samadhi* as joy gives way to peace.

The next four *jhanas* are said to be "formless", where the material meditation object is replaced by meditations on more ethereal things: *infinite space, infinite consciousness, nothingness,* and the last one that is a little too far beyond my comprehension even to name. I will do so anyway – it is *neither perception nor non-perception.* The descriptions of the four higher *jhana* states in the original Buddhist texts are fascinating and truly inspiring, but to repeat them here would serve little purpose. They are there to be consulted if your meditation takes you to those expansive realms, and my strong wish for you is that it does, but in such matters I am no guide. So, let's continue with consideration of just the material *jhanas*.

To reach each successive stage of *jhana*, a pleasurable factor from the previous stage needs to be relinquished. Unless and until we do this, we will attach to the pleasure and thereby impede our progress. We have previously discussed how meditation should not become a holiday destination from our everyday suffering, and this is precisely the message here. At this point in our practice, we have already learnt to slip several of our bonds on the path, so it is a matter of holding course and learning to let go of successively more. As we allow a progressively deeper settling of the mind, our awareness is experienced as both brighter and lighter, as the darkness and weight of delusion are abandoned. Through the experience of these more refined states of mind, we are able to see and feel delusion more clearly when it returns. It is as if it has form and mass that could not previously be discerned.

We will now briefly consider the journey through the second, third and fourth *jhanas*. Again, this journey is not a race. In the second *jhana*, the initial and sustained attention have both been left behind, and the meditator no longer dwells in the delight of focus on the meditation object, but now in the rapture that derives from the concentration. When we acquire the meditation object and hold it in our *samadhi*, we see the awesome, simply awesome, beauty contained within it, but this too needs to be relinquished. In the first *jhana*, concentration is still imperfect, in that it requires the effort of initial and sustained application, but in the second there is an established confidence in concentration. The effort is no longer separate from the *samadhi*.

As the meditator proceeds through third *jhana*, rapture is abandoned, giving way to pleasure and ease. However, even this more balanced quality of happiness still agitates the mind and can give rise to attachment, so this too must be relinquished on the way to fourth *jhana*, where only one-pointedness remains. One-pointedness is there as the end point of all four material *jhanas*, but only in fourth *jhana* is the attachment eliminated that may otherwise undermine it. In the fourth *jhana* there is nothing left to disturb the *samadhi*. The mind is purified of all attachment, and the remainder is a profound peace. Ultimately, this too must be let go of, because even such refined awareness entails that one is present to be aware, and so there is a remnant of self. However, here I am getting far ahead of my own direct experience and so it is wisest to leave this thread hanging.

Poison and Antidote

Thus, through deep meditation, we liberate the pure mind of awareness. The thinking mind is quietened, and the housebuilder is seen. Just as it was for the Buddha, the end of our suffering is now clearly in sight. When we emerge from our meditative state, we may find that the state of mind attained in meditation continues, sometimes very briefly, sometimes for longer. If we have managed to arrive at a deep state of awareness, this will feel very different from normal experience. We may see the world and our relationship with it more clearly and immediately, in a detached way, without clinging or resistance. When this happens, it will be a wonderful moment that we will not forget, and which will remove yet more friction from the perpetual motion that moves us on our path. We may speculate that we have become enlightened like the Buddha after his forty-nine days of meditation. If we do speculate thus, or indeed have any thoughts that analyse or try to prolong this state, then it is certain that we will find ourselves instantly back in a more familiar reality.

Often, of course, the contracted mind surges into consciousness as soon as our meditation is ended. What is it that causes our equanimity to be so acutely provisional? The answer lies in what the Buddha called the *defilements* of the mind. These are the primary causes of our suffering, and therefore need to be transcended before we can be free. If this is not done, the defilements instantly assail us as soon as there is a gap in mindfulness. They are not merely harmful mental formations of the sort we have already discussed, and neither are they limited to the hindrances and fetters that hold us back in our practice. Nor are they particularly personal, although each of us develops our own script for them. Rather, the defilements are deep and unwholesome urges of mind that we all share and which actually create our suffering in the first place. Whilst the aggregations, hindrances and fetters prevent us from advancing, the defilements actually draw us backwards. They are like gravity in that they hold us down, but as we draw further away from their source, their effect weakens.

Although *samadhi* meditation provides some relief from the defilements, both during absorption and as a result of the insights it may inculcate, it does not cleanse us of their origins. To be fully free from suffering, we must be free from the defilements altogether. Expurgation of the defilements can only be achieved through wisdom, and the Buddha was very clear that the cultivation of wisdom is as essential as meditation. He said that without *samadhi* there can be no wisdom, and without wisdom there can be no *samadhi*.

Three Root Poisons

Although it may be instructive to examine all the defilements listed in the *suttas*, and there are many, fortunately the Buddha taught a more direct route to insight on this subject. He asked the rhetorical question of what thing in the world arises with the sole intent of doing harm, and the answer to this question was that fundamentally there are three such things. He taught that all defilements are traceable to three "roots", which are often referred to as *the three poisons*, and sometimes *the three fires*. Translations vary for each of the three, but a personal view is that the most useful ones are *ignorance, attachment*, and *aversion*. The Buddha explained that from these three elemental poisons spring all the defilements, such as anger, hostility, cruelty, scorn, jealousy, avarice, conceit, arrogance, obstinacy, deceitfulness, hypocrisy, vanity, and carelessness. The three poisons stop us developing, and indeed tend towards retrograde motion. This is because they constantly seek pleasure and avoid pain, trapping us within a deluded search for gratification that can deliver no lasting satisfaction.

Many may be familiar with the Buddhist image of the *Wheel of Life*, which is painted at the entrance to many Buddhist temples and monasteries. This was conceived by one of the Buddha's chief disciples, Venerable Moggallana, and is a fascinating representation of the cycle of suffering, *kamma* and liberation. Some of the symbolism within the Wheel of Life is truly inspired and inspiring, but its interpretation is a subject in its own right, so for now we will focus only on the hub of the wheel. In the hub, the three poisons are represented by a pig, a bird, and a snake. These creatures represent ignorance, attachment, and aversion respectively, and they are shown in a tight circle, each biting the tail of the next in perpetual pursuit. There are good reasons for the nature of this pictorial representation, and the explanation is not nearly as unfair to pigs, birds and snakes as may first appear. However, that does not concern us here. What is important is the strong image of the central role of the three poisons in the whole cycle of suffering, and the tight, frenetic and conjoined cycle of their operation. Some sources indicate that this image was used by the Buddha himself in his explanation of how the defilements and the poisons are not static things, but are motivating forces within our minds. Their nature is always to be leading to something, urging our sense impressions to become feelings, our feelings to become concepts, our concepts to become thoughts, and our thoughts to become actions. Powerful imagery indeed.

Ignorance is something we have discussed extensively in these pages. It is fundamentally a lack of understanding of the nature of the mind and the way things truly are. It is the fundamental nature of the contracted mind. It is mistaking thinking for self. It is failing to see the impermanent nature of all things. It is the absurdity of seeking happiness through attachment to what we like and avoidance of what we dislike. It is seeing no need to change our outlook, and it is denying that we have choices in how we feel, think, and act.

Our ignorance creates a void that we fill with delusion, and the centre of this delusion is our concept of self, of *I, me and mine*. As soon as we adopt this distorted concept of a separate self, we are instinctively drawn to satisfying its hunger for pleasure, dominion, and permanence. We also become driven by the need to avoid the opposites of pain, diminution, and change. Thus the flames of attachment and aversion are added to the fire of ignorance, and they add further energy to the delusional blaze that now nourishes them. The eternal pursuit represented in the hub of the Wheel of Life is a hunger within us that can never be satisfied. To use an ancient simile that is common in Buddhist and other religious teachings, we are at times *hungry ghosts*. Such beings are also depicted graphically in the Wheel of Life, shown with huge bellies that require to be filled, but narrow necks that will not allow it. Hungry ghosts are one of the *realms of suffering* within the Wheel of Life. These realms symbolise different types of rebirth, where rebirth is the representation of cause and effect. The deluded premise of the contracted mind makes us hungry ghosts, based on a belief system that is manifestly false and a goal that is patently unattainable.

The Pali words that are translated here as "attachment" and "aversion" are often translated as "greed" and "hatred". Greed and hatred are of course forms of attachment and aversion, but these "a-words" are more evocative of the states of mind that can result if the poisons are not treated. Such extremes are particularly evident in our relationships with others. When we are attached to an outcome that gratifies the contracted self, this naturally curtails our ability to be compassionate and generous to those around us. As the greed of self is fed, so too do we lose the ability to be kind and forgiving. When we resist people and situations that conflict with our desires, then the opposite states arise and we can abide in anger, hostility, spite, and mean-spiritedness. We spin in the centre of the wheel of suffering, not even noticing that what we intend as forward motion is actually circular and often retrograde.

These three fires burn within us all, but the specific conditions and habitual responses that are personal to us will cause each to burn with a different intensity. The relative mix of the three will have a major influence on our personality. Personality is of course something that itself changes according to conditions, no matter how much we may like to think that our personality is stable and "ours". However, it is very beneficial to observe our own behaviours and thereby consider which of the three fires is driving how we create ourselves and the world around us. Although it is a common misconception of Buddhist practice that the goal is to eliminate personality altogether, this is certainly not the case; the goal is simply to be aware of it, along with all else.

Four Sublime Abidings

The Buddha taught that to overcome the defilements it is necessary first to purify the mind. Indeed, he described enlightenment itself quite simply as being a mind cleansed of ignorance, attachment and aversion. Of course, meditation is fundamental here, in that it delivers an understanding of the nature of mind that helps isolate the poisons so that they can then be made safe. In addition, he taught another way, to be used alongside meditation as another antidote to the poisons. The path to a pure mind is therefore not just "meditate and destroy", to quote an inspirational message I have seen in one Buddhist monastery. This complementary method is straightforward in principle, although challenging in practice, and consists of the cultivation of opposite states of mind for troublesome mental habits. Although the Buddha identified and taught opposing individual states for each of the defilements, fortunately just as he taught of root poisons, he also taught of elemental remedies to cleanse us of all defilement.

323

These fundamental antidotes are termed the *four sublime abidings*. Although translations of original Pali terms can be somewhat unsatisfactory, this is certainly not the case here. In Pali, these are the *brahma viharas*, and in using the term *vihara*, which literally means "dwelling", the Buddha was emphasising that we are not cultivating these sublime states as a temporary relief, but as an enduring place for the mind to rest. We are to live both *in* them and *by* them. The word "sublime" is also highly apposite, in all its senses – beautiful, perfect, pure, exalted, and morally worthy. Sometimes these four states are referred to as the *four immeasurables*, which introduces the important concept that they are limitless, but otherwise is somewhat flavourless as a translation. A key factor underlying the sublime abidings is that we are not to pick and choose who we wish to be free from suffering, and neither are we to place any limit on the good will that we can generate. Here again is the vitally important idea of *abundance* that we first met when discussing assertiveness and negotiation skills. The *brahma viharas* are boundless in every sense. Fortunately, the Buddha was sufficiently skilled in his descriptions of these states to speak of this abundance without reference to pie or cake.

Let's now consider each of the four *brahma viharas* in turn. Commonly accepted translations are:

Loving kindness
Compassion
Empathetic joy
Equanimity

Loving kindness is the simple wish that other beings may be well, regardless of their circumstances and of our own. It is important to understand that loving kindness is not at all the same as love, or at least not in the sense that the word "love" is most commonly used. When people speak of love, generally there is a strong sense of "I" that is accompanied by feelings of attachment and, if we are honest, a certain desire to possess. In romantic love, these aspects are particularly salient, particularly in the first flushes. In contrast, loving kindness is a selfless and unpossessing type of love. It is a simple, intentional state of wishing happiness towards another being; a projection of positivity devoid of any passion or desire for reciprocation. If we are feeling particular aversion towards another being, then a more realistic initial goal may be simply to wish that being to come to no harm. As there is no directly comparable translation, usually the Pali term *metta* is used.

Compassion starts with the wish that another being's suffering may diminish. It is an open-hearted response to the plight of another, and as such involves a softening of the boundary between self and other. When the heart is opened in this way and the hard edge of self is made fluid, then compassion naturally arises and flows both outwards and inwards. Another being's suffering can be understood and felt, because it is being experienced from their point of view rather than that of self. In compassion, we are necessarily less separated from other beings, and in this way are much closer to right view. When self becomes involved, compassion turns to pity, which is compassion's grotesque relative. Many wholesome states in Buddhist psychology have a close but unattractive sibling, and the ancient texts warn of these.

It is straightforward to understand the operation of

compassion when another being is suffering, but it is also important to understand that compassion can be appropriate when another being is happy. For example, if a person is happy in response to attaining an impermanent worldly condition that is subject to change, then they are in truth suffering and worthy of our compassion. In Pali, compassion is *karuna*.

Empathetic joy is the natural arising of gladness in the true happiness of others. Essentially, it is the opposite of jealousy. In sharing the joy of others as if it were our own, again we see the softening of the edges of self, which is a constant theme in the sublime abidings. The joy is essentially flowing between us and others without permanent abode in self or other. A frequent simile used to describe empathetic joy is that it is like the feelings of a parent when witnessing their child's accomplishments, not as a feeling of pride, which necessarily involves reference to self, but as a more basic sharing of joy. The concept of abundance is particularly significant here, in that the amount of joy that is available to be experienced is not limited by our own personal situations. So, even if we are in the midst of some sort of reversal in our lives, the degree to which we can experience joy in the fortunes of others is unaffected. This is perhaps the most difficult of the sublime abidings to embrace. As "empathetic joy" is a somewhat clumsy translation, and likewise the more common translation of "sympathetic joy", the Pali term *mudita* may be preferable.

Equanimity is a mental quality that can be described with many words – steadiness, balance, and serenity, for example. It means responding with the same calm acceptance regardless of what comes our way. All beings and all conditions are responded to like this, irrespective of their nature, and without heed to how closely they match with our desires, likes or dislikes. Through equanimity, everything affects our minds in the same measure, and our responses are smooth and level, without the extremes of attachment and aversion that are born of ignorance. This balance can only come from a deep insight into the nature of mind and the three characteristics of all things. In Pali, this is *upekkha*.

How To Be At Home Within the Sublime Abidings

Our goal is not to be occasional visitors or temporary residents within the sublime places of abiding, but rather to make them our natural habitat. As usual, the key to the door is meditation. So far, we have discussed using the breath as a meditation object, and in doing this we may have started to observe the natural arising of states that correspond to *metta*, *karuna*, *mudita*, and *upekkha*. The Buddha taught a more direct way to develop these states through meditation, and we have already gained some experience of this during the *Set* phase of our three-step practice. When setting ourselves for formal practice, we seek to cultivate and project feelings of gratitude, kindness, forgiveness and resolution before letting go and focusing only on the breath. It is on such resolutions that we will now focus, albeit with a new perspective.

The development of positive states through directed meditation is the basis of the method that the Buddha taught for developing a natural homing instinct towards the *brahma viharas*. This is what is called in Pali *bhavana*, which means "cultivation". The Buddha often used terms that would appeal to farmers and villagers, rather than to the noble circles in which he had previously moved, and here the analogy to the growing of crops is particularly apposite. We can encourage growth and create the right conditions for it, and as long as we sustain these conditions, then growth happens naturally. As a related aside, one of the analogies he used for delusion was that it is like a parasitic creeper that gradually takes over its host unless it is dug out at the roots. As another aside, this one not related, his previous princely lifestyle shows through in some of his other analogies; for example relating to horses, chariot-driving, and archery.

We can meditate directly upon the first three sublime abidings of loving kindness, compassion and empathetic joy. These meditations are commonly called *metta bhavana*, *karuna bhavana*, and *mudita bhavana*. As we learnt in our *Set* phase, this is not a matter of treating these states as meditation objects, but rather *becoming the feeling* and then *projecting* it first into self and then progressively outwards. A helpful translation of *bhavana* in this regard is "becoming". The fourth abiding, equanimity, is different in that it is in essence a fruit of our entire practice, as we learnt in our discussion of the fourth *jhana*. It is an outcome, rather than something we specifically work on. Equanimity is therefore cultivated through the development of the other three sublime abidings, and of course through meditation on the breath.

Meditation on loving kindness is the most commonly practised of the sublime abiding meditations, and is the most straightforward to understand. Just as equanimity can be regarded as the fruition of the sublime abidings, loving kindness can be regarded as the origin. Once a habitual affinity with loving kindness begins to develop, this will naturally lead to the arising of compassion and sympathetic joy. *Metta bhavana* does this through making the edges of self porous to the positivity we generate, such that it spills out to touch others. Like two pools expanding until they flow into one, the overflowing of loving kindness allows ripples of energy to travel without interruption between sources that were previously separate. Waves of loving kindness are perfectly formed to carry upon them the riders of compassion and sympathetic joy. Hence, it is on *metta* that we will concentrate our right effort.

So how do we go about meditation on loving kindness? Essentially, we go through the same *Ready* routine that we have adopted to this point in our sitting practice, and then use the intentions we generate in our *Set* phase as the meditation itself, albeit in a more structured and focused way. Our end point is a profound state of positivity towards all beings everywhere, in which we unconditionally wish them wellness and freedom from suffering. This is a long way from where most of us will find ourselves at the beginning of our meditation, so we approach it incrementally.

We have considered kindness to self repeatedly up to this point, and here I will emphasise this fundamental point again, because so many of us make the mistake of considering it more righteous to be gentle only with others than to extend the kindness to include ourselves. It is *essential* to begin with a heartfelt wish for our own wellbeing, because without loving kindness towards ourselves, there will always be an element of pollution in the attitude we can express to others. This can be a difficult thing to do at first, but the Buddha was very clear that we should not neglect our own spiritual welfare in favour of that of others. All beings everywhere deserve our wish that they be free from suffering, and cruelty to ourselves does not accord with this. We are, after all, part of this beautiful planet that we wish to be free from all suffering. Self-denial is often held to be a virtue, but is certainly not so in the Buddha's teaching if it also leads to self-harm. Loving kindness, like all of the sublime abidings, is not finite, so directing it towards ourselves is not a selfish act because there is no resulting diminution in the amount of *metta* available to others. Neither is it conditional – it is not a case of wishing *metta* to this person but not that person, or those cuddly animals but not those biting insects. It is for all beings, everywhere.

Start Small, Head for Big, and Don't Stop

So we make ourselves ready for meditation, and then start by thinking "May I be free from suffering", strengthening this feeling with an internal smile, or visualising our own face smiling back at us. After a few repetitions, and when the feeling of strong intentional willing has been truly experienced, we can start to extend the scope of the wish. The traditional method is to go through a set of steps that start in safe places by projecting loving kindness to those that we love, then to those that we respect or to whom we have reason to be grateful, then more neutral but familiar targets, then those to whom we feel enmity, and gradually on to all beings everywhere. The practice is always strongest when we use all our resources, such as feeling the goodwill we wish to project by generating an internal smile, or visualising the faces of the targets of our goodwill beaming back at us in gratitude. We are bound to feel some resistance in the course of this meditation, perhaps a feeling of personal unworthiness to receive loving kindness, or perhaps a reluctance to wish kindness to a loved one who has disappointed us, or a perceived foe. This is of course something we merely note without further reaction. It is unremarkable. It is ordinary. It is no cause for thought or analysis. Like everything else, it just *is*.

An example meditation framework may be as set out below, where we abide in each step for a couple of minutes, all the time being aware of the breath, using the in-breath for the wish and the out-breath for the projection.

May I be free from suffering.
May *<this loved one>* be free from suffering.
May *<these other loved ones>*...
May *<this person to whom I owe a debt of gratitude>*...
May *<this known neutral being to whom I bear no enmity>*...
May *<this person to whom I bear enmity>*...
May *<these neutral beings close by>*...
May *<those in my local area>*...
May *<those in a wider area>*...
Expanding to...
May all living things everywhere be free from suffering.

PART SEVEN

MIND-MADE IS
THE WORLD

Thinking and Oblivion

Throughout our history, many great thinkers have devoted considerable energy to the matter of how we can collectively improve our relationships with each other and with the planet we inhabit. There can be no doubt that this is a worthy topic for sincere reflection, indeed maybe it is the most valuable of all questions. However, rather than being just a subject for wise contemplation, such thinking can become an end in itself if due care is not exercised. As we have repeatedly observed in this book, we humans have a tendency to try to think our way out of problems that themselves emerge solely from thought. So, when we think great thoughts we can create great problems.

Thoughts can organise themselves beyond the formations of a single mind. Systems of thought, or ideologies, have been at the heart of much of human conflict, perhaps all of it, throughout the short history of our so-called sophistication. Although it is perhaps unfair to do so, one may single out as a recent example the ideas of Karl Marx, or Marxism as these ideas came to be known, once humanity had formed itself into sections that either embraced or rejected Marx's views. For much of the 20th century, world peace was gravely threatened by what was essentially a difference in political opinion about how to deal with Marx's writings – whether they should be promoted or suppressed. Indeed, in October 1962, at the very moment of my own birth, this schism came within a hair's breadth of leading to nuclear war between the USA and Russia during what has come to be known as the Cuban Missile Crisis. For almost two weeks, the world held its breath whilst a dramatic political staring contest played out between the two nations' leaders, John F. Kennedy and Nikita Khrushchev. Fortunately for us all, agreement was reached and the military might that had been assembled in an advanced state of readiness was stood down. Of course, my intention here is not to comment on Marx's ideas, which are as they are, it is just to observe what can happen when we attach to views, whether positively or negatively.

Of course, our timeless fascination with better alternative worlds is not limited to constructing realities that are intended to become material. An examination of the art, poetry, or literature in almost any period of our modern history will find a good smattering of imaginary perfect worlds that were created just for their own sakes. These are often referred to as "Utopian" visions, after a book by Sir Thomas More in the 16th century that described an imaginary island in which was realised a social, political and moral ideal. Unfortunately for Sir Thomas, some of his ideas were different to those of Henry VIII of England, and this led to the author's execution. Attachment to ideas is inevitably linked to unpleasant consequences, as the Buddha observed as the second of his four "noble truths". Beheading may be a swift solution for dealing with identification with self, but is not the lasting solution that humanity requires.

Clearly, the majority of the self-improving thought of our species is not directed at constructing an ideal world through a single collective vision of perfect conduct.

Rather, the dominant focus is similar to the everyday model of mental health, where we try to identify ways of influencing only the symptoms of an underlying problem, but do not consider the ways in which the problem may be of our own making. The example of mental health was carefully chosen, as not only is the response the same, but so is the underlying cause: self-view. In a troubled mind there may be dark thoughts and reduced serotonin, but in our troubled planet there are such things as weapons, oppression, destruction of nature, war, prejudice, cruelty, extinction, rampant consumerism, famine, food that does not nourish, and values that do not enrich. This whole mass of suffering is created by thinking minds with self-view, and it is impossible to defend any other explanation. Self-view that pursues such ends can only lead to our own extinction, and this too is irrefutable. We are well down that road already, and more thought cannot solve our problems if our thoughts are tainted by the same delusions that created them. If we turn our thinking minds towards the underlying cause of these effects, we can see it clearly, but our minds are much more comfortable when the explanation is out of sight. So too with the looming spectre of our self-destruction: it is always there, but we have learnt to filter it out.

Most of us leave it to others to work out the answers to the profound problems in how our species relates to itself and to the planet it inhabits. Things are easier that way. Most of those others respond to our predicament with thought, and most of that thought will relate to amelioration of superficial indicators rather than to the wider root cause. Although we would like to think otherwise, the priorities for such investigations are generally set by the availability of issues in the popular media rather than any hard analysis of what the imperatives should actually be for the future of our planet and its inhabitants. Priorities are also unduly influenced by self-interest at the level of nations. The frequent exposure of certain issues in the media, for example, global warming, creates a delusion that these are the most pressing issues that face us. Such availability biases are covered well in Daniel Kahneman's book *Thinking, Fast and Slow* that we discussed earlier.

When we respond to problems with intricate systems of thought, whether these problems be on a personal or global scale, we generally just tighten our bonds. To react to all problems instantly with thought is a habit that may in the past have served us well as a species, but now we need a lighter touch. An analogy here is that once upon a time it was beneficial for us to eat sugary and fatty foods whenever the opportunity presented itself, but now the evolutionary legacy is causing problems and we need to work on a new relationship with what we consume. The Buddha saw our destructive propensity to excessive thought, and developed a highly effective system of training that leads to liberation, enabling action based on wisdom and compassion rather than self-view. However, despite the attractiveness and potential of the Buddha's training, his teachings did not spread to the West, and instead a different faith was acquired there around the same time. This Western devotion was the veneration of thought and intellect. A short time after the Buddha's death, Plato wrote his famous book *The Republic*, and to this point it has certainly had more influence on Western minds than anything in the *suttas*. This is gradually and surely changing, but it needs further impetus if we are to advance as a species. Like food that is bad for us, thinking is hyperpalatable.

There is no doubt that there will be a measure of thinking required if we are to turn aside from the highway to oblivion. However, where the three fires rage, thinking just fans the flames. The agenda for thought needs to be set by wisdom and by restraint, and to achieve this we need to reset our whole relationship with thought. Before we can fully tackle the question of how humanity can transform its relationship with the mind's troublesome new guest of the self, it is useful to be able to relate to where we are currently and how this came about in evolutionary terms. It is also helpful to acquire a sense of proportion. Without such a perspective, it is difficult to comprehend the momentum that a negative outcome for humanity has gained through the hyperpalatability of thinking and self-view, and therefore how things may turn out if a change does not come soon.

Evolution of the Species – The State of the Art

The Journey to Self

About 50,000 years ago, *Homo sapiens* perfected evolutionary adaptations that were to endow it with an advantage so massive that it would lay claim to dominion over much of creation, and even come to believe that it had an enduring mastery over all of it. Such lofty self-view is not without a certain validity from the perspective of the contracted mind, but is premature at best. There is some debate about the specifics of how we came to have such a defining effect on our planet, and we will touch on this as we proceed with the explanation, but the evolutionary bottom line is that it is because somehow we acquired the abilities to *plan* and to *communicate*. These advances came at a potentially terrible price, in that they developed like viruses within the brain, gaining increasing influence over their host and smothering the natural wisdom that may otherwise recognise their self-destructive tendency.

Our stay on this earth has been comically short considering how highly we tend to regard our success. Very nearly all life that there has ever been is now extinct, and before becoming extinct much of it achieved far greater longevity that we have managed so far, or indeed are likely to manage. There is a great deal of life around today that was here before us, and that will still be there if we do manage to turn the lights out on our own species. It can be helpful to study the history of our kind relative to others, as this gives a perspective on our "success" that cannot be readily communicated in any other way. For those who have read Douglas Adams' wonderful series of books starting with *The Hitchhiker's Guide to the Galaxy*, the fabulous device called the *Total Perspective Vortex* serves a similarly humbling, but in my view essential, purpose. This apparatus was invented by a man in mocking response to his wife's insistence that he should get "a sense of proportion". Using a theory no less preposterous than any idea in modern physics, Trin Tragula was able to extrapolate a model of the entire universe from a piece of fairy cake, and he placed within this representation an infinitesimally small dot bearing the legend *You are here*. Despite its inventor's original purpose, the Total Perspective Vortex was adopted as an instrument of torture, after it turned out that a true sense of proportion is something that our minds actually cannot bear. The serious point here is that the contracted mind cannot accept the insignificance of its cherished concept of self, and that Trin Tragula's wife's point was as true about our entire race as she considered it to be about her husband.

Chicken or Egg: Communication and Problem-solving

Although we have described the limitations of the thinking mind extensively up to this point, we have only considered the *what* and the *how* of the problem. Our nature is such that the question of *why* we are as we are will naturally arise in our minds, and it is to this question we will now turn. While the Buddha taught that questions that do not lead to advancement in our practice are not beneficial, and indeed that to act well is more important than to have a reason, he also taught the value of wise reflection. Is speculating about the origins of the concept of self just useless thinking, or is it genuinely helpful contemplation? I would offer the view that the answer is certainly the latter, and so on this basis we will set out on the next step of our journey together.

Douglas Adams' concept of the Total Perspective Vortex provides a useful aid to understanding the insignificance of our own place in the universe, but it is also beneficial to add to this an understanding of the similarly marginal worth of the perception of self in our own minds. To do this, we need to take an evolutionary perspective, and in doing so it becomes surprising that the concept of self acquired such dominance in the first place. The old joke states, "If you want to go there, then don't start from here", but here is where we are, and the only place that we can ever be. It is straightforward to argue that since the Buddha's time we have made it significantly harder to achieve liberation from the bonds of the contracted mind, particularly in the West, but at the same time it is plainer than ever that there is a need for a change on a global scale. Figure 6 shows the journey to the emergence of self in our species, and we will now travel that path together before we discuss what to do next.

Figure 6 shows two arrows on the left, one illustrating significant stages in the emergence of language, and the other depicting key steps in the origin of our ability to plan

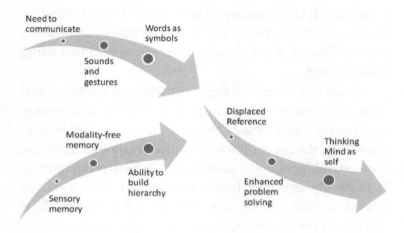

Figure 6 – Journey to the Self

and solve problems. These two evolutionary strands appear to have been the main contributors to the ultimate appearance of the idea of self in our minds. Although in scientific literature this progression is not generally shown in this way, it is unlikely that there would be any strong objections from scientists that things arranged themselves more or less thus. What would certainly get academic juices flowing is any discussion of the relationship between these two input arrows. It is generally accepted that there is a link between thinking and language, but there is no consensus on the nature of the relationship, and no real evidence to decide upon the validity or otherwise of the divergent and passionately held opinions in this area. Indeed, there has been so much controversy about the evolution of language that in 1866 the Société de Linguistique de Paris banned all debate on the subject, and the London Philological Society did likewise some six years later. It is interesting to note that debate in scientific literature did not really get going again for a hundred years following these somewhat amusing and bemusing silencing orders.

So, we will approach the explanation of the two input arms of Figure 6 with the intent of steering clear of any controversy that may detract from our objective. Essentially, the question we will avoid is whether language evolved independently, or emerged as a by-product of an increasingly complex brain. Less vexed, but also best skirted around, is the question of what intermediate systems of communication may have preceded complex spoken language. These are certainly fascinating scientific questions, but they will not take us anywhere nearer to enlightenment, so we can safely set them aside.

We can all agree that language is one of our species' many remarkable abilities and is, as far as we know, unique to humans. Moving along the top arc of Figure 6, we can suppose that in our evolutionary past there was a need to communicate to regulate social activities such as hunting and care of offspring, and that this would have led to a simple lexicon of meaningful sounds or gestures, or both. Communication would also have been beneficial in transmitting learnt knowledge from one individual to another. This much seems relatively straightforward and ordinary as a means of advancement, although again there is little accord on how it may have happened, and plenty of unresolved debate regarding the relative contributions of sounds and gestures. The final step on this arc is the most significant for our purposes, and is where humankind acquired its unique advantage. This is where we learnt to use a sound, or word, to *represent* something, as opposed to merely pointing to it in its presence or mimicking it with sounds or gestures. This is the beginning of using words *symbolically*.

Now we will move up the lower arc of the figure, in which we will trace the acquisition of another species-changing capability that is either the basis of, or related to, our acquisition of language. As we have already discussed, whichever is the case, it matters not. Before we do this, we will travel straight to the end of the arc and discuss the importance of hierarchy. Understanding something of the end of the story will enhance our ability to grasp the significance of the steps on the way. Let's fast-forward 50,000 years or so from this point in the diagram to the late 1970s, where the late and pioneering British psychologist Donald Broadbent was overseeing the work of a graduate student doing experimental research into consciousness. The research focused upon a commonly held view in cognitive psychology that the experience of consciousness results from an information processing limitation in our selective attention. What this research suggested was that human memory features a module that allows the storage of two items, plus the relationship between them. In conversation, Broadbent would often refer to "Flint's Conjecture", after his graduate student who made an interesting speculation. This was that a basic mechanism with three "slots" of abstract working memory and the ability to make associations between stored items is sufficient to build hierarchy, and therefore is the basis of the human ability to learn complex relationships, including language. Not only this, but that it is also the basis of our conscious experience, which derives from a limitation in selective attention. Although Broadbent would often refer to this idea, as he had an intuitive conviction that it had great significance, he did not return to its investigation during his lifetime.

According to this notion, the conscious thinking mind is a mechanism for operating on independent representations and creating a new representation that preserves the relationships between them. To build hierarchy, this process simply needs to nest inside itself, i.e. when the relationship is stored, then the original two slots are cleared and new elements can be combined with the stored relationship. Hierarchy is formed through the ability to embed one structure within another of the same type. We won't labour this point, but language has this type of hierarchical structure.

In 1956, the psychologist George Miller famously (at least to psychologists!) proposed that human short-term memory can retain a small but predictable number of items. This became known as *the magic number seven, plus or minus two*, to reflect the fact that experiments showed that subjects could retain between five and nine items in short-term memory. Since that time, psychologists have extensively refined Miller's model, accounting for some of the seven slots with various visual and auditory buffers, together with intriguing rehearsal loop capabilities to prevent items in memory from decaying or being overwritten. However, in the period of over half a century since Miller's research, what has remained constant is that at least three of our short-term memory slots are considered to be available for general problem-solving. Broadbent would have argued that this is no coincidence, as three slots are all that are needed to process hierarchical relationships.

We discussed earlier the extraordinary feats of learning

that our minds can achieve without thinking. In particular, we talked about how we are able to assimilate the things in the world that frequently occur together, and which are therefore likely to have a relationship of causality or at least connectedness. Such a learning strategy does not, of course, guarantee that it will always discover nature's laws, but is nevertheless remarkably effective. The evolutionary advantages of the emergence of an additional "working memory", guided by selective attention and under conscious control, are clear. Without such a capability, evolution would have been able to progress by blind trial and error alone, and only recognise an advantage if it were to deliver immediate benefit. The addition of the facility to direct our attention and to analyse the contents of our awareness, together with some general working space available to assemble structure, allowed us to start to formulate and test hypotheses in our heads. It also enabled us to exert some scrutiny and executive control over what was being learnt passively. This allowed benefits to be gained beyond our immediate situation.

There are three key factors that would enable us to take best advantage of such an adaptation. Firstly, it seems likely that the more curious the mind, the bigger the advantage. Secondly, owing to the limited nature of this function, there is a need to be selective, and therefore the ability to select well from the environment would be at a premium. Thirdly, and most importantly, in order to use this facility to plan and test hypotheses about the world around us, what is needed is *a representation of self* in the environment. Through developing these three capabilities, our species set itself up for an extraordinary evolutionary leap.

Let's now set aside our discussion of hierarchy and working memory, and travel back to the beginning of the arrow to trace the journey that our species might have made all those millennia ago. It is easy to get lost in speculation about how our problem-solving ability evolved, but one thing is certain – something amazing happened that set humans apart. Staying away from those areas where academic dragons breathe the fire of opposing perspective, the facts about how we got from basic environmental sensitivity to the concept of self appear to be as set out below. For now, we will limit our discussion to the three senses of sight, hearing, and mind, because these are the senses which are most often used to interact with the physical world, and which have therefore attracted the greatest amount of research from psychologists.

Forms in the world that impinge on our sight and hearing are retained in a visual or auditory buffer for a short while, until they decay and die or are replaced by the next sight or sound. This most elemental type of memory is shown in Figure 6 at the beginning of the lower arc. Sensory memory is fleeting; visual memory will decay within a second or so, and auditory memory within a second or two longer. A remarkable thing is that our species developed the ability to attend to and transfer items out of sensory memory into an area of memory that is not related to any of our senses, and so not subject to the same interference from additional sensory stimulation. Within this area of abstract working memory, we could actively rehearse and retain these items for longer, and so, in the most vital sense, they were available for further processing.

Another significant, and probably contemporaneous,

facility was that we also became able to call up items from long-term memory into this working area. This ability to hold symbols representing the present and the past for a short time in a working memory opened up two tremendously potent possibilities; firstly, the ability to combine elements in memory to produce something new, and secondly the facility to think about the future. We learnt to build up complex models of the outside world, and of our inner mental life, which, crucially, contained within it a representation of ourselves. This enabled us to construct composite mental models of possible responses to situations, allowing us to identify the most appropriate action.

In our evolutionary past, it is likely that we used this new facility whenever we needed to. Of course, the problem that the Buddha identified is that we came to exercise this thinking facility not only when it is required, but also when it is not. Moreover, we came to start using it even when we do not will it. It is as if it started to evolve further despite us, but more on this later.

Misplaced References – Not Here, Not Now

We are now at the meeting point of the arrows in Figure 6 and heading for the concept of self. As can be seen from the figure, self emerges following the acquisition of advanced analytical ability and language. As the sense of self developed, and along with it the tendency towards selective attention, it is likely that wider awareness diminished in equal measure. It is probable that initially this sense of self was more of an indirect "me" than a strongly subjective "I", in that initially it may have mainly served the purpose of social integration and cooperation. According to this view, the sense of "me" would have been a relative and inclusive concept, distinguishing self in the context of others, rather than being separate and self-serving as it is today. So, the unspoken question would be along the lines of, "What is my part in this?" rather than, "How can I change this to benefit me?" Unfortunately, the expansion of our mental abilities along one trajectory led to a contraction elsewhere as the "I" became more dominant, acquiring control of our attention and making it increasingly selective. Eventually, at the end of this part of our evolution, our sense of self acquired such dominance that it is reasonable to say that we actually became habitually unaware of anything else. In the expansion of our self-identity, our awareness of the present moment was overrun.

So, at this crucial point in our journey, we had increasing sophistication in both communication and memory, an accelerating facility to solve problems, an emerging concept of self, and an increased selectivity in our attention. We also had a mind that was capable of considering and representing itself, not just in the present but also the past and the future. Where did we go next? To unravel this, let's return to the evolution of language, at the point on the figure marked "Displaced Reference". Language is generally accepted to be *referential*, i.e. its contents refer to the world that is "out there". In addition, there is a related property of language that was named *displaced reference* by the American linguist Charles Hockett in the 1960s. This refers to the ability that language gives to describe something that is neither here nor now, i.e. something that can be there and then. Displaced reference allows us to conceptualise and communicate about people, objects and events that are remote from us in time and space. Indeed, the degree of displaced reference is unlimited – we can even conceive and talk of things that do not exist.

Of course, it may be that displaced reference is not so much a property of language, but a consequence of the elevated potential of the complexity of our brains and information processing capability, and we have already acknowledged the evolving mind's potential in this respect. As we have already agreed, intriguing as this aspect of the evolutionary debate may be, such matters do not concern us here and so we will move swiftly on. In addition to the ability to represent ourselves in the analysis of our options in the here and now, it is clear that there would be a huge advantage in also being able to project ourselves forward or backward in time, or laterally in space, in order to plan and to learn. As noted before, it is likely that the more curious the mind, the greater the benefit, and the more complex the self-referential scenarios that could be constructed.

So we arrive at the end of the arrow. Language has been acquired to communicate with others, and an advanced problem-solving mechanism has developed within the brain. Language has also been adopted within this problem-solving mechanism, and the concept of self has developed and started to wrap itself around this new facility. It seems logical to suppose that the more inquisitive individuals will have been endowed with the most potent sense of self and the most urgent need to control. For these most enterprising minds, it would seem reasonable to speculate further that selective attention may have become increasingly self-centred, and therefore that the beginning of a distortion that eventually became our modern delusion can be traced. *Misplaced* rather than displaced reference, in other words.

The Inner Voice

The evolutionary argument for language acquisition is most straightforwardly made when the purpose of language is regarded as being to communicate between minds. This may well have been the evolutionary impetus, although we will never know for sure. In some way language got wrapped up with our problem-solving ability, whose function is analysis of options, self-direction, planning and choice. The details of this union are unknown, but the most salient thing from our point of view here is something that is much more resistant to a plausible explanation – *somehow, language turned up inside our heads*. This is something we may take for granted, but it is nevertheless remarkable that we have an inner as well as an outer voice, and both speak in the same terms.

Of equal significance is the fact that this language came to speak with the voice of self. We cannot "hear" it as such, it has no sound or accent, but nevertheless it is as salient and present as any external voice. Indeed, it is more so; even when we are attending to another who is speaking to us, still the internal dialogue continues. Often we pay more attention to this internal dialogue than to the one in which our conversation partner expects us to be engaged. Aside from the subjective experience, which of course is deeply personal for each of us, the most convincing demonstration that this voice is like the language we hear is that psychological experiments reliably show that it is disrupted by human speech. The phrase that every parent will have uttered when looking after children – "I can't hear myself think" – provides less scientific, but perhaps more compelling, evidence of the same point.

So, there is a relationship between language and thought, and the thinking mind has a voice. For the contracted mind, this voice is a "force intensifier", in that it adds to the subjective experience of a continuous self. There is little more that can reliably be said about this inner voice, because it is uniquely experienced by each one of us. This is necessarily so, for two reasons. The first reason is that our internal language is free to evolve within each individual to take whatever form is suitable for that person. In contrast, the external language that is communicated between minds evolves in an inevitably more cultural manner because, of course, to be of any use, its meaning must be shared. Ultimately, we cannot really know whether our own internal language is experienced in the same way as anybody else's, even somebody we know intimately. We cannot "hear" anybody else's mind; we can only observe their behaviour.

The second reason that our internal language is profoundly personal is that it not subject to censorship – inside our own heads we can really be ourselves. We do not hold back our inner voice in the way we do with our outer voice, as we do not have the need to present ourselves in any particular way. Even if there were systematic research into this inner language, it would probably be pointless, not only because of its intensely personal nature, but also because of the fact that the subject and object in the analysis are one and the same.

An Unforeseen Problem

At the point that our species completed its journey through Figure 6, we had become endowed with a powerful mechanism for analysis, learning and self-direction. We could communicate with each other about the past, present, and future, and could hold similar dialogues with ourselves inside our own heads. We were able to represent ourselves, others, and objects in our inner and outer dialogues, and could create scenarios that had not yet occurred, or might never occur. However, with all this sophistication came a problem, or rather a cluster of related problems, and from this predicament one of the world's major religions was born.

We acquired a tendency to live inside our own heads, and in doing so started to confuse the contents of the mind with the real world. The inner dialogue acquired an all-consuming dominance that snuffed out our awareness of the present moment, and created an unhealthy emphasis on the idea of a self, whose initial curiosity led to self-view and from there a hunger for self-preservation and self-aggrandisement that could never be satisfied. This insatiable appetite meant that much of our newfound and highly adaptive analytical ability would devote itself to a maladaptive tendency, as our minds started to try to steal the march on other minds. Of course, those other minds were busy doing exactly the same thing. Our increased sophistication turned the social animal into a selfish hungry ghost.

There can be no doubt that the emergence of the thinking mind led to our runaway success as a species, but it may also have sealed our fate. Fortunately, the outcome is still in our own hands. Since the Buddha's time, thinking minds have sought to improve their lot, and created advancements to meet that end. Unfortunately, some of the recent workings of man are so terrible that they could wipe out all life on this planet, except perhaps the most creatively resistant bacteria. We stand collectively at the turning point, holding not just the means of our own destruction, but also the key to the liberation from all suffering. However, our naturally joyful and compassionate minds have been overtaken by a tyrannical former servant that is determined to stop us from seeing that we have this choice. We faced the same dilemma in the Buddha's time, and he clearly knew this. He showed us the way to liberation, but here we still stand.

The Limits of Rationality

We have curious and questioning minds. As children we learn about the world through almost insatiable questioning of adults. Although we may no longer irritate our parents by constantly asking them "why", we nevertheless retain much of this curiosity. The astounding scale of humankind's achievement is a testament to this – we could not transplant a human heart or discover Jupiter's many moons without asking the odd question.

Science cannot realistically avoid a bias towards investigating the universe from a limited perspective, i.e. what it means either to the individual scientist, or to humanity in general. This point of view is highly restrictive because, of course, we are all necessarily part of what we study, and this renders some of our attempts to understand things distorted at best and pointless at worst. As with the voice inside our heads, perhaps there are some things that our thinking minds simply cannot know because our connectedness to the entity that we are observing is too intimate. At the level of the atom, everything is as one, and indeed even at the level of DNA we can rejoice in substantially less uniqueness than we may otherwise think. If we accept the Buddha's teaching that the mind of awareness is actually without any limitation at all, it is ironic that we spend so much of our time trying to force our limited thinking minds to understand that which they can never truly grasp.

At the turn of the 20th century, physicists felt that they were close to a rational explanation of all things, and all that remained to be discovered was the detail. However, more or less straight away in that century things started to get decidedly weird, both at the sub-atomic level with quantum theory, and on a grander scale with the theory of relativity. Soon, science arrived at a point at which its concepts simply could not be thought or even imagined by the thinking mind. As the century progressed, and continuing up to the present day, the strangeness escalated rapidly. "Real" science left science fiction for dead in the wonder and ingenuity of its ideas, and the layperson could no longer reliably judge the plausibility, or otherwise, of the fantastic theories that proliferated. One model of multi-dimensional space seems just as crazy as the next to the uninitiated, and probably to many physicists. Physics seemed to be starting to brush shoulders with mysticism, which incidentally is the premise from which my own interest in the Buddha's teachings began, many years ago. Theories could be proven and accepted, but could not be thought. Some questions had answers that were so unpalatable, e.g. "both yes and no", and "neither yes nor no", that actually the questions lost meaning in any conventional sense.

The Nobel Prize-winning Danish physicist, Niels Bohr, famously spoke in eloquent terms about the behaviour of atoms being best described in terms similar to that of a poet, using simile and allegory, or in other words descriptions that evoke an understanding rather than directly demand it. The problem is that at the atomic level, particles cannot be described as independent things, but rather need to be explained in terms of their relationships with other things, including our own consciousness, and even then only with spectacularly complex theorising. It is often said that we are not spectators in the theatre of reality, but instead are actors within it. At the beginning of the period in which physics started to lose its rationality, Bohr's German contemporary, Werner Heisenberg, theorised that there are some things that we simply cannot know with certainty, at least not without making other things less certain. "Empty is the world", the Buddha said in the Dhammapada, which is one of the most popular and accessible ancient texts. By this he meant that nothing has lasting reality – it is all process, it is all change, and the "reality" of what we observe is an illusion. We are part of this flow, and our views and choices are as insubstantial as everything else. Like contemporary quantum physicists, the Buddha knew that consciousness creates the universe, not the other way around.

This intense period in physics that led up to the development of the most destructive weapon yet conceived, is both fascinating and important to consider. This is particularly so in light of the fact that the liberated energy that hideously killed the residents of two Japanese cities was a tiny fraction of the energy available to be released if we knew how. Our own bodies are made of atoms, just as is literally *everything* else, and so each of us is made of bonds that, if broken, could wipe out a substantial part of humanity. Maybe at the beginning of the 20th century we were more or less at the pinnacle of what we needed to discover about the physical world, and should have stopped there. Humanity has witnessed, to its eternal cost, the fact that splitting the atom was ultimately one of the worst things we could ever do. Like the dwarves in Tolkien's *The Lord of the Rings*, we delved too deeply and awoke a latent menace.

Our thinking minds have got to the bottom of how much of the universe appears to operate now, but still some allegedly fundamental questions remain. One of these questions concerns the nature of consciousness itself, for which scientists do not even have the beginnings of an explanation. However, what if we were collectively to decide that these questions are not so important after all, and that actually we can get along perfectly with what we already know? Indeed, what if the collective mental health and continued existence of our species were actually to depend on such a decision? In *The Hitchhiker's Guide to the Galaxy*, Douglas Adams parodied our search for the answer to the "Ultimate Question" of "Life, the Universe and Everything", with the famous answer of "42". Of course, this answer then led to another urgent pursuit, to determine what the question was. Fortunately, we already know what the ultimate question is, and its answer needs no verbal response. It is this: *What is in this moment?*

In other words, what if the primary focus of our thinking minds were now to be to start addressing this question through cultivating right view and right intention? What if some of our currently misdirected thinking energy were now directed towards right effort? What if we decided to follow the Buddha's guidance to pull out at the root the three poisons of ignorance, attachment, and aversion?

Self As Science Fiction? You Bet!

This book actually started as a novel with a somewhat far-fetched theme. The initial premise was that the thinking mind is evolving as a separate species that can, in certain circumstances, jump from its human host and become instantiated in other compatible hosts, be they carbon or silicon based, for better or for worse. The naked ambition of self was to provide the energy, some mathematical and computational arm-waving was to contribute the means, and so the stage was set for the drama to unfold. This has been an ongoing project for some years now, and indeed is still a planned venture, albeit one requiring reserves of imagination not yet discovered. However, I set this endeavour aside when I realised that first there was a much more important story to tell, which is this one.

It is perhaps ironic given the self's expansionist tendencies, that if we free ourselves from the yoke of self-view, our experience of the world expands dramatically, and along with it our sense of connectedness to all that it contains. So, travelling beyond the confines of self can already be achieved, but only on the cessation of self. Then, our awareness comes to be like the air, light, and gravity that surrounds us – something limitless that is not "mine" or "yours", but just *is*. During the Buddha's ascetic life before his enlightenment, he learnt meditation from some renowned masters, and attained higher *jhana* states under the tutelage of the great teacher Alara Kamala, who declared to the Buddha at one point "As I am, so are you; as you are, so am I." In other words, pure awareness is not a personal experience.

Although my original ideas for a tale were fantasy, it is nevertheless instructive to focus on the five key aspects of self that qualify it for the role of villain in a science fiction novel. The serious point here is, that although these five elements are somewhat sinister, they are certainly not fantasy and therefore they give us reason to be highly circumspect regarding the contents of our own minds.

Firstly, self is a *usurper*. It has already taken over our minds. On the basis of all we have discussed so far in this book and learnt through meditation and reflection, it is clear that there is much more to mind than self, but nevertheless self is often all we can perceive, and also frequently all that other people perceive of us. Of course, there are those who have trained their minds and managed to deal with self, but for most of us we are overrun for much of the time.

Secondly, self is a *survivor*. Although a traditional Darwinian view of evolution focuses on "survival of the fittest", it is, of course, true that no individual, no matter how fit, has ever survived longer than a human lifespan.

What has survived is self. As Buddhist monks chant daily, we have not gone beyond death. We have learnt how to prolong life and put off the final moment, but in many ways this has just created a new set of challenges of dealing with very old and frail bodies and minds. The same monastic chant also wisely reminds us that we have not gone beyond old age and sickness. The following verse from the Dhammapada is not amongst its most jolly, but describes our condition as well today as it did in the Buddha's time:

> *Behold your body – a decorated doll*
> *a mass of sores*
> *sick and full of craving*
> *in which there is nothing lasting or stable.*

Despite the fact that no individual self has transcended death, self is nevertheless resident in every functioning mind that has ever been since we reached the end of the path described in Figure 6. Although it likes to present to us the illusion that we are all different, in fact this shared delusion is one of the things that makes us all the same. Self is now wired in, and has continued to evolve from its initial functions in planning, communication and problem-solving to become the dominant agent of human change. Although so much has altered in the health, longevity and appearance of our physical form since the Buddha's time, it is straightforward to argue that all of this comes from the activities of self and the thinking mind, not from Darwinian random mutation. Now that the self is more deeply entrenched and it has various technological augmentations at its disposal, the contracted mind has largely, if not totally, usurped any process of Darwinian evolution for our species. Cultural change now happens at such a rate, and with such an impact, that the natural process has been short-circuited.

Thirdly, the self is an *invader*. It has expansionist tendencies, or in other words it has a desire to be more than it is. This is a very important point, and is at odds with the Darwinian view that all advancement happens by chance. Humans, at least in the "developed" world, have a deeply held inner purpose that their lives should be "moving on" in some way, and they take steps to make this so. No other life on this planet seems to perceive a problem with its lot, such that it is inspired to want to be "heading somewhere". Even the urge to be different from our fellow beings seems to be unique amongst humans. It is, of course, natural that beings should have a desire to seek food, shelter, a mate, and so on, but when this instinct is taken over by self, as has happened to *Homo sapiens*, it becomes very much more than the sum of its natural parts. We can clearly see the self as an invader in the way that some people will forcefully try to impose their ideas on others, as if trying to create copies of self running on other hosts, displacing the previous self.

Fourthly, self is a *subjugator*. It captures and binds together thoughts into formations, and then marshals any resource at its disposal to turn these formations into fears, complexes, irrational beliefs and all sorts of escalating and destructive mental habits. The Buddha used analogies liberally, but here a modern analogy might help, and it is certainly in keeping with our current science fiction theme. The forces that bind the *khandhas* together are like those that bond together the components of the nucleus of an

362

atom. To break these bonds requires an intense focus, but when they are breached the energy of awareness is set free with stunning power.

Fifthly, self is a *deceiver*. It is a master of disguise and calls itself friend, ambassador, ally, counsellor, and saviour. Its deceits are so cunning that most of the time they go unnoticed, and the housebuilder that the Buddha saw so clearly is free to go about its business without interruption. We have already remarked upon how straightforward some of the insights of the Buddha's path actually are, and how we regularly fall into the same obvious delusion over and over again, but so subtle is the veil that is drawn over our suffering, that we do not see it.

Usurper, survivor, invader, subjugator, deceiver – these are not necessarily the words that a visitor would wish to be placed on their calling card. Fortunately, despite all of this naked ambition, self is merely that much – *a visitor*. To use the analogy of the computer underlying the everyday model of mind, we can show through meditation that self is merely a guest program that can be run on the host computer of the mind. When we are meditating well, self shifts from a foreground process to a background process, and then gradually shuts itself down. The guest eventually either leaves because it is being ignored, or sits down quietly to be part of the serenity that abounds. As the great master Ajahn Chah once said, its departure is encouraged if we do not set out a chair for it.

Returning to our science fiction theme, what if such an artful entity as self has duped us into being hosts for its ambitions and has now started to outgrow us and seek new hosts beyond the human realm? What if the runaway train of technological advance actually has a driver, and the thinking mind is purposefully extending its empire, ultimately to take up new residence and assert its rights as an independent species? This may be straying somewhat into fantasy (and there is a book in there somewhere!), but no matter how unlikely it may be, we should perhaps not take a chance given how much there is to lose.

Withdrawing from this somewhat whimsical tangent, there is a serious point to be made here regarding the nature of our response to self. We can make this point as a logical argument, using the form of reasoning that has come to be known as *Pascal's Wager*, after the 17th century French mathematician and philosopher who first expounded it. Adapting Pascal's method to the Buddha's teaching, we end up with the following logic:

If we cultivate right view and right intention, and the Buddha's path leads to liberation, then there is everything to gain (we are liberated).

If we cultivate right view and right intention, and the Buddha's path does not lead to liberation, then we have lost a finite amount (we have spent time meditating and reflecting, and we have renounced some unskilful practices that we could otherwise have been indulging in).

If we do not cultivate right view and right intention, and the Buddha's path leads to liberation, then there is everything to lose (we are caught in an endless cycle of suffering).

364

We have to make a decision, because choosing not to decide equates to making a decision. The outcome cannot be determined by reason alone, and so we are obliged to make a wager.

The form of Pascal's Wager applies well to our choices regarding the Buddha's teaching, and more specifically to right view and right intention, which create the impetus for us to begin and then maintain the practice. Logically, it is plain that we should cultivate these elements of the path, because in doing so we can either gain everything or lose a finite amount, whereas in not doing so we can lose everything. For those who favour the more literal meaning of "rebirth" within the Buddhist teachings, then of course the potential gain is even greater relative to the potential loss, as the liberation from suffering will extend beyond our current lifetime. Regardless of our stance on rebirth, the only logical option is to pursue the practice with commitment, because to opt to abandon it in the wager makes no sense. This is clearly true regardless of the science fantasy and 17th century wordplay, but adding a little drama in the final part of a book is surely excusable.

Psychological Evolution –
The Art of the Possible

The Buddha said that the human condition is the only one from which a living being can become enlightened, and therefore it is one of unique responsibility. This is the basis of the hope that the Buddha saw for us all, and we need to take it very seriously. Six "realms of existence" are shown within the Wheel of Life, one of which is the human realm. We have already discussed one of the other realms – the hungry ghosts; a realm in which many of us spend much of our time. Beings are reborn into these six realms, conditioned by their *kamma*. It is easy to become distracted by the debate about what to take literally and what is symbolic within the Wheel of Life, particularly regarding rebirth, but fortunately the Buddha would not have encouraged such debate. Rather, it is likely that he would have stressed that the important consideration is how we use the symbolism to move our own practice forward. So, the "correct" interpretation is the one that works for us towards that end. We would no more wish to be born into the next moment as a hungry ghost than we would to become one in a future life following the death of the body. Essentially, the Wheel of Life is a psychological map, and we should take from it a single question: *what can we do with our human condition that is beneficial, given the endless cycle of cause and effect?*

This is the question that we will now seek to answer.

It is the fundamental question of psychological evolution, which some may choose to call spiritual evolution. Again, what is important is not the label but the outcome. The key message is that humanity has reached a crossroads psychologically, and although it was the thinking mind that got us to this point, the role it must now play to ensure our survival is a very different one. As we have already discussed under the attention-grabbing headline of "oblivion", the word "survival" is not chosen lightly here, and the stakes really are that high. As long as the illusion of self remains in control of the thoughts and deeds of our species, destruction is near inevitable. Many of the so-called advances of the modern age, not least the advent and persistence of nuclear weapons, show that we are already seriously pushing our luck. If the natural wisdom and compassion of the mind of awareness can be re-energised on a global scale, then there will be harmony; but how can this change be brought about to save a whole species?

Of course, evolutionary change does not happen in an instant, but takes extended periods of time. Up to now, it has happened only in a blind way, without life having any intention other than to survive and perpetuate. Since living things first emerged on our planet, potentially favourable new traits have appeared at random in the development of each species, and where they have conferred some immediate benefit, they have emerged as adaptations in future generations amongst successful members of that species. Those creatures possessing the beneficial mutation would then have an advantage over those without it, and so their "fitness" would be increased, where fitness is defined as the ability to produce more surviving offspring. That is how evolution has worked for us, and for all living things, up until this point. However, to ensure our longevity, things now need to be different, in two fundamental respects. Firstly, the change that we must now make requires *intention,* i.e. it must be deliberately willed and actively seen through. Secondly, the benefit to humanity will be *deferred,* in that the full benefit will not be immediately apparent.

It is clear that change of this type cannot occur through the natural process of evolution as we know it, but fortunately in the Buddha's teaching lies the means to bring it about. Although the path of meditation, restraint, and reflection is a long-term commitment and ultimately has a goal, we have now learnt firsthand that it delivers benefits from the outset – it is "beautiful in the beginning, beautiful in the middle, and beautiful in the end". As we have already observed, the immediate rewards of the *dhamma* are sufficient to strengthen our intention to continue with our practice, creating and energising the perpetual motion of increasing gain. When this happens, it is readily apparent that the positive effects are not just personal, but extend to all beings with whom we come into contact. This may start in a small way, perhaps with a fly whose life we spare, or an increased focus on the provenance of the food that we consume, or considering another's perspective in a disagreement. As a result, we start to live our lives with more freedom from remorse, and we feel the return of good will from those to whom we have shown it. Such is the nature of *kamma*. It does not take too much imagination to see how ultimately such positive energy could transform all things.

So, here we stand, still at the turning point. Although

when the Buddha set in motion the wheel of *dhamma* he could not have foreseen the specifics of the devastation we would be able to bring about some two and a half millennia later, he certainly knew that humanity has the capability both to destroy itself and to liberate itself. He saw that there was hope for our species back then, and fortunately there is still hope now, despite the fact that the three fires of ignorance, aversion, and attachment rage even more fiercely in modern society. What the Buddha set out all those years ago was not just a guide for living in his time and in times to come, but was actually the blueprint for the next step in our evolution – a psychological evolution. It is apparent that his teaching is now reaching Western as well as Eastern minds, both explicitly through the rise of Buddhism in the West, and more subtly through its influence on such diverse fields as psychological therapy and corporate training. The hope is that it may reach enough minds to prevent the extinction of our species by its own hand.

This Is Not Ancient India

Since the Buddha's time, life in the so-called developed world has changed beyond measure, and in the last half-century the rate of change has increased sharply. We will now consider together the proposition that with this acceleration seems to have come an amplification in the strength of the sense of self that the contracted mind presents to us. This growing dominion of self has been the driving force in much of the resulting change in our culture, and it is essential that we become aware of how this is taking place within us. As we noted earlier, the self is an artful confidence trickster with expansionist tendencies, and in modern times it has found a most effective means to feed its habits. Although the root poisons of ignorance, attachment, and aversion are in all likelihood no different today than they were at the time of the Buddha, and it is probably reasonable to assert that we are no more or less driven to act for good or for ill, this deeper-seated nature of self makes the outlook for our species decidedly bleaker. This means there is a more urgent need to recognise the evolutionary fork in the path that lies before us and act accordingly.

The strengthening grip of the self has its origins in the Scientific Revolution when Descartes came up with his famous *Cogito ergo sum*, although veneration of thinking had begun much earlier. The more recent quickening can be traced to a culture-changing union of three innovations; two distinctly modern, and one ancient. Both of the newer advances took an existing major technology that was already familiar to large organisations and made it *personal*. The first of these was the development of the personal computer, which was introduced in a popular and accessible form in the late 1970s. The second was the emergence of high-capacity digital communications targeted at the individual subscriber a couple of decades later. The joint fates of these two technologies were inextricably bound together with the invention of the World Wide Web at the beginning of the 1990s. The Internet had been around for some years already, but these new innovations made it "ready to hand" for ordinary users, which created an insatiable demand for access at all times and in all locations.

There had hitherto been considerable inertia in the adoption of the Internet, owing to the rather technical nature of its interfaces and its history in defence and academic institutions. As interfaces became more intuitive and responses more instantaneous, we entered a period of change in which each new innovation seemed to lead inevitably to the next at a rate not previously experienced. Computing and communications had not only become personal, they had become commodity appliances that required very little skill to operate. What lit the metaphorical touchpaper for the technological explosion that followed, was the ability for these new advances to exploit the ancient technology of written records. This convergence was of great consequence for our psychological evolution, and our future still hangs in the balance as we explore the options it has brought us.

The emergence of writing and drawing as a means of recording and communicating the wisdom of our species actually emerged remarkably slowly in our history. It can be traced from the earliest symbolic systems some five millennia before the Buddha's birth to printed books almost two millennia after his passing. However, the mass accessibility of written material in book form has until very recently been somewhat limited. Now, in a flash, almost the entire wisdom of humankind, plus an insanely large corpus of not-so-wise opinion, has become available to our minds through the Internet. So too has the ability to reach out and communicate instantly with individuals and communities right across the globe.

These are culture-defining changes, and they have led us to a progressively more private existence, where personal contact with others is reduced, and goods and services are increasingly tailored to our own specific needs. Notice how the elderly within our society, who are used to a more challenging relationship with technology, feel ever more isolated and left behind. Contrast this with the way the very young can interact readily with the gestural interface of a tablet computer whilst they are still struggling to make themselves understood through language. We have disappeared into ourselves, and as a result, the culture of "me, me, me" is more dominant, and indeed more accepted, than it has ever been before. Self is selfer than it has ever been.

Although feeding the hunger of self is inherently dangerous, not all change is bad, because not all minds are bad. Today, anybody who wants to learn about the Buddha's teachings can simply search and find a wealth of information, including written and recorded teachings from the wisest of monks and other practitioners of *dhamma*. Excellent translations and explanations of the *suttas* are also freely available. Equally, somebody who wants to learn how to do something much less wholesome with their life can do that too, usually with even greater ease. The Internet can be used for helping to develop our wisdom, for feeding the root poisons, or just for wasting time. It serves as an amplifier and multiplier for the hindrances, and it is common to speak of the Internet as a "vortex" into which we can become drawn. When this happens, we emerge some time later, blinking into the sunlight and wondering where the time has gone.

The Internet search engine has become an extension of our sixth sense of mind, and like that sense, it can be used to take us towards liberation or to carry us away. Just as we can observe the operation of the defilements within us by watching where our senses are carried by our unguarded attention, so too can we gain insight from what we seek to present to our minds via the Internet. So, the Buddha's advice to "guard the sense doors" should apply here too, and vigilance should be maintained over portals to the virtual world as well. If our curiosity is left unchecked in this new realm, we can feed and strengthen unhelpful mental formations at a rate not previously possible before the Internet age.

Although it would be preposterous to say that the Buddha foresaw the development of the Internet and its search engines, it is fascinating that in the largely autobiographical Ariyapariyesana Sutta he distinguished between two types of search; *noble search*, and *ignoble search*. Noble search, he said, seeks out those things that are uncreated, unexcelled, and not subject to birth and death. Ignoble search delights in that which is impermanent and of no intrinsic value. Ignoble search, together with our increasingly private and tailored experience of the world, is the essence of the modern problem that has led to the increasing power base of self. In addition, social networking allows us to speak to more and more people, without the constraints that ordinarily apply to face-to-face interaction, and therefore the need for right speech here is particularly acute. As ever, the choices are our own, and our responsibility is to be aware that we are making them.

What is remarkable is that despite such dramatic change in the world and how we relate to it, the Buddha's teachings are as applicable today as they were when they were first expounded. However, there is one area in which I can't help but wonder whether the Buddha would reinterpret his teaching to take account of a more complex society that has bred a more deep-rooted self-view. This relates to one of his specific instructions to monks who were having difficulty freeing themselves of the defilements. Where restraint and meditation were not quite doing the job in uprooting a particular defilement, the Buddha would teach *transformation* of that defilement as an alternative to letting go. At the more extreme end of the spectrum of transformational techniques, he taught of the "austere" or *dhutanga* practices, which were directed at dealing with stubborn defilements, and some are still practised today. One such practice from the Buddha's time was for a monk to go and live in a charnel ground, which in ancient India was a place where corpses were taken to rot or be eaten. Charnel grounds were not like tidy graveyards, but were gruesome and dangerous places, where creatures lurked that did not care whether they dined on dead or living flesh, and human ne'er-do-wells went about their business without fear of being observed.

The grisly sights in a charnel ground were held by the Buddha to be a good way not only to understand death and the nature of the body, but also to transform sensual desire. In the *suttas*, the Buddha urges his monks to contemplate these repulsive scenes and reflect that all bodies, no matter how attractive they may appear, are of this nature. In the Buddha's India, culturally people were fearful and superstitious about death, and so a charnel ground would have seriously challenged their mindfulness. To illustrate, some translations of ancient words that were used at the time to describe the potential companions for monks in charnel grounds are "sorcerers", "cannibal witches", "zombies", and "demons". Were the

Buddha alive today, my view is that he would regard the practice of his path in the modern world outside the monastery as a particularly extreme form of *dhutanga* practice, equivalent in transformational strength to living in a charnel ground, teeming with ghoulish characters created from increased self-view.

Not only do the Buddha's teachings carry the same power and relevance today that they did in his time, but even now they appear to miss out nothing. No matter what situation we face, or what comes up in our minds, the answer is always *sanditthiko*, right there in the moment. It is a truly remarkable achievement that one man could have such lasting and world-changing insight, but of course he would not have wished us to attach to such a view. Today's most pressing and precious task is the same as it was back in ancient India – the cultivation of an awakened mind, a *buddha mind*, to end our suffering.

Of course, liberation from our own personal suffering is not sufficient to save our planet, but it is the largest step we can take in that direction as an individual. The skilful and harmonious behaviour encouraged through the Buddha's path is directed to both self and other, and the definition of "other" must necessarily include those beings yet to be. We humans have climbed to the very top of the food chain and although our achievements in thought, word, and deed are considerable, we nevertheless have a deep and abiding responsibility not to abuse our position, and to leave a positive legacy for all beings. What has changed since the Buddha's time is that the task has become harder, and never has it been more important to keep an eye on self.

A Buddha Mind for Our Time

The change needed for our species can only be brought about through *intentional cultural evolution*, although fortunately to do this we need only focus only on our own behaviour. The rest will follow naturally, but what we do not have is time. In the distant past, evolution did not seem to be in any particular hurry to move along, and billions of years elapsed on our planet before life of even the simplest variety came to be. Our own species took so long to get going that we *Homo sapiens* have not even lasted for one per cent of the time the dinosaurs were on this earth, in fact nowhere near even one fifth of one per cent. More humbling still is the amount of time that we "modern" *Homo sapiens* have been milling about on this planet thinking we are in charge, which is a considerably more trifling percentage. A comparison with the longevity of dinosaurs has not been made here just to inculcate a much-needed sense of humility with respect to our planet, but also because it will automatically bring to mind ideas of extinction through spreading activation, and thereby sensitise us to thoughts about the demise of our own species. These great creatures eventually became extinct because of something cataclysmic that happened to the earth, snuffing out their line, along with a great deal else. It was something that they could neither predict nor prevent. This contrasts sharply with the potential destiny of our own species, because in our case extinction is likely to be at our own hands. What is more, our folly is likely also to wipe out more than our own species, just as we have already brought about the extinction of many other species through our self-centred behaviour. The development of nuclear weapons is a case in point; so many nations have now developed these terrible devices that there is clearly a pressing need to make decisions with different types of minds.

One of the key meditations used in the Buddhist tradition is referred to as "reflection on the qualities of the Buddha", in which each of nine qualities is systematically called to mind, considered, internalised, and experienced. This is intended to help develop our right view and right intention, by reflecting upon how this ordinary (if somewhat privileged) man gained ultimate enlightenment through impeccable wisdom, mindfulness, and restraint. Although there is considerable merit in expounding this list of nine qualities, for present purposes we are going to concentrate on only one. The others are there to be discovered if we so desire by skilful use of our mind sense-extension, the Internet search engine. This particular characteristic of the Buddha, a personal favourite, is called *sugato* in Pali, and like so many Pali words of the period it does not have a single-word translation in a Western language. It means something along the lines of "well faring", or "going to a good destination". *Sugato* is a quality that we need to develop both individually and as a species.

Luckily, there is no need for theories of social organisation, prescriptions about the behaviour of large corporations, or indeed any other view about the conduct of others in order to be one who is *sugato*. Although we are moving on to a level of consciousness that is global, the means of getting there is entirely within the reach of each one of us. All we need to do is to establish a personal base of wisdom, mindfulness, and restraint within our own thoughts and deeds, and in this way live harmlessly on our planet. Rather than seeking to influence the actions of others in a direct and controlling way, we should let our own conduct inspire their respect and curiosity. Setting an example is a highly efficient way to communicate, and if our skilful comportment arouses the inquisitiveness of others, then it may be appropriate to pass on what we have learnt. On the other hand, if another person has not specifically asked to hear our story, then it is probably more beneficial to work on our own practice than try to influence theirs. No blood has ever been spilled in spreading the word of the Buddha, and we need to keep it that way!

The Buddha encouraged us to associate with "wise friends" who are engaged on the same path of peace. Indeed, in the Maha Mangala Sutta, he is asked about the way to the highest blessings, and his answer begins with an exhortation to "associate with the wise", showing how much value he placed on choosing our companions well. He described such spiritual friends as being virtuous in thought, speech, and action, and energetic in their pursuit of liberation. If we cannot be with such people, the Buddha taught that we should seek solitude instead. This may seem like tough advice, but the Buddha was emphatic about it. If we associate with those engaged in unskilful practice, then because the idea of a fixed and immutable personality is an illusion, the unwise actions of others will condition similar behaviour in ourselves. Such is the nature of *kamma*. Essentially, this is all the social organisation that is needed – we should associate with good and vigorous people, strive to be this way ourselves, and resolve to be available to those who wish to follow the same path.

The nature of the change that is needed for humankind is not so much a change in the sense of moving away from something, but more a natural culmination, or a growing-up. We are not renouncing or resisting anything, but rather we are moving on. In the West in particular, we tend to "push" with ideas, but now we need to let go, and therefore the increasing maturity that our species needs is more of a flow and not a push at all. We spoke earlier about the Buddha's frequent analogy of crossing a river to find our liberation, and this is the river of attachment and suffering into which, according to the *suttas*, thirty-six streams of desire will carry us if we are heedless. We also learnt that he taught ten "perfections" when we were discussing the specific perfection of *dana*, or giving. It is illuminating that the Pali word *parami*, which is generally translated as "perfection", has another sense, which is "crossing over". So, in adopting perfections such as generosity, we are crossing over from unskilful and unhelpful states of mind and ways of behaving to those that are beneficial. This is as true at the collective level as it is at the individual level, and the perfection of giving is a superb example, because without it the Buddha's teaching would not have been preserved and passed down the ages. Through this kindness, many have already reached the further shore.

Whilst we are talking of the perfections, although earlier I resisted the temptation to enumerate the list of ten, I will do so now as the time is right. Like so many aspects of the journey to the further shore, the perfections are both cause and effect: we cultivate them to assist us in attaining a pure mind, and they naturally arise at times when our mind is pure. We will not go into a discussion of each one, as they are intrinsically embodied in everything we have discussed so far about the path, and in just listing them the beauty of each word is so clearly evident. Whenever our practice is becoming weak or rigid, it can be immensely healing just to consider each one for a moment. They are:

Giving
Morality
Renunciation
Wisdom
Effort
Patience
Honesty
Resolve
Kindness
Equanimity

So what is it that must be done in order to ensure that we play our part in the cultural evolution that is now a necessity for our species? The answer is simple: we just follow the path described in the Buddha's teachings and do the best we possibly can. In the terms of Pascal's Wager, we bet our future on the Buddha's path; not just our own future, but the future of all things that live and the planet they inhabit. We do not have to "be" or "become" anything to do this, we just need to recognise the value in the path to a sufficient depth to step out upon it. We do not need to "be a Buddhist" to follow the Buddha's example, and indeed when one considers closely what the word "Buddhist" really means in the context of this remarkable man's teachings, we can see that the label is in any case of no importance. Doubtless we will develop a certain sense of gratitude towards the Buddha as we learn more of the path, but how such gratitude is expressed is a personal choice and needs no self formed around it.

In specific terms, the best way to describe what needs to be done is simply to return to our lists (and be thankful that we decided to be sparing with the lists we selected for consideration!). Below are the lists that we have discussed together so far, and if we understand them well we are properly equipped to be called *sugato*:

Three characteristics of all things
Three root poisons
Three divisions of the eightfold path
Four foundations of mindfulness
Four sublime abidings
Four material jhana states
Five hindrances
Five aggregations
Five jhana factors
Eight path elements
Eight worldly winds
Ten perfections

Just contemplating this list of lists shows how the Buddha's teachings flow into each other in a beautifully interconnected way, such that there is really no beginning, end, or natural progression. His proclamation "I teach suffering and the way out of suffering" described the beginning and the end well enough, and it is a personal choice which elements of the teachings speak best to us and therefore mark out the route that we might take. Nothing matters other than the outcome.

A View From a Lake

The word *Utopia* in Sir Thomas More's book title is generally held to be a pun, exploiting the fact that the Greek words for "good place" and "no place" are pronounced in the same way. Sir Thomas is not, of course, around to explain his intention, but the punning title serves us well here. The Utopia we seek is not another place – it is the present moment, which is actually the only place it could possibly be. Our choice is how perfectly it is experienced, and how perfect it is experienced to be. Reality can only be as it is, and our responsibility is to behave well in this very moment, the only moment there is, for the benefit of ourselves and all things that live or are yet to be.

Thought is a wild thing that needs to be tamed, and is best employed simply to generate the resolve and wisdom we need in order to accept and respond appropriately to the next moment. Particularly in the West, our propensity to think has clouded this simple vision, and we spend much of our mental life travelling in time. We need to think less, and when we do think we need to know we are thinking and thereby think better. So too with speech, and so too with actions of the body. The awareness, wisdom and morality that can be cultivated by each of us now needs to arise at societal level. For one person to renounce killing or false speech is a beautiful thing, but for a culture to do so could save the world. We need to part with the small stake of right view and right intention, and accept the wager that will lead to our liberation.

As for me, I worked at a business park on the River Thames in England for over seven years, and attended there almost every day, give or take a couple of extended periods of hospital treatment and several holidays. I was Chief Engineer of a large UK public sector technology system, indeed the largest that has ever been or probably ever will be. I would set my alarm for a time just before dawn, and then commute to take up my parking place at work. Before starting work, I would walk to a nearby lake, on whose border there was a bench, and there I would sit. The lakeside was not always calm. There were flies and mosquitoes whose persistence I learnt not to resist, and there was the whooping encouragement of the morning boot camps working out in the parkland that surrounds the lake. These stirred some very negative views in my mind, because of course people are more challenging than insects.

The swans, coots and moorhens would swim past on the lake, stirring the waters a little, but leaving stillness behind on their passing. One coot became so accustomed to my sitting that he would often leave the water and walk up to stand by my side for a while. Perhaps there was even an energy to which he was drawn. His company was so frequent that I gave him a name, "Moorhen", which may have confused him somewhat, as may my arbitrary choice regarding his gender. It was a name that came from my ignorance, although once my ignorance had been corrected by a friend, it amused me and so he remained "Moorhen". All coots look the same to me, and so wherever I meet one in the world, it is Moorhen and I greet him fondly. Much of this may sound like the beginning of an insipid metaphor about stillness of water, or about bias in the process of attribution, but it is not. The view from the lake is not a metaphor; it was real. It was Moorhen's view. It was of a man meditating to improve himself and his relationship with the world. It was of a being who wished him no ill will, and to be at all times free from suffering.

Each man or woman who does this contributes to the perpetual motion that will save our species and our planet, and possibly nearby worlds as well.

The sight of somebody meditating needs to become commonplace.

It is not just for the birds.

Acknowledgements

The Buddha encouraged us to associate only with wise friends, or else to seek solitude. I have followed this advice to my perpetual advantage, and would like to thank the wisest of all friends, my wife Maria (SuperMaz). She has inspired, assisted, and tolerated me in infinite measure. She has made this beautiful world a more wondrous place.

I would like to express heartfelt gratitude to all who have taught me about the mind. Even with a doctoral degree in psychology, my understanding did not come together until I started to visit Amaravati Buddhist Monastery in the late 1980s. The influence of the monks and nuns there, and in particular the remarkable Ajahn Sumedho, can be clearly traced in the pages of this book. In all my later meanderings seeking truth, I have not encountered a more direct inspiration.

In addition, I give thanks for the translations and writings of Bhikkhus Bodhi and Thanissaro; Ajahn Munindo's way of expressing things; Xanthe's surfing instruction, which improved my mind more than my surfing; Mr Christopher Milford, for my life (twice); everyone who has made the effort to learn Pali; gifts given to sustain the tradition; and Oxford University, where it all began.

Finally, I bow to the Buddha himself.